Advances in Contemporary Educational Thought Series
Jonas F. Soltis, Editor

The Cultural Dimensions of Educational Computing:
Understanding the Non-Neutrality of Technology

C. A. Bowers

Power and Criticism:
Poststructural Investigations in Education

Cleo H. Cherryholmes

The Civic Imperative:
Examining the Need for Civic Education

Richard Pratte

Responsive Teaching:
An Ecological Approach to Classroom Patterns
of Language, Culture, and Thought

C. A. Bowers and David J. Flinders

A Critical Theory of Education:
Habermas and Our Children's Future

R. E. Young

Education as a Human Right:
A Theory of Curriculum and Pedagogy

Donald Vandenberg

EDUCATION
AS A
HUMAN RIGHT

*A Theory of Curriculum
and Pedagogy*

DONALD VANDENBERG

TEACHERS
COLLEGE
PRESS

Teachers College, Columbia University
New York and London

Published by Teachers College Press, 1234 Amsterdam Avenue
New York, NY 10027

Library of Congress Cataloging-in-Publication Data

Vandenberg, Donald.
   Education as a human right: a theory of curriculum and pedagogy/
Donald Vandenberg.
      p. cm.
   Includes bibliographical references.
   ISBN 0-8077-3029-7
   1. Education—Philosophy. 2. Education—Curricula. 3. Moral
education. I. Title.
LB880.V34E34 1990   90-35561
370'.1—dc20   CIP

Printed on acid-free paper

Manufactured in the United States of America

96 95 94 93 92 91 90   8 7 6 5 4 3 2 1

1-27-91

Contents

Foreword by *Jonas F. Soltis*   ix
Preface   xi
Acknowledgments   xv

PART I   **Value and Moral Education**   **1**

CHAPTER 1   Education and the Moral Crisis   3

Evidence of Nihilism   4
The Moral Crisis   7
Preliminary Definitions of Moral Terms   10
Value and Morality   12
The Existential Context   15
Conclusion   17

CHAPTER 2   Ethics and the Hidden Curriculum   19

Deontology   19
Ross and Intuitionism   20
Kant and Rationalism   24
Kohlberg and Education   28
The Community Under Law in the Counterculture   30
The Community of Scholars Under Law   32
Existential Considerations   34
Moses and Revelation   38
Conclusion   41

CHAPTER 3   Value and the Hidden Curriculum   44

Teleological Ethics   44
Pop Hedonism and Education   45
Utilitarianism and Education   47

Pragmatism and Education 54
An Immanent Critique of Teleological Ethics 56
Jesus and Self-realization 60
The Hidden Curriculum 62
Conclusion 65

CHAPTER 4 Value, Ethics, and Education 67

Values in the Cosmos 68
Human Dignity 72
Moral Agency 74
Moral Freedom 77
Equal Freedom 78
Moral Equality and Brotherly/Sisterly Love 80
Marx's Criticism of Human Rights 82
Human Rights in the Hidden Curriculum 83
The Existential Connection 86
Response to the Moral Crisis 89
Conclusion 92

CHAPTER 5 Learning to Value Things in Classrooms 94

Learning Values from the Teacher 95
Learning Values from Classroom Procedures 99
Digression on Method: Utilitarianism 101
Value Clarification 104
Discussing Moral Dilemmas 109
Learning Human Rights and Obligations 111
The Transpersonal Standard 115
Conclusion 116

PART II Cognitive Education 121

CHAPTER 6 Education and the Intellectual Crisis 123

The Critique of Science 123
The Technological Consciousness 125
The Reproduction of the Social Structure 127
Limitations of Philosophy of Science 129
Knowledge of the ACTS and Disciplines 132
Education in Advanced Industrial Society 134
The Concern for the Environment 135
Conclusion 136

CHAPTER 7   Interpretive, Normative Theory of   138
             Education

             Doing Philosophy of Education   *138*
             Normative Evaluation   *139*
             Interpretation of Practice   *141*
             Interpretation Through Texts   *142*
             Critique of Propaganda   *147*
             Conceptual Analysis of Educational Language   *148*
             Normative Educational Questions   *149*
             Doing Philosophy of Education Existentially   *151*
             Theory of Intellectual and Moral Characteristics *153*
             Conclusion   *154*

CHAPTER 8   Knowledge in the Curriculum   155

             Historical Conceptions of Science   *155*
             Conceptual Didactics: Peters and Hirst   *157*
             Perceptual Heuristics: Spencer   *163*
             Experimental Heuristics: Dewey   *167*
             Interpretive Didactics: Broudy   *171*
             Conclusion   *176*

CHAPTER 9   Knowledge in Education   182

             Co-intentional Dialogics: Freire   *182*
             Conceptual Dialogics: Greene   *187*
             Education in the Cosmos   *193*
             Elements of Common, General Education   *200*
             Conclusion   *216*

CHAPTER 10   Knowledge in Pedagogy   222

             Generic Claims About Human Nature   *223*
             The Existential Context   *224*
             Greene's Pedagogy   *229*
             Witnessing the Truth   *236*
             Domain- and Lesson-specific Phenomenological   *241*
                Research
             Conclusion   *245*

             References   249
             Index   261
             About the Author   271

Foreword

Think about education as a universal human right. Donald Vandenberg does, and it leads him to propose a universal curriculum for
everyone. Accepting cultural pluralism and multiple intelligences as
facts of life, he nonetheless talks sensibly about what knowledge is of
most worth for all human beings. He offers a curriculum and form of
pedagogy for the city and countryside, for modern and Third World
nations, for living life to its fullest as best we can in an imperfect and
incomplete world on a planet we all inhabit together.

Not since John Dewey has there been a more fundamental and
comprehensive development of the idea of education and its relevant
pedagogy in response to the difficulties of the times. In Dewey's day,
with the movement toward urbanization and industrialization, the ordinary ways of living and the material conditions of everyday life were
changing rapidly and jarringly. Today the changes in everyday life could
be laid at the feet of the continuing technological revolution, but many
see their roots in the nihilism entailed by following Enlightenment
thinking to relativistic conclusions in ethics and epistemology.

In order to deconstruct this nihilism, Vandenberg wisely goes back
to the philosophical tradition in ethics, taking the attitude that the likes
of Rousseau and Kant, Kierkegaard and Mill have something to say to
us, even though powerful philosophical arguments are frequently produced against their views. He mines their ethical theories for ore that
he forges into a useful contemporary formula containing respect for
persons, human dignity, human rights, cosmic sensitivity, and social
responsibility. He describes the morally ideal school setting as a "community of scholars under law" and the classroom as the place for
learning the values of things.

He then turns to make and justify choices in cognitive education
upon this normative base, reflecting in a similar extractive fashion on
the curriculum and teaching ideas of Peters, Spencer, Dewey, Broudy,
Freire, and Greene. His method is hermeneutic and eclectic in the best

senses of these terms. It is the problematic of our moral and epistemic relativism that orients his arguments and constructions, not a particular approach or view of philosophy. His distinction between the conceptual and perceptual, like Dewey's between the logical and psychological, allows him to make clearer what it means to learn in meaningful ways. His broad inclusion in the human curriculum of ACTS (arts, crafts, trades, and sports) along with the disciplines opens up the idea of worthy learning and human endeavor in a most democratic, egalitarian, and satisfying way. He also offers an ecological view of the religious aspect of existence. Finally, he specifies the elements of a common, general education in the multiple realities of the manipulable world, the play world, the natural and social worlds, the lived world, and the worlds of books and numbers. For him, teachers should be models of valuing and witnesses of truth in these various worlds of human experience.

This is a book for all who want to look at the ideas of our heritage in a new light. It speaks to the heart of the educational process and to the most intractable problems in education with a sincerity and vision needed today. Vandenberg does indeed advance educational thought with this superb effort.

Jonas F. Soltis
Series Editor

Preface

When the human rights movement of the 1960s was concerned with obtaining equal opportunities in education for disadvantaged minority groups, it was for the most part assumed that the knowledge in the curriculum of advantaged groups should be available to everyone. The question of the sorts of knowledge that should be in that curriculum as everyone's human right was hardly raised. Nor have the heirs apparent to the human rights movement, the critical theorists, responded with an epistemically grounded, constructive alternative that specifies the kinds of knowledge to which everyone is entitled to access. Their critical pedagogy revives the Enlightenment faith in the transformative power of education, but "the Enlightenment heritage must be repossessed and reinterpreted" (Greene, 1986, p. 440). Its particular concepts of rationality have led to the present crisis and are untenable. Our appropriation of the Enlightenment should not be based on such figures as Descartes, Spinoza, Voltaire, Newton, or Kant, but on a composite made up of Thomas Jefferson, Benjamin Franklin, and Thomas Paine (Brinton, 1967). To avoid anti-intellectualism in the deconstruction of the Enlightenment, it should occur within the horizons of the Enlightenment faith in the value of the diffusion of knowledge through the education of the people, guided by the ideal that "knowledge of the nature of all things is Enlightenment's goal" (Bloom, 1987, p. 256). Knowledge about things in the world is tremendously important existentially, for it is among them and by means of them that we find out who we ourselves are (Ortega y Gasset, 1933/1958, p. 21). If we have to become postmodern, it is only to become post-postmodern.

It is within this context that I have formulated in the following pages a theory of the curriculum and pedagogy for common, general education. The idea for the project arose initially during my undergraduate years. Simultaneously a member of the No-nonsense Generation of veterans of the Korean conflict and of the Beat Generation of the postwar years, I was often confronted by professors who were not always aware that their knowledge was about life. After entering the field of philosophy of education, I tried formulating a normative theory of education to counteract the depersonalization of modern society, using resources that made sense to me. After existentialism and phenomenology, it was human rights ethics. Now, to investigate the role of knowledge in existence and education, it is textual hermeneutics.

Main ideas for the book's structure, such as exploring multiple perspectives from the past to respond to the moral and intellectual crisis, developed during the years I read Maxine Greene's *Teacher As Stranger* with experienced teachers in Queensland, Australia. Although my use of phenomenology, but not existential philosophy, to study educational problems had preceded hers, I became dissatisfied with the approach. It is correct to be concerned with the student's being because of twentieth-century nihilism, but we followed too closely Nietzsche's and Heidegger's metaphysical interpretation of nihilism as the oblivion of being. We must now ask why they did not formulate an ethics and theory of knowledge to overcome moral and cognitive nihilism. We should therefore consult modern ethical theories and exemplars of Western educational theory to repeat Greene's work with greater concern for retrieving the Enlightenment heritage and with greater receptiveness for their genuine insights into the human condition. Greene's acknowledged urban consciousness, furthermore, needs supplementation with a consciousness that is as autochthonous and ingenuous as it is urban and sophisticated. The investigation is therefore hermeneutical in the sense explained in Chapter 7. Its method combines linguistic, conceptual, existential, and phenomenological analyses with dialectical reasoning in order to consider educational phenomena in their substantive, normative dimensions. It involves an intensive reading of the original texts to develop from the primary sources an objective theory of value, obligation, and knowledge that can enable us to transcend moral and cognitive relativism in education.

The idea of investigating value and moral education before cognitive education comes from Michael Degenhardt's *Education and the Value of Knowledge*. We have to be able to say things are good before we can say knowledge is good. Part I of this book therefore inquires into how we can know values and obligations and how this knowledge should affect education. After a brief analysis of the moral crisis, it seeks a resolution by examining the great ethical theories of modern times. Each theory is related to the hidden curriculum because basic value and moral sensibility develops through the way classrooms are run. These perspectives are synthesized in the human rights ethics of Chapter 4. The synthesis is applied in Chapter 5 to the curriculum and pedagogy in order to respond educationally to the moral crisis.

The synthesis also provides a justification for the claim that education is a human right. Then Part II tries to ascertain the knowledge that belongs in the curriculum in the education of everyone when education is considered to be a human right. After a brief survey of the intellectual crisis, it seeks a solution by deconstructing the nihilism in the curriculum proposals of major Western theories of education. The deconstruction is a mild ideological critique that extracts the aspects of the theories that contribute to our understanding of the role knowledge should play in human existence. These aspects are synthesized in Chapter 9 to establish the contours of the main content of the curriculum that is everyone's human right. The synthesis is applied to pedagogy in Chapter 10 to respond to the intellectual crisis.

If the book makes any progress toward overcoming nihilism, it is due to the greatness of the theories it dares to de-ideologize even while learning from their understanding of the role of knowledge and education in human existence. Any originality in the volume lies in three aspects. First, the fact that it consults the great historical works only after discussing the contemporary questions of the content of moral and cognitive education allows a sympathetic reading of the primary sources in an effort to discover what can be learned from the original texts. Second, this in turn allows for a more profound consideration of the real problems than is possible with secondary sources and commentaries. Finally, it also allows the cumulative syntheses to form a historically based, ontologically grounded, normative theory of education that is beholden to no particular philosophical school of method or doctrine.

Acknowledgments

Part of Chapter 4 was read to the Philosophy of Education Society of Australasia at its 1985 Hobart meeting and published as "Human Dignity, Three Human Rights, and Pedagogy" in *Educational Theory* (Vandenberg, 1986). I thank this journal for its kind permission to use this material, which is copyrighted by the Board of Trustees of the University of Illinois. The axioms used in the same chapter, however, were developed for use in West Orange High School, New Jersey, thanks to an invitation from Dr. Ruth H. Legow for me to give a talk there. Some of the ideas of Chapter 9 have been excerpted, rethought, and rewritten from papers published in *Philosophy of Education, 1983, Teachers College Record*, and *Phenomenology & Pedagogy* (see Vandenberg, 1984a, 1987a, 1988). I thank the Philosophy of Education Society and the editors of these journals for their gracious consent to use these materials in this way.

The significance of human movement for all knowledge was first brought to my attention by Stephen Smith. I trust that all other debts are adequately documented in the text. I am grateful to the universities of Queensland and Illinois for, respectively, a study leave and a pleasant environment in which to complete this book. I am also thankful for the editorial advice of Jonas Soltis, the collegiality of Ted D'Urso, and the enduring support of Erma, who is the wind beneath my wings.

Part I
VALUE AND MORAL EDUCATION

CHAPTER 1

Education and the Moral Crisis

Education is an aggregate of phenomena that can be viewed from many perspectives. Historically, education is the transmission of the human heritage in order to maintain and enhance the level of civilization a given society has attained. Anthropologically, education is the humanization of the young that occurs in the dialogue between the generations and that enables the young to attain adulthood and a place in adult society. Sociologically, education is the socialization of the young into the societal roles and values believed necessary and desirable for a society's continued existence. Politically, education is the preparation for citizenship in the state or nation. Economically, education is the acquisition of the knowledge, skills, and values necessary for gainful employment and for training the workforce. Existentially, education is becoming aware of the possibilities of being that enable one to achieve an adult presence to the world as a morally and socially responsible person with one's own value and dignity. Cosmically, education is the journey of becoming at home in the universe.

Education is all these things and more. Each point of view accentuates certain aspects of knowledge and value at the expense of others. The recommendations for knowledge, value, and morality for the school curriculum inherent in each perspective cannot be implemented in a balanced way unless the claims about the nature and aim of education are properly adjudicated. This requires an investigation of the epistemic basis of formal education. It also requires judgments of value, for, regardless of whether the objective is civilization, adulthood, social continuity, vocational competence, skilled labor, human dignity, or cosmic belongingness, it is a highly prized good. To judge among these valuable things requires an investigation into the axiological basis of education that is specifically guided by the question of the epistemic warrant for judgments of value. How can we know value? How can we know what is good?

It is widely believed that there is no such knowledge and generally assumed that everyone is entitled to his or her own values. The right to freedom of thought, conscience, and expression is understood as the right to have any beliefs one wants about the good and the right, regardless of their cognitive warrant or defensibility. According to some commentators, the general belief that there are no intersubjectively valid, objective standards of value is so pervasive it amounts to a moral crisis in Western civilization. If philosophers, for example, reflect their culture, and if moral relativism is nihilism, then, because many philosophers believe that moral judgments are somehow arbitrary, "our age is truly nihilistic" (Olson, 1967a, p. 515).

Moral relativism is frequently accompanied by a similar unbelief in the existence of truth in the cognitive domain. Indeed, in his 1969 treatise on nihilism, Stanley Rosen claims that the moral crisis in philosophy is reducible to a crisis in reason. When the philosophers who defend reason reduce its role to the logical patterns of inference from "empirical facts" and deny its efficacy in judgments of value, they are hoist with their own petard. If we cannot speak reasonably about what is good, we cannot speak reasonably about the goodness of reason (p. xiv). Nihilism, according to *Webster's New World Dictionary of the American Language* (1974), is "the denial of the existence of any basis for knowledge or truth" and a general rejection of morality and religion. Because we have to be able to say some things are good before we can say that knowledge is good, we will postpone consideration of nihilism in the cognitive domain and begin with moral nihilism.

EVIDENCE OF NIHILISM

This is one of the most turbulent, catastrophic centuries in the history of the human race. There may be no problems of values in small, country towns where isolation from the mainstream of life enables people to maintain firm convictions of right and wrong and an adequate program of moral education for their young. What can be said about education in values and morality in these isolated pockets of the world, however, is of little help in the schooling of urbanized children and youth. The mass media and mass transportation have urbanized many small towns, moreover, so that urbanization is no longer a matter of geographical location. There is nowhere to go to escape the problem of values and morality of the contemporary world and the pervasive nihilism of Western civilization.

Nihilism shows in the rising rates of divorce, child abuse, delin-quency, drug use, alcoholism, abortions, and violent crimes constantly reported in the media. Authoritative sources of accurate data can be consulted by anyone who wants to prove something. Conservatives cite such data to support the need for repressive measures; liberals, to show the need for institutional change. Because figures lie only when liars figure, the value of such data ought not to be underestimated. It is difficult, for example, to convince children and youth from single-parent homes of the genuine value in a lifelong marriage or in the sexual morality associated with it. Their experience prevents them from thinking objectively about it. Even if they can imagine a satisfac-tory marriage, they cannot appreciate its value and probably lack the personality structures and social skills necessary to realize one in their own lives. Increasing divorce rates thus decrease the possibility of successful inculcation of the values of lifelong marriage and its correla-tive sexual mores.

Just as marital values are likely to lack credibility to the young from single-parent homes, so, too, do many other traditional values lack credibility in the eyes of the young growing up under the threat of the annihilation of the human race. It may be myopic to be overly con-cerned with the superbomb, however, for, had it been invented, it would have been used in World War I. There is no difference in principle between the artillery shells of 1917 and self-guided missiles with multi-ple, nuclear warheads; nor between the deaths of the 55 million people killed in World War II and the destruction of 4.5 billion people—except the latter has not happened. The rhetoric of the fearmongers and demagogues, however, creates the impression that World War III has already happened, much as science-fiction movies create the impression that extraterrestrial beings have already visited the Earth. The fantasy makes it difficult to appreciate the reasons for the arms race, accept mutual deterrence as a fact of life, and realize that it has in fact prevented the outbreak of a third world war. The reports of the possi-ble self-destruction of the human race have been greatly exaggerated. What has been called the *big change* occurred between 1914 and 1918, when it became readily apparent that the massive destruction of a "world war" was possible, given the technology. Sensitive observers of the human comedy changed their images of the kind of creature the human being is. The great theologian, Paul Tillich, for example, walk-ing on the battlefields of World War I, decided Nietzsche was right: God is dead. Former idealists became political realists as they accepted the necessity to confront power with power.

The changes in international relations in the aftermath of the two world wars were accompanied by a virtual second industrial revolution and changes in the intellectual climate that are perhaps best signified by the emergence of the Lost Generation, the Beat Generation, the Angry Young Men, the Me Generation, the counterculture, and the Yuppies. This intellectual climate, as articulated by the intelligentsia in social commentary, *belles lettres*, and the arts, contains very few attempts to know the good or the right in conventional terms. Dada, surrealism, the stream-of-consciousness novel, abstract painting and sculpture, theater of the absurd, pop art, punk, acid rock, deconstructionism, postmodernism, and so forth, including the avant garde in almost all genres, show the surrender of the easy moralism that celebrates and reinforces what arty, "bohemian" people used to call "bourgeois values." In spite of the slight shift toward upbeat things during the 1980s, one can no longer go to literature or the arts for knowledge of the good and the right.

When Nietzsche noticed that God was dead a full century ago, he was not speaking about deity but about us. A survey of Western civilization shows that God is no longer working through historical events. There is no evidence for the existence of God. The import is similar to Dostoevsky's statement, "If there is no God, all things are possible." Because moral values had been legitimated in Western civilization by the Judeo-Christian religions, a widespread loss of belief in God can result in widespread moral relativism and amorality. Dostoevsky's point, too, is not about God but about individual morality. People who obey moral rules only because they are believed to be divinely ordained are left rudderless when they lose faith in God. Dostoevsky examined this predicament in fiction; Nietzsche, in life. People act as if they no longer believe in God. What values might they believe in? Nietzsche and Dostoevsky can be ignored, but they are harbingers of something that is happening to Western civilization. Urbanization and the specialization of labor have secularized life. Religion no longer supplies its unifying, pervasive rationale. Even religion has become secularized and reduced to a leisure-time activity, good for Sundays only. Just as Tillich decided Nietzsche was right during the first world war, so did the clergy who fought in the French Resistance find it right to lie, cheat, steal, wound, and even murder as they adopted situation ethics during the second world war. It is therefore quite understandable that the young who are brought up in the apparent imminence of a third world war frequently find that "all things are possible." The fault is not theirs, not any more than it is the fault of youth from single-parent homes if they are unable to perceive the value of a lifelong marriage. There have been few models of virtue available. So pervasive is the nihilism, we do not know what such a model of virtue would resemble.

Nor has there been an abundance of guidance from philosophers. After Kierkegaard and Nietzsche, European (Continental) philosophy often became oriented to some version of existentialism and relativism in values, while many English-speaking philosophers adopted some form of positivism. This belief that factual statements should be tested by empirical observation, while value statements are subjective, leaves a philosopher with little to do except examine the way in which these meaningless value statements are used to express approval, utter commands, and prescribe actions. The untenability of the fact/value dichotomy has not prevented many philosophers from accepting it. At any rate, until they began working in areas of applied philosophy such as environmental and medical ethics, they have not generally written for the public since the second world war. Because they have generally not addressed public issues or commanded public respect for their opinions on values, they have contributed to the general nihilism by default. Many people have therefore turned to ersatz religions, astrology, gurus, therapists, and the authors and celebrities commodified by the mass media for guidance on questions of what is good and right.

The phenomenal urbanization, secularization, and democratization of society, moreover, leaves people rootless and anomic, lost in the normlessness that makes them vulnerable to dictators, fashions, media hyperbole, peddlers of the latest brand of snake oil, and the problems that result in the ever-increasing rates of alcoholism, drug use, divorce, teenage pregnancy, and violent crime. If these rates continue to rise, the moral crisis they manifest may result in the decline of Western civilization as we know it.

The problem is not only how we can know what to value, what is good, and what is right. It also involves the substantiation of beliefs about value and morality. It requires the formulation of an educational program that sophisticated, cultured people will accept for their children, that teachers can implement in the classroom, and that is also credible to children and youth in an age when everything seems to coalesce in the encouragement of hedonism and relativism.

THE MORAL CRISIS

Because of the kind of evidence cited, many people believe there is a moral crisis at the heart of Western civilization. By this they may mean any of the following: (1) No one knows what is right and wrong.

(2) There is widespread disagreement about what is good and right and not enough common values to hold society together. (3) There may be adequate agreement about what is right and good, but it is badly mistaken. (4) Society is in the midst of a confusing transition to a new form of civilization, which creates a pervasive puzzlement over the loss of the values of the old form and the emergence of the values of the new one. (5) Human society as such is disintegrating. Such talk might lead one to conclude that the end of the world is at hand, or it just may be that talk about a moral crisis is upmarket, nihilistic chic.

Allan Bloom's (1987) best-selling commentary on the state of higher education in the 1980s, *The Closing of the American Mind*, for example, opens with this claim: "There is one thing a professor can be absolutely certain of: almost every student entering the university believes, or says he believes, that truth is relative" (p. 25). This includes truth in both moral and cognitive domains, for Bloom later chides the liberalism of John Stuart Mill and John Dewey for lacking a concern for natural rights and for fostering the attitude of openness toward the new that effectively closed the "American mind" to fundamental principles, their supportive moral virtues, and the books that might expand and change one's own point of view (pp. 29, 34). Clarence Karier (1987) similarly complains that, because of television's massive stunning of the American mind, "America has entered a world of nihilistic values and irrational discourses in which image was more important than substance" (p. 259), leading, among other things, to the acceptance of charismatic leaders who manipulate the tribal symbols of the mythical frontier hero (p. 259).

These claims from opposite ends of the political spectrum warn us that allegations of a moral crisis may be scare tactics to prepare the way for the solution the crisismonger has in mind (Weaver, 1972). It is not surprising, for example, after reading a chapter on the need for a prophetic voice in education in David Purpel's *The Moral and Spiritual Crisis in Education* (1989), to find that Purpel's list of "what everyone should know" includes "the Sermon on the Mount, the Ten Commandments, the Declaration of Independence, the Gettysburg Address" (p. 129). Conspicuously missing is the Constitution of the United States and its First Amendment regarding the separation of church and state. Sometimes the crisismonger is simply having a personal moral crisis in public. It is nevertheless clear that the moral context in the last quarter of the twentieth century is quite different from previous eras. The difference constitutes the century as a period of expanding nihilism. To call it a "moral crisis," however, assumes that values are historically and culturally relative after all. If values are objectively or intersubjectively valid, there cannot be a moral crisis, although widespread ignorance of these values manifests a crisis in civilization. In other words, the conditions of life in an advanced industrial society may destroy the credibility of the knowledge of the good and the right, but they cannot alter what is good or right. If, for example, it was wrong to punch someone in the face in Chicago in 1894, then it was wrong to punch someone in the face in Japan in 1943, in New Orleans in 1990, and in Rome in 395. The legal and cultural rights and wrongs change, but not the moral rights: It is always wrong to hurt another person. Right and wrong do not change, although our knowledge of them does, and so does the believability of that knowledge.

A moral crisis can be sharply distinguished from a lack of credibility. A crisis is a critical turning point. If there is a moral crisis, things should get better or worse rather quickly. The present crisis, however, is a slow one. We may not be around to tell if it gets better or worse. We can live with a lack of credibility. At most it indicates the need for a different educational emphasis. Although neither is credible, many people believe in UFO's and astrology. That such people cannot convince skeptics indicates a lack of credibility, but nothing more. It can be tolerated. The matter changes, however, if one believes that peace can be maintained only through the mutual deterrence of superbombs or only through the creation of nuclear-free zones around the world. Both sides want peace, but neither believes the other wants it. This is not a moral crisis but a lack of credibility.

Those who claim there is a moral crisis sometimes support their case with the claim that this is the first time in human history that it is possible to commit the suicide of the whole species. It may be technically possible, but until it occurs we cannot know if it is humanly possible for one of the superpowers to initiate the use of nuclear weapons in any way that would eventually result in destroying everyone. As for accidental initiation, this can be added to the probability that one will get hit by a truck while crossing the street next week or suffer some other fatal accident. One should live so long as to die by nuclear bombing. The worst fate anyone can fear is one's own death. The horror of mass destruction can cause great consternation only on the assumption that one is not personally involved. This is in bad faith, resting as it does on the lie told to oneself that displaces the fear of one's own death by projecting it into horror over World War III. The threat of this war, however, does not make life, always a very fragile thing, any more endangered than it has been. The uncontrollability of human events has always been part of the human condition. This is precisely why knowledge of the good and right is so very important. It is why moral courage is so important. Nietzsche also said that living means being endangered. Without moral danger, there can be no moral choices, no morality, no moral character, and no moral heroes.

In the final analysis, it might not matter educationally whether there is a moral crisis or a general lack of credibility of the knowledge of goodness and rightness. Without credibility, education in moral values will fail. A widespread educational failure will eventually develop into a moral crisis in society. It is Bloom's (1987) and Purpel's (1989) thesis, from opposite ends of the political spectrum, that this has already occurred. The question of the credibility of values, however, is merely a variation on the theme of how we can know what is good and right. Before we turn to the classical, modern theories to synthesize their resources, we will need some preliminary definitions to provide a general framework for the inquiry.

PRELIMINARY DEFINITIONS OF MORAL TERMS

There are no neutral or objective definitions in ethics. The very choice of terms in the definition engages one in substantive theory building. Perhaps we can start with a definition given in *Teacher As Stranger*, where Maxine Greene (1973) says,

> Wherever they make choices with values and preferences in mind, people are engaging in moral behavior. *Moral*, therefore, applies to many kinds of valuing, to judgments of good and bad, right and wrong; and to the relationships between those judgments and the actions of men and women. (p. 214)

This is a very good beginning, but not all choices involving values and preferences are moral choices. To isolate the moral realm, a distinction between moral and nonmoral choices should be added. Examples of nonmoral choices might be choosing between a sapphire and emerald engagement ring, an incandescent and fluorescent desk lamp, or between steak and spaghetti for dinner. One can consider these choices in terms of good and bad. Some people find sapphires better than emeralds, fluorescent lamps bad for their eyes, and steak better than spaghetti, or vice versa. These are value choices, concerned with nonmoral values. They may be perfectly free choices, rather than resulting from psychological or social conditioning, but within the isolated contexts stated, nothing moral is involved in the choices or their consequences.

Some ethical theories, however, would broaden the context of these apparently innocuous choices. Suppose the lamp purchaser discovers that the tungsten in the lamp was produced by slave labor or under conditions of apartheid. Then the choice of the lamp becomes a moral choice. Because they violate human dignity, one ought to refuse to support slave labor or apartheid by refusing to purchase the lamp. Similarly, the choice between steak and hamburger for spaghetti may be related to the differential price structure of an exploitative economic regime. One might decide one has a duty to boycott the expensive cut to avoid supporting that system. For other people, the relation of these choices to the rest of their budget may be more to the point. They might decide on the cheaper lamp or meat to save money for their children's shoes. It would be immoral to buy the expensive things and neglect the obligations to one's children.

The moral domain, in other words, is concerned with obligations, with "oughts" and "shoulds," with doing the right thing in regard to other people. The examples appear to be nonmoral choices only when abstracted from the social and historical context. Their moral dimensions appear once the relation to other people is restored. The question now is whether all morality falls within the realm between people and, conversely, whether all relations between people fall within the domain of morality. We might entertain the possibility that the domains of morality and the interhuman are coextensive. Because not all value choices involve other people, we should note the distinction between moral and value choices.

A second fundamental distinction is between subjective and objective rightness. Someone found legally innocent of murder because the gun discharged accidentally is thereby judged to be subjectively blameless, although objectively wrong. An act is right subjectively if the person intends to do the right things (or means no harm). It is objectively right, however, only if the overt action is right. For example, if the check one sent to the electric company is lost in the mail, one is subjectively right. One did the right thing, but the consequences did not follow as expected. The action is not objectively right. Suppose one is writing two letters, one to the electric company saying they will have to wait for their money, the other to one's aging mother, intending to send her some cash in her hour of need. Suppose things get mixed up, the cash is sent to the electric company, and it is accepted to pay the bill. The action vis-à-vis the electric company is subjectively wrong but objectively right.

Some ethical theories emphasize the subjective rightness of acts and discuss matters of moral motivation, such as acting on principle, out of a sense of duty, in good will, in response to felt obligations, following moral rules, and so on. These also emphasize doing the right thing. Other ethical theories claim that good intentions actually lead to a nasty place. These theories are concerned with the objective rightness of acts and their consequences, emphasizing the realization of the good, or value.

VALUE AND MORALITY

The distinction between goodness and rightness is fundamental. Giving some attention to the use of the words *good* and *right* in ordinary language and a context more significant than lamps or hamburger will show it is not invented by philosophers. The context used here is one of the more obvious focal points of the moral crisis—the ethics of sex education. A number of statements are made to note the use of the word *good*, establish the whole picture, and show that everything that is good is not necessarily morally right. Sex is good. Sex with a person of the opposite gender is good. Sex is good whether it is premarital or postmarital. Sex within marriage is good. Sex outside of marriage is good. And so forth.

Perhaps the point of these kinds of sentences is clear enough. Another set can be added. It is good if one's initial sexual experience occurs on one's wedding night. It is good to have faith in one's mate's sexual fidelity. It is good if a couple with children remain together the twenty or so years needed to raise them to maturity. The nuclear family is good. The extended family is good. Remaining sexually loyal to one's mate for one's whole lifetime is good. Reciprocated loyalty is good. It is good to remain together with someone for forty years after one has vowed, "'Til death us do part."

This second set of sentences shows that the others are simplistic and naïve. Judgments of value have to get complicated to take into account a number of facts. One can agree with all the sentences in both groups, but not act on them all. Some are mutually exclusive. An open-minded tolerance allows one to give intellectual assent to all by adding in some cases, "But it is not for me." One can agree that virginity at marriage is good even if one was not a virgin or never married, just as one can say it is good to remain married to the same person for forty years even if one is single, divorced, or widowed. Similarly, one can agree that sexual loyalty in marriage is good even if one is not loyal, or that extramarital sex is good even if one is steadfastly loyal. Such intellectual agreement is not hypocrisy unless it is accompanied by a pretense to virtue not possessed.

The illustration makes a number of things apparent.

1. So long as we are merely talking about what is good, making verbal value judgments that are not directly related to our own conduct, we can be very open and generous with what we claim to be good. We can honestly believe that all of the sentences in both sets are true. They are in fact judgments of the value of something, and they are all true. They all disclose value.

2. When it comes to actual conduct, however, we are forced to choose between incompatible goods. Within the framework of these sentences, we would not have to choose between good and bad. The choices between goods are difficult enough to make.

3. One may have already acted within this area before becoming aware of the choice. Some people, for example, do not consciously choose to remain virgin until marriage because they do not think about it until it is too late. Others remain virgin until marriage through lack of opportunity.

4. We can claim that some old-fashioned things like premarital chastity, marital fidelity, and the choice of a lifelong mate are still good, regardless of any so-called revolution in sexual morality. They may not be the *only* good, but if they were once good, they still are good. Claiming that they are good, furthermore, does not entail saying anything else is bad or wrong.

5. Although we can claim that these old-fashioned things are good and also that de facto relations are good, we cannot choose both. One cannot have a de facto relation as a young adult and then settle down to a traditional marriage wherein one's initial sexual experience occurs on one's wedding night. Nor can one engage in a traditional marriage and then switch over to the other morality. The choices are incompatible.

6. They are existential choices. Making them decides who one is. If one is not able to choose decisively with one's whole being, then this, too, is who one is.

7. All of the sentences are true because of the connection of goodness with pleasure. If one agrees with all the sentences, it may be that one acknowledges that anything yielding pleasure is good. If something is good, or has value, this means that someone can realize its value in some act in which there is an actual, felt appreciation or conscious awareness of its qualities. *Pleasure* is one name for some of the feelings that accompany this value realization.

By changing a few words, all of the foregoing value sentences can be made to relate to food: Shrimp are good. Shrimp are a good appetizer before a main course of roast beef. Shrimp are good as a side dish. And so on. Most of the same things follow. The choices are between alternative goods. One cannot have two appetizers because the second would not be an appetizer. Nor can one have two main dishes, for then neither is the principal course. Nor can one eat a meal twice to try it the other way the second time. This analogy shows that the sentences are solely concerned with goodness and value realization.

Morality has not yet been considered because no attention has been given to right and wrong. We can add a few more sentences to our statements about coitus. We might say that, no matter how good premarital sex is, premarital chastity is right. No matter how much sacrifice it may entail, fidelity in marriage is right. Why? Premarital sex eliminates the possibility of having the first sexual encounter with someone who is so beloved that one has chosen to live the rest of one's life with that person. Both things are good, but one prevents the realization of the other. It is right to choose the greater good by letting the choice of mating coincide with the choice of a mate. Similarly, one can appreciate the value of fidelity in marriage only after one has been married some twenty or thirty years. It is wrong to deny oneself this good. If this seems argumentative, it nevertheless shows how everything changes with the introduction of the words *right* and *wrong*. It is much more difficult to show the truth of sentences such as, Premarital chastity is right. This does not by itself say premarital sex is wrong, but, if it is, it is due to obligations one has to one's future mate and to one's children. There may also be an obligation to one's future self. Can one refuse these and still get married in the sense of choosing a lifelong mate?

The use of the word *obligation* was unnecessary so long as the language game remained with the word *good*. The addition of the word *right*, however, raises the question of why something is right or wrong. It brings in the obligations to the greater value, to others, and to oneself. It brings the discussion into a different realm of meaning, that of morality. It makes most sense to use it with the word *good*, but it can be used alone. More conservative people might very well talk about sexual morality in terms of right and wrong without mentioning that sex can be good even when it is wrong. They might even be offended by the first set of sentences and want to claim that premarital chastity is right without reference to the good that can be realized through it. A whole set of mores, completely specified in terms of right and wrong, can develop. A codification of these mores into moral rules omits much of the context and may seem unrealistic when it is not.

The illustration therefore serves to distinguish the use of *good* and *bad* from the use of *right* and *wrong* in moral language. It does not try to indicate what is right, but only to show the different perspectives. We might claim it is always right to maintain chastity until marriage and to remain faithful to one's spouse, and we might even make these claims publicly defensible. What has been said might make them credible. It probably cannot be claimed, nor made credible, that it is wrong to engage in premarital or extramarital sex. They may very well be wrong, but one does not have to believe them wrong to claim the other things are always right. To say that premarital chastity and marital fidelity are right in terms of attempting to realize a lifelong mateship, especially when there will be children, is like saying it is always right to drink milk and eat whole-grain bread and plenty of fruit and vegetables. To say these are right does not imply it is wrong to drink and eat other things.

The illustration shows one other thing. If a high school student comes to a teacher after school for confidential advice regarding premarital sex, the teacher is always right to *advise* that it is always right to remain chaste until marriage, just as it is always right to plan on a lifelong mate and accept the responsibility for children if one's mating results in them. This does not mean these things *are* always right. It means they are always the right advice to be given by teachers within the pedagogic relation to the young. They will make up their own minds in any case. To be credible, however, the dialogue about the matter may have to recognize the truth of the first set of sentences given to illustrate the relation between morality and value. Morality sometimes requires the sacrifice of one good for another.

THE EXISTENTIAL CONTEXT

That this advice about advice is not a mere lapse into conservatism can be shown by a brief consideration of the existential context. Someone teaching postpubescent youth in high school, asked for advice regarding sexual morality, ought to remain within the conditions of dialogue. When asked for advice in a one-on-one situation, it is as wrong to be nondirective as it is to be authoritarian. Both are antidialogical. Some talk about sex being good might avoid alienating the young person. In any case, it is the truth. When truth is open, the talk about what is right will not be rejected out of hand. The shift to what is right without denying that other things might also be good might allow the young person to understand the distinctly moral realm. If the student objects that the institution of marriage is disintegrating, as evidenced in divorce rates and so on, it is right to indicate it is changing to a superior form of equality and companionship, which is much more difficult to maintain. The question then is whether one is going to do one's utmost to become the kind of person who can do one's full share to hold a marriage together. In other words, mating can be explained as an existential choice made with one's whole being that makes possible the genuine being together of the kind found only in a lifelong marriage. This existential possibility requires a great deal of one.

After one acknowledges the basic hedonism found in the youth culture, one should trust youths to want to become all they can become. One should trust them to be able to reason the issue through with enough depth to come to understand that choosing among several goods leads into questions of right and wrong. Then one can justify what is right in terms of what is valued as good. One should also be careful not to claim more than one can. A claim that premarital chastity is right does not have to be accompanied by claims that anything else is wrong. This might cause one to lose credibility, especially if the assertion is not true.

The general procedure can be applied elsewhere. Smoking is both good and bad. There are genuine pleasures to be obtained from it, but, because of the evidence regarding lung cancer, one is always right to refrain from smoking. One is always right to recommend refraining, even if one smokes oneself. The same can be said of drinking. There is some good in drinking alcoholic beverages, and some bad, but it is always right to abstain and to so advise. The same holds true for marijuana, of course, and for other drugs. These suggestions should probably not be used with youth who have not yet come into contact with the moral situations involved. It is imprudent, if not immoral, to raise questions about their morality with people who are doing the right thing already. For example, if there is a rather consistent agreement with the institution of marriage in a conservative community, it continues to be right to choose a mate with one's whole being for one's whole life even if it is advocated for the wrong reasons. Thus any pedagogical recommendations flowing from the illustration are inappropriate in situations where the so-called moral crisis has not yet occurred. The school is always right to provide a protective environment until young people are mature enough to address the problems of the adult world without error. Where the moral crisis has occurred, however, then clarity on the values involved through a focus on the word *good* can establish a basis for the subsequent consideration of right and wrong. This allows the students to make a transition from the esthetic to the ethical phase of existence, to use Soren Kierkegaard's (1843/1987b) terms. This is not only a moral but a very existential thing to do.

It is too soon, however, to introduce Kierkegaard. The distinctions we have made between *good/bad* and *right/wrong* are those of ordinary language. They do not depend upon any ethical theory, although they could not have been made without knowledge of the two main branches of ethics. The view that holds that the domains of right/wrong and morality are coextensive—that is, that morality is concerned with matters of right and wrong conduct—is called *deontology*, or *deontological ethics*. This view is also concerned with subjective rightness, problems of moral motivation, and the mental processes involved in moral choices. It will be considered in Chapter 2. The other view reverses things and hardly considers the right in the pursuit of the good. Because this concern with the good and the bad has been linked with objective rightness, value theory, and the consequences of choices, it is called *teleological ethics*. It will be considered in Chapter 3.

CONCLUSION

Certain features of contemporary society are frequently referred to as evidence that Western civilization is in the midst of a moral crisis. Prophets such as Nietzsche (1885/194-) have even wondered if the human race has evolved sufficiently to deal with the problems it confronts and whether it is now necessary to evolve to a new level of existence. Moral values certainly have had a difficult time since World War I because of the continued threat of planetary war; the lack of support by professional philosophers and the intelligentsia; the breakdown of religion and the secularization of society; and the rising rates of divorce, drug abuse, alcoholism, and other symptoms of personality disintegration, anomie, and nihilism.

The situation is worsened by the phenomenon of the self-fulfilling prophecy. If enough people believe there is a moral crisis in the sense of a genuine loss of knowledge of what is morally right and obligatory, their own demoralization can precipitate one. The prevalence of nihilism therefore makes it more important than ever for people engaged in the education of the young to remain of good cheer and confident in their hope for the moral regeneration of the world. The major ethical theories of modern times will be examined in this spirit to see what orientation they can supply for the moral and value education of the young. The two main kinds of ethical theories—deontological and tele- ological—will be considered in connection with their implications for managing classrooms because this so-called hidden curriculum forms basic moral sensibility insofar as formal education can develop it. After the two kinds of theories are synthesized in Chapter 4, they will be applied in Chapter 5 to the pedagogy of enabling the young to learn to value things.

CHAPTER 2

Ethics and the Hidden Curriculum

Children learn standards of right and wrong conduct in the way classrooms and schools are conducted. These are distinctly moral learnings if, as they learn how they are expected to behave, their understanding of these expectations is that they are obligations and duties. Because they are not part of the curriculum that children go to school to study, these acquired behavior patterns are often referred to as the *hidden curriculum*. William Heard Kilpatrick (1951) more appropriately called them *concomitant learnings* to indicate that moral and other learnings occur concomitantly with direct instruction in the overt curriculum (pp. 227f., 246f.). Although Part I of this volume develops a basis for the moral and value judgments necessary to establish a normative theory of the content of the overt curriculum for common, general education, the ethical theories considered are applied intermittently to this hidden curriculum. It may provide the most significant moral learning that occurs in schools, for students learn to conduct themselves appropriately in class regardless of the teacher's view of the moral crisis. A teacher who may not know what is always right in adult life, moreover, is compelled to encourage students to do what is right within the classroom. The following investigation of deontological ethics to find out what is right should at least increase the depth of this understanding.

DEONTOLOGY

For its definition of *deontology*, the *Concise Oxford Dictionary* (1976) contains this entry:

> **deonto' logy** *n.* Science of duty, ethics; hence deontolo' gical, *a.*, deonto' logist *n.* (f. Gk. *deont-* part. st. of *dei* it is right + o + logy)

It is quoted here because deontology is sometimes defined as being related to duty and obligation without reference to what is right. There can be a duty or obligation, however, only if the existence of the right thing to do precedes the duty or obligation. Examining roots of words can be misleading, but in this case the root is in agreement with common sense. It is one's duty to do what is right. One is obligated to do what is right. To know what one's duty is, or what one's moral obligations are, requires one to know what is right. The dictionary consequently defines *duty* in the moral sense as the "binding force of what is right." To say that deontology is the science of duty therefore means it is the science of the binding force of what is right. The second definition simply identifies deontology as ethics. *Ethics* is given as a synonym for *deontology*. It is elsewhere in the same dictionary defined as the "science of morals, moral principles, rules of conduct, whole field of moral science." Then it says that morals are "concerned with goodness or badness of character or disposition, or with the distinction between right and wrong."

It may not be too helpful to resort to the dictionary as an authority in philosophy, but some philosophers who make a great deal out of ordinary language refer to deontological ethics as if there can be another kind. The other kind will be considered in the next chapter, but it can also be claimed that there is no other kind and that it is redundant to refer to deontological ethics. Deontology is ethics. It is the theoretical attempt to formulate ideas of right and wrong in the quest for an understanding of duties and obligations. It is the theory of rightness as such.

Deontology is compatible with four ways by which rightness is alleged to be known: intuition, reason, observation, and revelation. We will study in turn the original writings of the major Western representatives of all four ways. Then these ways of knowing the good in teleological ethics will be considered by examining the original writings of their major representatives in the next chapter. The goal is not to pit the theories against each other but to extract their partial truths in a sustained effort to obtain knowledge of right and wrong by accumulating understanding from a variety of sources worthy of our attention.

ROSS AND INTUITIONISM

Perhaps the most famous statement of intuitionism is that of Thomas Jefferson in the Declaration of Independence:

> We hold these truths to be self-evident,
>> that all men are created equal,
>> that they are endowed by their Creator with certain unalienable Rights,
>> that among these are Life, Liberty and the pursuit of Happiness.
>> That to secure these rights, Governments are instituted among Men, deriving their just powers from the consent of the governed.
>> That whenever any Form of Government becomes destructive of these ends, it is the Right of the People to alter or to abolish it, and to institute new Government . . . to effect their Safety and Happiness.

It may not appear to be self-evident that all people are created equal. In context this means that everyone is equally entitled to the human rights specified, that government should help people realize their rights, and that no hereditary monarch or aristocracy has a right to govern without the continuing consent of the people.

Perhaps the most defensible statement of intuitionism in ethics, however, is William David Ross's (1930) *The Right and the Good*, to which our discussion will be restricted. Like Jefferson, he appeals to self-evidence:

> That an act, *qua* fulfilling a promise, or *qua* effecting a just distribution of good, or *qua* returning services rendered, or *qua* promoting the good of others, or *qua* promoting the virtue or insight of the agent, is *prima facie* right, is self-evident; not in the sense it is evident from the beginning of our lives, or as soon as we attend to the proposition for the first time, but in the sense that when we have reached sufficient mental maturity and have given sufficient attention to the proposition it is evident without any need of proof, or of evidence beyond itself. It is self-evident just as a mathematical axiom, or the validity of a form of inference, is evident. The moral order expressed in these propositions is just as much part of the fundamental nature of the universe (and, we may add, of any possible universe in which there were moral agents at all) as is the spatial or numerical structure expressed in the axioms of geometry or arithmetic. . . . In both cases we are dealing with propositions that cannot be proved, but that just as certainly need no proof. (pp. 29–30)

Ross does not use the word *intuition* but speaks of the apprehension of the rightness of certain types of acts. It is more like insight, understanding, or perceptual awareness that develops through moral experience and reflection than like a sudden inspiration or "bolt from the blue." Only a limited number of kinds of actions, furthermore, possess this prima facie rightness. If we combine the ones mentioned in this passage with those Ross stated earlier (p. 21), we have the following prima facie duties: promise keeping, truth telling, repairing wrongs, returning the equivalent of services received, distributing goods according to merit, helping others (or oneself) to develop virtue or intelligence or to realize pleasure or happiness, and not injuring others. These can be called the duties of fidelity, reparation, gratitude, justice, beneficence, and nonmaleficence to correlate them with the dispositions (or virtues) needed to carry out the prima facie duties. As Ross puts it, we should, for example, have a "disposition to fulfil promises and implicit promises *because we have made them*" (p. 22).

Ross's (1930) analysis of promise keeping will suffice to show what he means by claiming there is an immediate apprehension of the rightness of certain types of action (and not the rightness of any kind of action). There are three issues involved. One is whether, given that keeping a promise is a prima facie duty, it is ever right to break one. If it is, the second issue concerns morally adequate grounds for breaking a promise. The third is the proper understanding of the rightness in so doing. Ross's example is that one has promised to meet someone at a specified time for a rather trivial purpose, but an emergency arises in which one can help someone involved in an automobile accident. Doing so will cause one to miss the appointment. One understands intuitively the rightness in helping in the emergency even if it means missing the appointment, thereby breaking the promise (p. 18). By calling promise keeping a *prima facie duty*, Ross does not mean "at first sight" but a conditional duty. It is a duty that is not to be denied on a whim, for reasons of self-interest, or after further deliberation about the wisdom of the promise or the desirability of its consequences. It is a duty one is obliged to carry out unless a greater duty intervenes. In the example, the relief of suffering is "more of a duty" than keeping the appointment. One is confronted with two duties, the rightness of each of which is immediately apparent (p. 20). It would not be morally correct to break the promise if the appointment concerns an important matter and the suffering that can be alleviated is slight. Because it is appropriate to apologize for not having kept the appointment, it remains true to say one should not have broken the promise. One is thus confronted with two prima facie wrongs and should choose the lesser evil. Ross claims, furthermore, that keeping a promise normally comes before an act of benevolence. The latter becomes more of a duty only when the good to be achieved is great and the promise relatively trivial (p. 19).

The illustration shows that it is right to keep promises, even though in some cases they ought to be broken. The exceptional cases prove the rule. They are not counterexamples that require rejection of the insight that promise keeping is a prima facie duty. A prima facie duty is neither an actual duty in a particular situation nor an absolute duty. Just because it may be right to break a promise to fulfill a greater duty, however, is no reason to believe it is right to break one merely to do what one wants to do or because one has changed one's mind. Keeping promises remains the prima facie duty.

Ross (1930) appeals to ordinary experience in the lived world. He claims that if one asks the ordinary person why he should keep a promise, he would say because he made it. This would involve reflecting on the past, not on the future or the consequences of fulfilling the promise (pp. 17, 37). He would simply perceive the rightness of keeping the promise that was made because it was made. It is this perception of rightness that makes Ross's view intuitionistic and deontological. If we understand what a promise is, then, after we make one, we feel obligated to keep it. To make it is to accept an obligation to do something such that making it is acknowledging the rightness in subsequently keeping it. Intuiting the rightness of keeping one is therefore nothing in addition to knowing what a promise is. Anyone who can distinguish between a deceitful and genuine promise while making one is quite aware that a promise is the sort of thing that should be kept. It is self-evident.

Ross (1930) seems correct to claim that the prima facie duties are self-evident in the sense of being immediately known without rational demonstration or empirical evidence. They are known by acquaintance. An appreciation of their value, or goodness, however, requires experience on the receiving end. If one benefits when someone else keeps a promise involving some personal sacrifice, one appreciates the value of promises. It is like friendship, the value of which may be realized most fully when friends remain steadfast when it is in their self-interest to forsake one. The same thing holds true for the other prima facie duties. Truth telling, for example, the rightness of which is perceived in the implicit promise made when entering into conversation (p. 21), is appreciated when one hears the truth that has been difficult to express.

When Ross (1930) claims that the specified prima facie duties are part of the moral furniture of the universe, and of any possible universe that contains moral agents, it is tantamount to saying that these duties are the necessary conditions, or constitutive elements, of moral life. The acceptance of their obligations is the necessary or constitutive condition of moral agency. Providing insight into their rightness is therefore the task of any education that seeks to develop moral agency. Their consideration as part of the necessary conditions of morality, however, brings us to Kant's theory.

KANT AND RATIONALISM

According to Immanuel Kant (1788/1949), the human being belongs to two worlds. In the phenomenal world, behavior is subject to causation by the same laws that govern the rest of the natural world. In the intelligible world, conduct is guided by reason. The human being is empirically bound but transcendentally free. So long as actions are guided by desires and inclinations and concern for their consequences in terms of one's own pleasures and happiness, they are caused by organic factors and have no moral value. Action guided by a moral rule that is provided by reason without regard for one's desires and inclinations is freely chosen and has moral worth. Because only action guided by a moral rule (such as keeping promises or telling the truth) escapes the determinism of the material world and has moral worth, such rules are the necessary conditions of morality. To be a moral agent, one has to act on such moral rules as reason dictates from duty, without concern for consequences (pp. 200–205).

Kant means one should do one's duty out of a sense of duty and not out of a selfish concern for consequences. One should tell the truth out of respect for the principle of truth telling, not because honesty is the best policy for achieving self-serving ends. The correct reason for speaking the truth is its inherent rightness, which one knows when one realizes that it can logically become universal law. Lying cannot be practiced universally because if everyone lied, no one would believe anyone. Then no one could deceive anyone with a lie. Lying can succeed only by taking an unfair advantage of the general expectation that people speak the truth. Speaking the truth, however, is universalizable. Everyone can do it without logical contradiction. Reasoning out whether one's action is guided by a moral rule that can be universally practiced therefore lets one know if it is a valid moral law (Kant, 1785/1959, pp. 18–19). When acting on this moral law that reason dictates, one is transcendentally free. Choosing to do one's duty because of allegiance to a moral law therefore enables one to act autonomously and on a level of equality with all other rational, moral beings. Following such moral laws admits one to the moral community. Such moral laws are therefore a necessary condition of moral agency. They are the laws of freedom (1788/1949, pp. 140–141). For Kant (1785/1959), then, to do what is right, one should "act as though the maxim of your action were by your will to become a universal law of nature" (p. 39).

Kant's (1785/1959) examples of universalizability illustrate distinctions between duties to oneself and to others and between absolute and conditional duties. He holds that it is morally wrong to commit suicide, even when continued living will bring only wretchedness. If a system of nature had a law that would destroy life by the very feeling that urges the improvement of life, it would not continue to exist as nature. On the other hand, the preservation of one's own life regardless of its wretchedness is universalizable. The duty to honor the humanity in oneself by continuing to live in such a situation is unconditional. A similar unconditional duty to others is illustrated in consideration of whether it is right to promise to pay something back, knowing one will never be able to, in order to borrow it. If one tried to universalize deceitful promise making, no one would believe promises and they would become ineffective. Promise keeping, however, is universalizable (p. 40).

Concerning conditional duties toward oneself, Kant (1785/1959) claims that neglecting to develop one's talents and abilities cannot be a universal law of nature, "for, as a rational being, he necessarily wills that all his faculties should be developed, inasmuch as they are given to him for all sorts of possible purposes" (p. 41). Neglecting to develop one's talents involves, presumably, not learning how to read and write, not acquiring knowledge or vocational skills, and so on. Because unskilled adults are parasitic upon people who have developed their abilities, the quoted sentence obligates one to undergo general education. Concerning contingent, meritorious duties to others, Kant admits that the human race could exist without giving attention to the welfare of the less fortunate, but he maintains that it is impossible to will a universal neglect of others without self-contradiction. The person willing it sooner or later will need and want the love, sympathy, and help of others (p. 41). The duties of self-improvement and beneficence are teleological, oriented toward the goals of self-improvement and the happiness of others, so they are imperfect duties, contingent upon circumstances. These ends, furthermore, are not selfish or in conflict with the perfect duties to oneself and others, before which they should always give way.

It is wrong, for Kant, to violate one of the unconditional duties in order to respond to the obligations of the conditional duties. One's actions would have no moral worth if one lied, stole, broke a promise, or hurt another person merely to develop one's abilities or for the sake of some benevolent act. The perfect duties are categorical, without exception. The rejection of Kant's theory by those philosophers who believe there are situations in which it is right to lie or break promises for benevolent reasons arises from a misunderstanding. A reconsideration of the breaking of a trivial promise to relieve suffering will show Kant's point. Whereas Ross (1930) says one has an obligation to relieve the suffering out of a greater duty, what follows from Kant's (1788/ 1949) view is that this would replace an unconditional with a conditional duty. This takes it out of the moral realm and into the empirical realm, where the worth of the action should be judged by its consequences. These are not its moral worth but the good actually obtained. Kant's own example is that if one lies to a murderer who comes to one's door looking for an intended victim who has taken refuge in one's house, one is legally responsible for the consequences, even if the murderer catches the victim, who has secretly left one's house, and murders him. If one tells the truth and the murderer enters the house and finds the victim and murders him, one is not responsible for the victim's death. One is not guilty; the murderer is (p. 348). Kant does not claim that one should tell the truth in such a farfetched situation. He claims that one should always tell the truth, for the moral law is categorical. When one does not, it becomes an empirical situation that should be judged by the consequences, for which one is criminally liable.

The reasons have to do with Kant's (1785/1959) theory of moral motivation, personal dignity, and self-respect. One should always "act so that you treat humanity, whether in your own person or in that of another, always as an end and never as a means only" (p. 47). What it means to be an end in oneself is the same thing as what it means to be human. For Kant, it is to be endowed with reason and the capacity to become a free, self-determining, moral agent. At this point, Kant's rationalism is often emphasized at the expense of his egalitarian, democratic aspects: "This principle of humanity and of every rational creature as an end in itself is the supreme limiting condition on freedom of the actions of each man" (p. 49). This may make it seem as though only people with the intellectual ability to cope with high-level abstractions can think through the moral laws, like Plato's guardians, but Kant's expectation is that ordinary people can do it. From the idea that all human beings are ends in themselves follows logically "the idea of the will of every rational being as making universal law" (p. 49).

Kant (1785/1959) is concerned not only with individual morality and ethics but also with a community of ends in themselves and a philosophy of law. In the moral community, each of these ends in themselves should be deciding upon which moral rules are universalizable and therefore worthy of respect. When all pursue their own desires and inclinations, chaos results. When they consider their actions impartially to ascertain which are universalizable, they are coming to know the moral rules that everyone should choose because they are the rules that everyone can follow simultaneously, independently of idiosyncratic desires and inclinations (pp. 51–53, 82). It is as if a misbehaving pupil were asked, What if everyone in class did that? Because the requirement of justice is to "act externally in such a way that the free use of your will is compatible with the freedom of everyone according to universal law" (1797/1955, p. 35), the laws of freedom are the laws of equal freedom. One knows a rule or law is worthy of one's respect if it is understood to be necessary to establish equal freedom. Such respect is for Kant the sole moral motivation, for it prompts one to do one's duty out of duty:

> Respect for the law is not the incentive to morality; it is morality itself, regarded subjectively as an incentive, inasmuch as pure practical reason, by rejecting all the rival claims of self-love, gives authority and absolute sovereignty to the law. . . . Respect for the moral law is therefore the sole and undoubted moral incentive. (1788/1949, pp. 183–184, 186)

Thus an act is right for Kant if it is done purely out of duty understood as obedience to universally valid moral rules that is given freely out of respect for them (1785/1959, pp. 13–17, 58; 1788/1949, pp. 187–188). In his words, "Duty and obligation are the only names which we must give to our relation to the moral law" (1788/1949, p. 189).

It should be noted that the prima facie duties in Ross's (1930) theory are all universalizable. Ross has undoubtedly taken the categorical imperatives from Kant and softened their rigor by calling them prima facie duties to account for genuine conflicts of duty. For Kant it is always one's duty to obey the moral law, that is, the universalizable principles that are perfect duties toward other people, such as truth telling and promise keeping. Ross leaves it open to refuse one duty in order to fulfill a greater one, as when the people who harbored Ann Frank lied to the Germans to protect the Franks. In Ross's view, furthermore, one can have respect for a Kantian moral law when one has insight into its rightness even if one cannot personally perform the logical operations that prove it is universalizable. Intuitionism and rationalism as ways of knowing what is right are therefore compatible with each other on the level of moral conduct. At least our exemplars agree on the reality of rightness as a unique, irreducible element inherent in certain kinds of moral acts. They can be synthesized for educa-

tional purposes through Kohlberg's stages of moral development, two
of which are deontological.

KOHLBERG AND EDUCATION

The empirical psychologist Lawrence Kohlberg (1984) claims that
reasoning according to the universal moral principles Kant thinks belongs to all morality is an activity that occurs at the highest stage of
moral growth. Each of Kohlberg's three major stages of moral development (premoral, conventional, and postconventional) comprises two
distinct stages, for a total of six stages. In the two premoral stages, one
conforms to moral rules to appease someone with power and to gratify
one's desires, respectively. One might say it is good to share things, but
only because this avoids a fight, for example, or only because the
recipients will also share when it is their turn. At the two stages of
conventional morality, one obeys moral rules to gain social approval and
acceptance and because one perceives them to be intrinsically right,
respectively. The latter or fourth stage is therefore deontological. In it
moral rules and laws are accepted as being right simply because of their
inherent rightness, which is self-evident. At stage five one supposedly
believes that moral rules and laws are not right in and of themselves
but represent matters of agreement. They are arbitrary in the sense
that they could be different, so long as people agree on a set of rules.
Kohlberg's stage four is thus like Ross's (1930) theory, while his stage
six reflects Kant's theory, since it is deontological on a rational level. An
anomaly is that Kohlberg claims that to get to stage six, one has to go
through stage five, which is teleological ethics, a layer of utilitarianism
sandwiched in between the main fare of deontology at stages four and
six.

The stages are for Kohlberg an invariable sequence. One cannot go
from stage two to four, from three to five, nor from four to six,
without going through the intervening stages. Furthermore, one cannot understand more than one stage "ahead," although one will concede the argument to someone speaking at the next higher stage. If a
teacher talks about moral problems at stage five to students at stage
three, they will not, according to Kohlberg, understand properly and
will categorize the remarks in terms they do understand. To promote
the moral development of students at stage three, the teacher has to
appear to them to be at stage four. A teacher at stage six, however,
might reason that it is one's duty to educate students at stage one to
live up to the standards of stage three or four and might even use

operant conditioning to promote the requisite learning. This is Kant's own solution. Like Piaget (1965) and Kohlberg, he thinks that children and youth are not capable of reasoning at the level of universal principles. Learning in the moral domain is necessary, however, before they reach the age of reason. To avoid the negative effects of indoctrination, only those values that reason will dictate when they become old enough to reason should be inculcated. This is the classical justification for moral training, as distinguished from moral education. It is Kantian to use operant conditioning, provided it is abandoned when the pupils attain stages three or four and become amenable to the reasoning that will lead to higher stages. This is also approximately Richard Peters' (1966) recommendation in *Ethics and Education* when he claims that one has to enter the palace of reason through the courtyard of habit (p. 314).

This application to pedagogy, however, involves rampant schematizing. It is quite fallacious. Kohlberg's theory is not about stages of moral development; it is about stages of conceptual development in the moral domain. It is cited to represent observation as a way of knowing what is right. The theory is based on quasi-observational data gained through verbal responses elicited by a set of moral dilemmas. All Kohlberg observed was moral talk spoken in the presence of a researcher. He did not observe moral talk in actual use or moral conduct itself. He clearly believes that the more one knows about what is right, the higher the stage of verbalizable, cognitive development in the moral domain. His conclusion that the fourth and sixth stages are intuitionistic and rationalistic, respectively, therefore lends observational confirmation to the theories of Ross and Kant. It suggests they grasped something essential in the epistemology of moral obligation.

In other words, when Kohlberg asked the question, How do we know what is right? he, like Plato, gave more credence to the elite. His method, nothing more than an elaborated opinion poll, let him isolate the intellectual elite and discover that they employ a Kantian rationalism to reason out what is right. To get there they have had to go through an intellectual phase of intuitionism. His theory should be applied only very carefully. It should not be used to extend intuitionism beyond the specific moral acts that Ross called *prima facie duties*, nor extend rationalism beyond the universalizable actions Kant called *moral laws*, without additional philosophical justification. With this caveat, Kohlberg's framework can allow for a transposition of deontology to a developmental and educational perspective.

People in every one of Kohlberg's stages are apparently willing to obey the same moral rules; only the verbalized reasons for following them differ. These reasons might also differ sharply from the actual motivation for obeying the rules or for acting in accordance with them. Kohlberg has no evidence that children obey rules out of fear of reprisal, self-gratification, or social approval. They say they do when talking about moral dilemmas presented to them verbally, but this is evidence for it only if they possess the self-transparency and self-elucidation that children by definition do not possess. It is quite compatible with his theory to hypothesize that, regardless of their ability to verbalize about abstract moral matters, children will obey rules out of love, trust, and a sense of fairness. If so, then to promote their moral development in classrooms, teachers should gain their love and trust and appeal to their sense of fairness when introducing rules of conduct. One might ignore their stage of conceptual development and insure there is insight into the rules' rightness. Such insight does not necessarily require the discursive, conceptual understanding inferred from the data collected by Kohlberg. Such insights develop moral sensibility, the basis for any subsequent moral reflection that will have epistemic value.

THE COMMUNITY UNDER LAW IN THE COUNTERCULTURE

Moral sensibility is overlooked by conservative applications to education of Kant's ethics and his concept of the community under law. Kant's kingdom of ends, wherein individuals legislate for themselves, assumes everyone's reason will dictate the same moral laws and thereby implement the general will recommended for democratic governance by Rousseau (cf. Cassirer, 1932/1961, pp. 260–262, 274), whose bust Kant had in his library. Kant (1788/1949) also wrote a very famous essay called "Perpetual Peace," which suggests that his ideal of personal autonomy in a community under moral law is distorted by the interpreters who emphasize the duty to obey statutory laws. The expression of the community under law in the U.S. counterculture that emerged in the antiwar protest movement of the late 1960s is more compatible with the spirit of Kant's deontology, for there it remains in contact with the imperative to treat individuals as ends in themselves. This is the idea of fraternity—or brotherhood and sisterhood—that entered into democratic ideology from Christian sources in the seventeenth and eighteenth centuries. It is embodied in Kant's principle of respect for persons.

Kant's idea of individuals as ends in themselves refers to the transcendental ego, as distinguished from the phenomenal self that is observable by the methods of the natural sciences when applied to the study of human beings by physiologists, psychologists, and social scientists. The person who should be respected—the end in itself—is the entity that sets its own goals. It is the invisible unity of self-conscious consciousness, the interiority that manifests itself outwardly, in speech and action, to ordinary awareness in the lived world. The imperative to treat this end in itself, what Sartre (1943/1956) calls the for-itself, as a moral agency is at the heart of what Charles Reich (1970) calls "Consciousness III" in *The Greening of America*. Reich claims that this "Consciousness III postulates the absolute worth of every human being—every self. . . . Consciousness III refuses to evaluate people by general standards, it refuses to classify people, or analyze them" (pp. 242-243). This is Kant's idea of treating people as subjects rather than as objects, but it is related to the emotional substratum that is created by dialogical, I-Thou relationships. These enable one to feel respect for others and obligated to them. The counterculture consequently emphasizes the importance of love, similarly to the Christian maxim about loving one's neighbor, without the sexual repression. This provides the emotional support for the good will Kant claims enables one to do one's duty solely because of its perceived rightness.

The deontology in some areas of the counterculture is more apparent from the perspective of Ross's prima facie duty of nonmaleficence. Some counterculture people have claimed to know intuitively that we should not hurt each other, but with an emphasis upon sympathetic and compassionate feelings toward the problems of others that is exemplified in Kant's conditional duty of benevolence and Ross's prima facie duty regarding the fair distribution of good. This should be contrasted with the use of rationality to justify these duties, for there is in the counterculture a very deep distrust of logic and rational thought of the kind often associated with Kantian ethics. The deeper trust in one's own feelings is a confidence in the conceptually vague but perceptually sharp insights of moral sensibility (Reich, 1970, p. 278). This has been known as intuition in the history of philosophy, even by Kant.

In concluding his exposition of the counterculture under the name of "Consciousness III," Reich (1970) claims that it

> rejects the idea that man's relation to man is to be governed primarily by law or politics, and instead posits an extended family . . . without individual "ego trips" or "power trips." But it is a complete misconception to suppose that this community is not governed by law. . . . On the contrary, the community of Consciousness III has a far more genuine concept of law. (pp. 417-418)

Reich has been discussing the people who have been seeking alternative ways of living, explaining that they are very communally minded and manifest actions that "bespeak a community that does have law, in the sense of standards that are universally respected" (p. 418). Laws that merit universal respect are precisely Kant's quest, and his moral law is exhibited in the counterculture, according to Reich:

> We have already described those basic laws upon which Consciousness III rests. Respect for each individual, for his uniqueness, and for his privacy. Abstention from coercion or violence against any individual, abstention from killing or war. Respect for the natural environment. Respect for beauty in all its forms. Honesty in all personal relations. Equality of status between all individuals, so that no one is "superior" or "inferior." Genuine democracy in the making of decisions, freedom of expression, and conscience. If this is not a community of law, what is? (p. 418)

Spokespersons for the so-called counterculture do not speak of a community of law, but these are Reich's very words. The community under law described in this passage is what Kant had in mind, expressed on the level of moral and esthetic sensibility. The difference is that for Consciousness III it has to be enclosed within "an atmosphere whose dominant mood is affection" (p. 422).

THE COMMUNITY OF SCHOLARS UNDER LAW

Every classroom can be such a community under law. So can every school. Educational applications of Kant's and Reich's ideals differ according to their differences regarding the community under law. Kant's depends upon respect for the moral law, whereas in the counterculture it is based upon affection and respect for persons, according to Reich. Although Kant is the basic philosophical source of the principle of respect for persons, he himself subordinates this principle to the claim that the only unqualified good is the good will that fulfills its obligations out of duty to obey moral laws out of respect for law. This is reversed in the counterculture, at least according to Reich, where the good will fulfills its obligations out of respect for other human beings, thereby acting in accordance with those moral laws, if not out of obedience to them.

The application of Kant's view to education does not in itself violate the principle of respect for persons and treating each person as an end if it is true that children and youth who cannot reason are not yet such persons and ends in themselves. If they are not, then externally imposed discipline is justified by the need for the young to learn to respect the moral law in order to achieve freedom and autonomy. This application can be combined with Kohlberg's theory by explaining to students how the rules of the classroom and school define their obligations to the community of the classroom or school, thus enabling them to develop the cognitive operations of stage four.

The application through the countercultural interpretation does not necessarily involve the same kind of talk about good reasons to explain rules and help students understand their rightness conceptually. Without underestimating the power of such objective thinking, what seems required, rather, is taking the concept of community seriously to develop moral sensibility on the affective and perceptual level, just as Dewey (1916) called attention to the classroom as a social situation. It should be more like an application of Ross's view because people in the counterculture frequently state their feelings on moral matters as if their self-evidence suffices. There is some justification for their viewpoint. When they say *feelings*, they mean the moral sentiments they have developed through experience, and the rightness of their sentiments is in fact self-evident. For example, they hold racism and sexism to be morally wrong (of course) and might refuse to articulate conceptually a reasoned justification for equality of treatment. There is indeed little point in presenting rational arguments on these issues to people who hold contrary views nonrationally. The feelings or moral sentiments involved, moreover, are generally in agreement with Kantian moral law and could be articulated in its terms.

Because the counterculture has appeared to be radical, it might be asked if an application of its precepts to the classroom radicalizes students. Reich's (1970) statement immediately following the previous quotation is quite germane: "This is law in the true sense, not in the perverted sense of mere coercion that we know today. This is a community bound together by moral-esthetic standards such as prevailed before the Industrial Revolution" (pp. 418–419). An attempt to change society back to the status quo ante would be ultraconservative. A nostalgia for the kind of integrated community that existed before the secularization and urbanization of Western society is clearly present in the rural communes of the counterculture. They have attempted to lead a self-sufficient, agrarian life similar to that existing before the industrial and technological revolutions. One might ask whether the vision of a community under law abstracted from the counterculture is viable in school programs today. Are not the industrial and technological revolutions here to stay? It is probably correct to assume that the specialization of labor that accompanied these revolutions and the consequent urbanization are irreversible changes. The schools can do little to restore the lost community. This is all the more reason for them to embody a sense of community during the developmental years of the young. It is the "high touch" that John Naisbitt (1984, ch. 2) claims should accompany the implementation of "high tech."

The idea of a community of scholars under law, moreover, is an effort to implement deontological ethics (or, simply, ethics) in the hidden curriculum. The goal is not to promote community but to provide a context conducive to learning the moral obligations students have to each other. The students in a classroom or school should have one goal in common: the maximum learning of everyone. Within this goal they share the duties of perfecting the talents and abilities within themselves and others (Kant) and of promoting insight and virtue within themselves and others (Ross) insofar as these can be achieved through school learning. The prima facie duties of beneficence and nonmaleficence oblige students not to interfere with each other's learning. If it is to be a Kantian community of scholars under law, furthermore, the rules that define their obligations to each other are those that are necessary to establish the equal freedom to learn. The question is how they can become aware of these rules in a way that promotes insight into the rightness of the obligations they specify. It can be hypothesized that a perceptual consciousness of each other in an atmosphere of affection will develop the respect for each other that is necessary to ground moral development in the conditions of human existence.

EXISTENTIAL CONSIDERATIONS

When the school is a community of scholars under law, students learn basic morality of a deontological kind as they learn to conduct themselves in accordance with classroom and school rules. It may not be very important who makes up the rules. When students do, it promotes a greater understanding that their purpose is to allow them to harmonize their efforts to maximize their learning. When teachers and administrators make them up, there is a greater chance that the rules will actually be needed to establish the equal freedom to learn. Regardless of who makes them, rules should establish the school as a community under law dedicated to learning. They should be the means whereby students learn their obligations to each other, rather than to teachers or the bureaucracy. The principles of developing the humanity in themselves and others derived from Kant and Ross already specify obligations to one's own becoming and are therefore existentially grounded. The question is whether the rules that function as moral rules of a deontological sort are compatible with the conditions of authentic existence.

Aspects of the thought of the protoexistentialist are pertinent. Kierkegaard's (1845/1967) distinction between authentic and inauthentic modes of existence involves three phases—the esthetic, ethical, and authentic modes. These can be understood as stages of life one goes through chronologically or as phases one slips into and out of, like degrees of being awake. The ethical, deontological mode is for Kierkegaard necessary to enable one to emerge from the esthetic mode on the way to the authentic, which he refers to as the *teleological suspension of the ethical*. Authentic existence itself is not deontological for Kierkegaard, but it can occur only after the ethical stage. One must get up to legalism, as it were, before going beyond it. If these categories are cast into a developmental pattern, childhood is the esthetic phase; youth, the ethical; and mature adulthood, the suspension of the ethical in order to become oneself by realizing one's very own possibilities. If youth is a life phase where deontological ethics are appropriate, then the individualism often attributed to existentialism belongs to adulthood, where complete responsibility for one's life can be accepted. This developmental pattern is compatible with Kohlberg's theory, for his premoral stages fall within Kierkegaard's esthetic stage; his stages of conventional morality make up Kierkegaard's ethical stage; and, finally, conventional morality is transcended in order to become oneself in Kierkegaard's suspension of the ethical.

When students in elementary and secondary schools are required to act in accordance with school rules, it helps them shift out of the esthetic mode of childhood play. On the one hand, the child should play in order to live the life phase of childhood fully, so youth as a life phase can be lived fully, and so on. On the other hand, the esthetic phase is largely one of hedonism in which one does what one wants for the pleasure in it. Kierkegaard (1843/1987a) refers to Mozart's Don Juan as an example, which suggests that living in this phase is sort of a playboy/playgirl existence. The experience of time displays the structure of its existence. Attention is captured by the qualities of things immediately present. Goals do not structure consciousness. Don Juan is completely indiscriminate: Any woman will do, for the personal relationship is very superficial. His concern is with immediate qualities and immediate enjoyment (his own), not with what will happen the next day or the next week, or when he will get old. The focus of consciousness is on the present. This phase of existence is experienced by almost everyone on vacations or do-nothing weekends, but some people's lives are spent predominantly in this phase. Its inauthenticity is manifested in its temporal structure, in which one has "time on one's hands," or "time to kill," facing a stretch of time and wondering what to do with it, not realizing that this time is one's life and that wasting time is wasting one's own life. Time is experienced "out there" as a vacant period one has to get through, without realizing one is called upon to do something. It is inauthentic existence because it lacks the striving necessary to become onself. In the esthetic phase one leads an undifferentiated, anonymous existence.

In the ethical phase, one's time is well organized. Kierkegaard's (1843/1987b) example is the shopkeeper who opens his shop so regularly that neighbors set their clocks by his movements. To organize one's day by the time of clocks is to operate in the ethical mode of existence because it is reducible to relating one's actions to those of other people. One becomes a creature of habit and lives every day the same, largely in what Heidegger (1927/1962) calls "average everydayness." Time is still experienced "out there," divided into hours as if they are real. One is punctual, but a clock watcher for all of that. Enclosed in the routine habits and decisions made long ago, one does not waken sufficiently to engage in conscious choosing.

The third stage is attained when contingencies disclose that one is obligated to make a unique response to a unique situation. Kierkegaard's (1843/1954) example is Abraham (pp. 67–77). From an ethical point of view, he took Isaac to Mount Moriah to murder him. From a religious point of view, it was to sacrifice him. In either case it was a suspension of the ethical. If it is a true account, it was one of the most decisive moments of human history. It founded Judaism, Christianity, and Islam. In this phase of existence, time is no longer reified and projected outside of oneself. One is constantly surprised at how quickly time passes because of the engrossment in what one is striving to accomplish. Kierkegaard refers to this suspension of the ethical as "teleological" because one chooses to do something with one's whole being, with the courage and integrity to make it an existential choice. It determines one's identity and one's future, which are about the same thing. In his words, the person must

> have power to concentrate the whole of life and the whole significance of reality in a single wish. If a man lacks this concentration, this intensity, if his soul from the beginning is dispersed in the multifarious, he never comes to the point of making the movement, he will deal shrewdly in life

like the capitalists who invest their money in all sorts of securities, so as to gain on the one what they lose on the other. (p. 53)

It is doubtful that many children and youth have the strength of character to concentrate their whole being in one act of consciousness, except when making an occasional career or marital choice. If not, the schools should be a community of scholars under law to insure that the individual goes through an ethical phase in sufficient depth to enable him or her to make existential choices as an adult.

In the ethical phase the individual subsumes idiosyncratic inclinations within a conformity to the rules that are the same for everyone, as Kant would have it, but this specific socialization is necessary for the very individualistic Kierkegaard. In his words,

> Faith is precisely this paradox, that the individual as the particular is higher than the universal, is justified over against it, is not subordinate but superior—yet in such a way, be it observed, that it is the particular individual who, after he has been subordinated as the particular to the universal, now through the universal becomes the individual who as the particular is superior to the universal. . . . This position cannot be mediated, for all mediation comes about precisely by virtue of the universal; it is and remains for all eternity a paradox, inaccessible to thought. (1843/ 1954, p. 66)

In the esthetic phase, one is just like everyone else, an anonymous, undifferentiated nonentity. If one subordinates one's "individuality" to the duties and obligations of deontological ethics—that is, to the universal—one does not become the universal. It does not exist. Only particular people exist. You and I and she and he exist. The ethical maxim does not exist. By subordinating oneself to it, by obeying it, one does not become the maxim. Nor does one remain the undifferentiated individual. One becomes someone, the particular person who fulfilled this obligation on this occasion. One becomes a specific moral agent. One becomes oneself.

Although it is customary to oppose Kierkegaard to Kant and rationalistic ethics because of his anti–Hegelian polemics, it is fairer to understand him as simply carrying Kant to the next step. Kant decontextualizes ethics. Kierkegaard recontextualizes the same ethics. Kant's principle of respect for persons that obliges one to treat others as ends in themselves also obliges one to respect them in their becoming themselves through rules that are the same for everyone. This lets them bring this end in itself into being, for it is as yet an unrealized possibility. Acting in accordance with universal principles particularizes the individual. This can be seen more readily in the subjective appropriation of moral principles explicated in Buber's examples, to be considered in the following discussion of revelation as a means of knowing what is right.

MOSES AND REVELATION

There is no evidence to show that there is a distinct way of knowing what is right by revelation understood as a supernatural event. To ignore the great historical importance of the belief that there is, however, begs the question. To claim there is evidence recorded in the sacred writings of one of the great world religions accepts them on authority and also begs the question. As Martin Buber (1936/1956a) suggests, the so-called revelation recorded in the Old Testament is

> the verbal trace of a natural event, that is, of an event which took place in the world of the senses common to all men, and fitted into connections which the senses can perceive. But the assemblage that experienced this event experienced it as revelation vouchsafed to them by God, and preserved it as such in the memory of generations, an enthusiastic, spontaneously formative memory. (p. 246)

The natural events occurring in the life of the Moses of Exodus and the following three books of the Bible will be investigated to ascertain whether he has any knowledge of morality. Then an account of contemporary moral experience shaped by the "spontaneously formative memory" of the moral statements of the textual Moses will be given before considering their meaning for the congregations that continue to regard them as divine revelations.

It is appropriate to begin with Moses if the reason for considering this alleged mode of knowing is its historical importance. We know virtually nothing of the divine statutes Abraham promised to obey, which makes the law of Moses the earliest source of Hebraic deontology. Although the statutory laws laid down by Moses are indebted to the Code of Hammurabi, they also embody the ethical obligations of restitution, reparation, compensation, impartiality of judgment, and equality before the law, which are not in that code. The ethic of the Ten Commandments, moreover, is related to the statutory law of Moses the way the Bill of Rights attached to the Constitution is related to the federal and state laws of the United States and the way the various human rights' covenants of the United Nations are related to the statutory laws of their ratifying nations. It is a set of moral standards to which common allegiance is professed that establishes a national ethos and serves as a criterion of the validity of statutory laws. It establishes the coherence between morality and law essential to constitute a community under law.

Although the Decalogue is frequently criticized for the negativity of its injunctions, these include prohibitions against false witness, stealing, murder, and adultery, it will be recalled. None of these are openly advocated by any moral code (or teacher), and three are prohibited by law in modern societies. As Ross (1930) points out, furthermore, these four maxims specify duties of nonmaleficence. The duty not to harm others is more basic than other duties because the restraint of one's own aggressive impulses is the first step toward the consideration of others that is the heart of morality (p. 22). Anyone who accepts that nonmaleficence is a prima facie duty should accept at least these four commandments as stating specific prima facie duties of nonmaleficence. What they add is unconditionality.

Their putative unconditionality can be exemplified in an account, consistent with phenomenological evidence, of experiences shaped by the memory of these maxims considered as verbal traces of natural events in which Moses participated. When Buber was challenged with a question from the audience about what would happen to the teachings if everyone accepted the situation ethics inherent in his philosophy of dialogue, he replied with an indirect communication ("Elements of the Interhuman," tape recording). Someone who came to him for advice regarding military conscription said that while mulling things over, the meaning of the words, "Thou shalt not kill," struck him in an almost bodily way. Buber explained how the commandment is only two words in Hebrew to show it was a matter of insight into an objective norm of rightness, not words, and to substantiate that the phrase was encountered as a command, which gave the young man a severe problem regarding the draft.

Another example is the case of the man who, on the eve of filing for divorce, wondered if he would be able to look the judge in the eye when he swore under oath that his marriage had broken down beyond repair. He realized this meant he doubted it himself and wondered if it meant he should not be filing the papers. Then, from deep within his being, causing him to shudder visibly, came the silent words, "Thou shalt not bear false witness," as he realized he might be able to perjure himself a little but he could not slander his wife. He understood as if for the first time the meaning of these words prohibiting false testimony.

These two encounters involve sudden insight into the meaning of words previously understood conceptually without full recognition of their existential import. The insight came so unexpectedly that the rightness articulated in the words presented itself forcefully, independently of conscious volition, almost as if it were a command spoken by someone else. The obligation disclosed itself as an overpowering prohibition that could not be denied. Something similar must have occurred with the intervention of Socrates' daimon.

Buber (1939/1965b) claims that such encounters occur only to people who are so unified they are able to respond to the concreteness of a unique situation with their whole being. It is ordinarily called *moral integrity*. It is a response to the uniqueness of the situation as such, not a conceptual, discursive deliberation over moral principles, that elicits the encounter:

> The command inherent in a genuine norm never becomes a maxim and the fulfilment of it never a habit. Any command that a great character takes to himself in the course of his development does not act in him as part of his consciousness or as material for building up his exercises, but remains latent in a basic layer of his substance until it reveals itself to him in a concrete way. What it has to tell him is revealed whenever a situation arises which demands of him a solution of which till then he had perhaps no idea. Even the most universal norm will at times be recognized only in a very special situation. (p. 114)

Whereas maxims are stated in the third person, the command disclosed in such a contextualized encounter addresses one in the second person, unconditionally: "Thou shalt not . . ." This understanding of the "spontaneously formative memory" enables Buber (1936/1956b) to claim, "The law is not thrust upon man; it rests deep within him, to waken when the call comes" (p. 321).

To remain within the phenomenological evidence, two things should be noted in this account of the sudden insight into self-evident rightness. In both instances, and in a third regarding stealing (Buber, 1939/1965b, p. 114), the insight concerns prohibitions of acts harmful to others. No warrant is given for alleged insights that would harm others. Second, what is encountered are the moral teachings of Moses. No warrant is given for divine revelation as a distinct mode of knowing. The mode of knowing is an existentialized, strong intuitionism wherein the immediate apprehension of the moral mistake one is about to commit is overwhelming. This in turn presupposes prior learning of the injunctions involved.

To obtain revelation as a distinct mode of knowing rightness, one has to belong to a congregation that interprets the verbal traces of selected natural events as the manifestation of God, whether recorded in the Torah, the New Testament, the Koran, the Book of Mormon, or the like. For a member of such a congregation it becomes one's duty to obey God's will as the congregation understands it. This involves matters of religious faith. It lies beyond the limits of philosophical investigation except to claim that they are natural events that the given congregation chooses to interpret as the revelation of deity, as Buber suggested. The principle of religious liberty makes it inappropriate to criticize what any congregation believes are the duties and obligations of revealed morality, provided they do not violate civil and criminal law and public morality. It is similarly inappropriate to criticize the right of any congregation to educate its young in church schools that satisfy minimal standards established by the state for all its citizens. The same principle, moreover, prohibits basing moral education in publicly financed schools on claims of revealed knowledge, for this would violate the consciences of students who do not belong to the congregation that is the source of such putative knowledge.

CONCLUSION

If there is a moral crisis in Western civilization, it is not because we lack knowledge of morality. We know it is right to keep promises, tell the truth, return services received, repair damage caused, distribute goods on merit, respect people as individuals and not merely use them for our own ends, abide by the rules of equal freedom, refrain from harming others, relieve suffering, and further the development of the abilities and humanity in oneself and others. If there is a moral crisis, it is because this knowledge is either sparsely or ineffectively distributed.

Because of the apparent lack of adequate diffusion of the knowledge of what is "always right," we have considered the theories in which Ross and Kant attempt to substantiate this knowledge. That this resort to theories of great historical significance is not merely an attempt to resurrect traditional values is shown by the comparison with the contemporary expressions of Kohlberg, Reich, and Buber. If Kohlberg's theory is in fact gender-bound because of the isolation of its inquiry to inferred cognitive operations, Reich's theory of the morality of the counterculture is gender-free, as any ethic must be. "Consciousness III" is Kantian in content, though not in mode of knowing. Its rejection of distorted, misplaced rationality parallels the feminists' rejection of logocentric, male-dominated thinking and may even be its original source. Its emphasis upon affectivity and insight suggests the timeliness of an approach closer to Ross's concern for the immediate apprehension of rightness.

The original writings representative of "intuitionism" and "rationalism" have been consulted to avoid the reification of general methods of knowing into the vacuous entities that inhabit the pages of secondary sources, commentators, and general accounts in metaethics. There is no claim made for their validity beyond the self-evident truths and categorical imperatives formulated by Ross and Kant and stated herein. To the contrary, actual moral reflection and moral conduct by existing moral agents is more complicated than either, as the consideration of Kierkegaard and Buber shows. The knowledge of the prima facie duties and imperatives is obtained through disciplined but decontextualized philosophical reflection, not within situated moral reflection. A fair, disinterested consideration shows that intuitionism and rationalism need each other. Knowledge of what is right should be both immediately apprehended and universalizable. As Kant (1781/1965) says, concepts without perceptions are empty and perception without concepts is blind. This is why to promote moral development concomitantly with instruction in the overt curriculum, the classroom should *be* a community of scholars under law.

So-called intuitionism and rationalism need each other because H. A. Prichard is right. He claims that moral philosophy is based on a mistake because "we do not come to appreciate an obligation by an argument, i.e., by a process of nonmoral thinking" (1912/1955, p. 475). The feeling of obligation and of the rightness of certain kinds of acts is irreducible and developed only on a pretheoretical level in the actual situations of the lived world. This mistake can be traced all the way back through the history of philosophy to Socrates, when, at the beginning of the *Republic*, he rejects the rightness of telling the truth and returning what one has borrowed by means of the fallacious counterexample that one should not return a weapon or tell the truth about where it is to a friend from whom one has borrowed it but who has gone mad (331c). This is true of course, but a morally sensitive, ingenuous person would simply tell him that because he might hurt himself with it, the weapon will be returned later when he is better. This is the truth and merely postpones returning the weapon, rather than violating the promise to return it by expropriating it. The counterexample does not prove that telling the truth and paying one's debts are not the prima facie duties that ought to be violated only for the sake of a greater duty. Philosophers who cite this incident seldom notice Socrates' later statement that the moral person would never commit sacrilege or theft or betray his friends, and "he would never break a solemn promise or any other agreement," which presumably would include returning borrowed items (443a). In the mistake of Platonic rationalism that objectifies and decontextualizes moral concepts and consequently assumes that insight into the good can be achieved only at the end of a lengthy period of conceptual education, we can see exemplified Heidegger's claim that Western civilization is the protracted movement toward nihilism that began with Plato (Dreyfus, 1981, pp. 510–511).

This is not to reject rationalism, either in moral philosophy or in moral education. It merely suggests that in either case the role of conceptualization is to explicate the prereflective insights into obligations that have been gained in moral experience on the level of moral sensibility. This is why the classroom should be a place wherein students become aware of their obligations to each other in the construction of an atmosphere conducive to the maximization of learning.

Among the obligations we know we have is the obligation to develop the abilities and humanity in oneself and others. This justifies common, general education, but deontology by itself will not allow for an adequate specification of the criteria necessary to indicate what might belong in the curriculum. Deontology needs teleology, for moral conduct needs goals, too. Deontological and teleological ethics will be synthesized in Chapter 4 after the latter receives our independent consideration in Chapter 3.

CHAPTER 3

Value and the Hidden Curriculum

The concomitant learning of obligations to other students in classrooms conducted as communities of scholars under law can occur with or without the general atmosphere of affection, of love and trust, that was added to Kant's perspective but not without his sense of fairness. His formulation occurs within a transcendental deduction of what must be presupposed about the human mind for conduct to be moral. His method prevents him from referring to the phenomenal world of the warm, friendly creatures who populate the Earth and the classroom in particular. An affectionate atmosphere should be added to the deontological model because the value domain is much broader than the obligations and duties that emerge from the rightness of certain kinds of actions.

TELEOLOGICAL ETHICS

Ethical theories that claim moral conduct involves the realization of value, or good, deny that rightness is an independent characteristic of certain kinds of actions. They claim an act is right if and only if it realizes value or produces good. Then *good* is defined to indicate the specific kind of benefit that should result from any action worthy of being called *moral*. The definition in *The Encyclopedia of Philosophy* (Olson, 1967b) begins,

> The common feature of all teleological theories of ethics is the subordination of the concept of duty, right conduct, or moral conduct to the concept of the good or the humanly desirable. Duty is defined as that which conduces to the good, and any statement enjoining a particular course of conduct as a duty or moral obligation is regarded as acceptable only if it can

44

be shown that such conduct tends to produce a greater balance of good than do possible alternatives. (p. 88)

Deontologists also hold that "duty conduces to the good," but the good is subordinated to duty in moral conduct itself, when one's awareness should be focused on the obligation at hand, not on foreseeable results. Often arising as a reaction against deontology, teleological ethics can be defined simply as nondeontological ethics. Because it claims that the issue is not how we know what is right, but how we know what is good and how to achieve it, its obvious correlate is empiricism (and vice versa). There are enough intuitionistic and rationalistic elements in its major representatives, however, to maintain the pattern of exposition through the four ways of knowing utilized in the previous chapter: intuition, reason, observation, and revelation.

POP HEDONISM AND EDUCATION

The hedonist claims an act is right if it produces pleasure. Any pleasure will do, although the more intense or prolonged it is, the better it is. The classical statement is the *Rubaiyat* of Omar Khayyam:

> A book of verses beneath the bough
> A jug of wine, a loaf of bread, and Thou
> Beside me, singing in the wilderness.
> Ah, wilderness were paradize enow.

Eat, drink, and be merry, for tomorrow you may die. Hedonists are not at all concerned with promises, truth telling, relieving suffering except their own, acting on principle, or fulfilling obligations.

Modern statements of hedonism begin with something like Hobbes's simple materialism (1655/1839, pp. 406–408). Everything in the universe is matter in motion. Human beings, as matter in motion, are motivated by fear of pain and desire for pleasure. Pain is bad and pleasure is good. Any act that produces pleasure is right. It is right to eat, drink, and be merry so long as one avoids indigestion, hangover, and pregnancy. Provided we avoid the consequences of overindulgence, whatever we do is all right if we enjoy it. In the slogan of the counter-culture, "If it feels good, do it."

Hedonists, then, reduce the question of how we know what is right to how we know what gives us pleasure. Apparently we know by immediate apprehension, or intuitively, what feels good. We know what we like by self-conscious awareness of our own feelings. Through experience, however, we can learn about the pleasures to avoid because their painful consequences outweigh the enjoyment, and so on. Other theories, however, agree that pleasure is good. It is hedonism only when it is claimed that only pleasure is good.

Summerhill (Neill, 1960) is often read as an application of hedonism to a real school. Neill seems to apply Freud's pleasure principle without regard to his reality principle. The first way to apply hedonism to the hidden curriculum, then, is through laissez-faire freedom. If the children are allowed to do what they want, they will choose whatever gives them pleasure. They will play and have fun. When they do not enjoy what they are learning, they will turn to something else and learn by trial and error to do what gives them pleasure. They would avoid the pain and suffering ensuing from imposed learning tasks. This was actually Neill's practice. Classes were scheduled every morning at his boarding school, but the students did not have to attend. Then afternoons were completely free for play, games, sports, arts, crafts, or whatever anyone wanted to do.

A more complicated application assumes that it does not always give pupils pleasure to make their own choices. If the criterion is not freedom but pleasure, the teacher should choose enjoyable activities for the class. The main principle of hedonism is acknowledged so long as classroom activities are fun, more like play than work. The fullest application is the claim that it does not matter what they are learning so long as they enjoy learning it. This assumes that the only criterion of goodness is pleasure. It is compatible with hedonism, moreover, for a teacher to adopt operant conditioning as a pedagogical method. Suffice it to say that B. F. Skinner's *Walden Two* (1948) seems to embody a determined, thorough-going attempt to develop a hedonistic society. At least operant conditioning can be used to develop a society in which people experience pleasure in almost everything they do. This may seem morally repugnant, but only to a deontological perspective. The moral dilemma, however, is choosing between a Summerhill and a Walden Two. This requires a criterion of value not available in hedonism.

The permanent truth of hedonism is that claims about value and goodness should have some relation to what people actually find to be of value in their experience because of the pleasure it yields. The subjective appreciation of value and good may be necessary in any adequate ethical theory. Unless something somehow and somewhere feels good, one can wonder how it can be considered to be good. Hedonism simply takes this partial truth and totalizes it. It is superficial and simplistic. Not just any Thou singing beside me will bring me closer to paradise. A jug of milk is better than a jug of wine. Then, too, we could accept hedonism and raise a generation of masochists conditioned to enjoy coping with wretched living conditions. Hedonism, moreover, is characteristically individualistic. Not only egocentric, it is characteristically unconcerned with other people's pleasures. The Marquis de Sade was a hedonist. That old fellow in the Country Western song who has withdrawn from the world and finds pleasure only in children, old dogs, and watermelon wine is a disenchanted hedonist. Hedonism's expression in the *Rubaiyat* stanza depicting the withdrawal of two lovers into the wilderness, away from the cares of the real world, is characteristic.

UTILITARIANISM AND EDUCATION

Hedonism became socialized in the quantitative utilitarianism of Jeremy Bentham, who, like Kant, is a major Enlightenment figure. Like Kant, Bentham (1789/1939) assumes that all behavior in the phenomenal world is caused, but this leads him to combine ethical with psychological hedonism in the opening statement of his *Introduction to the Principles of Morals and Legislation*:

> Nature has placed mankind under the governance of two sovereign masters, *pain* and *pleasure*. It is for them alone to point out what we ought to do, as well as to determine what we shall do. On the one hand the standard of right and wrong, on the other the chain of causes and effects. (p. 791)

Bentham's empirical claim, or explanation, is that all human conduct is caused by the desire to obtain pleasure and avoid pain, regardless of what we may think we are doing. His ethical claim is that the only valid criterion of rightness is the desire to obtain pleasure. This leap between what is and what ought to be is enabled by a fundamental value judgment that Bentham apparently believes to be a self-evident truth: "Pleasure is in *itself* a good—nay, even, setting aside immunity from pain, the only good; pain is in itself an evil—and, indeed, without exception, the only evil" (p. 815).

Bentham (1789/1939) complicates things, however, by distinguishing among physical, political, moral, and religious pleasures and sanctions. He gives little notice to the physical pleasures of individualistic hedonism and dismisses religious sanctions as no longer of interest to philosophers. He is concerned with political sanctions, administered through legislation and punishment, and with moral sanctions resulting from social approval and disapproval, such as love of reputation, honor, glory, and fame, and the fear of dishonor, disgrace, infamy, ignominy, and shame (pp. 800–802, 818). These horizons require Bentham to expand the idea of pleasure to include personal or public benefit, advantage, profit, convenience, emolument, good, interest, and happiness. The idea of pain is similarly widened to include personal or public mischief, disadvantage, inconvenience, evil, loss, and unhappiness (pp. 792, 805). The inclusion of this broader range of phenomena within hedonism leads Bentham to formulate the principle of utility,

> which approves or disapproves of every action whatsoever, according to the tendency it appears to have to augment or diminish the happiness of the party whose interest is in question; or, what is the same thing in other words, to promote or oppose that happiness. I say of every action whatsoever; and therefore not only of every action of a private individual, but of every measure of government. (p. 792)

An action is right if it is useful, and it is useful if it promotes the happiness of the individual or of any number of people whose interests are at stake.

One can know what is right by calculating the intensity, length, proximity, and certainty of the pleasures that will result as a consequence of the act, subtracting from them the pain that also results, and taking into account the pleasure and pain for each of the individuals whose interests are involved (Bentham, 1789/1939, pp. 803–804). This calculus is intended primarily for legislators, but it is also appropriate for ethics, which is defined as "the art of directing men's actions to the production of the greatest possible quantity of happiness, on the part of those whose interest is in view" (p. 846). The criterion of the rightness of an action thus becomes the greatest happiness of the greatest number, "for the dictates of utility are neither more nor less than the dictates of the most extensive and enlightened (that is *well-advised*) benevolence" (p. 827). By defining rightness as whatever promotes the greatest happiness of the greatest number of people, Bentham transforms hedonism into a powerful ideology of social reform. It justifies social legislation designed to improve the material welfare of the majority of the people.

The principle can be applied directly to the classroom. The class should study things that produce the greatest pleasure for the greatest number of students. This should be qualified, however, because immediate pleasure is not the only criterion of utility. Bentham words the proximity criterion as the "propinquity or remoteness" of a pleasure

(1789/1939, p. 804). He refers to the pleasure received when the act occurs, but there is no explicit or implied preference for pleasures that are realized immediately. This means that the selection of activities and curriculum content can include whatever is to the benefit, advantage, profit, and self-interest of the greatest number of students in the long run.

The criterion of certainty is also relevant if it is clearly determinable that learning some things is in the students' long-range interest because they help furnish marketable skills and therefore will enable more pleasure to be realized in adulthood. Too much emphasis upon remote pleasures, however, undermines the spirit of quantitative utilitarianism. It is right, instead, for the teacher to make the decisions to promote the greatest good of the greatest number so that most students will enjoy learning. Classroom rules should also be formulated and enforced in ways that create a pleasant learning environment for the majority of the students.

Although Bentham's hedonic calculus is supposed to be purely quantitative, he has subtly shifted the criteria of rightness from pleasure to happiness. This becomes clear in the theory of John Stuart Mill, who defended utilitarianism against its critics so thoroughly that it has been deontological ever since. Mill's (1863/1939b) effort to save utilitarianism depends on the "difference of quality in pleasures, or what makes one pleasure more valuable than another merely as a pleasure" (p. 901). Mill never says what makes one pleasure more valuable than another, but he does convincingly argue that there are qualitative differences between them that are testable intersubjectively. If one considers two pleasures and finds that most people who have experienced both consistently prefer one of them, then that one is a more desirable pleasure. Poetry is better than pushpin. His example can be extended: Chess is better than checkers, classical music is better than pop, grand opera is better than Broadway or Hollywood musicals, and so forth. It is for Mill "quite compatible with the principle of utility to recognize the fact, that some *kinds* of pleasure are more desirable and more valuable than others" (p. 901). Which kinds are more valuable becomes clear when Mill claims that people capable of appreciating both kinds of pleasures "give a most marked preference to the manner of existence which employs their higher faculties" (p. 901). (cf. the *Republic*, 581–588).

Mill (1863/1939b) illustrates this manner of existence when he claims that if one is intelligent, educated, and morally sensitive but dissatisfied with one's own life, one would not choose the life of a fool, dunce, or rascal even if one believed they were satisfied with their lives:

"Better to be Socrates dissatisfied than a fool satisfied" (pp. 901–902). Although Mill does not explain why some pleasures are more valuable than others, he does try to explain that the unwillingness to choose the "lower grade of existence" is because of "a sense of dignity, which all human beings possess in one form or other, and in some proportion to their higher faculties, and which is so essential a part of the happiness of those in whom it is strong, that nothing which conflicts with it could be, otherwise than momentarily, an object of desire to them" (p. 902).

Mill (1863/1939b) has already claimed that the higher faculties are those of the intellect, feelings, imagination, and moral sentiments, as distinguished from sensuous, physical structures (p. 901). He is not now saying they are chosen because they exercise the so-called higher faculties. He says it is due to a sense of dignity. By this he means a sense of human dignity because of the contextual correlations of sensuous, physical pleasures with the "lower animals." He says this sense of human dignity is an essential part of the happiness of people who have a strong sense of their own dignity, which in turn seems to correlate with the degree to which one possesses "higher faculties." People with a strong sense of their own dignity would never choose the less valuable of two pleasures except for temporary lapses in their dignity.

With this recognition of qualitative differences between pleasures, however, Mill (1863/1939b) has unwittingly abandoned utilitarianism. The criterion of choice between two qualitatively different pleasures is no longer pleasure but the factor that makes one more valuable. The rightness of a choice depends not on its yielding pleasure but on its compatibility with a "sense of dignity." The pleasures can be quantitatively equal, yet the one that maintains human dignity is and ought to be chosen. Mill's claim seems to be true. Perhaps people who choose to keep their promises, tell the truth, return services received, repair damage caused, and so forth, sometimes do so not because they sense it is their duty but to maintain their sense of human dignity, even when it gives them no pleasure and may even be mortifying to do so. Mill himself claims martyrdom can be morally justified if one sacrifices one's own life for the happiness of others. He even claims that the highest virtue is the readiness to make such a sacrifice (p. 908). He merely wants to deny that such sacrifice is good and to claim that the principle of utility does not necessarily involve the agent's own happiness but "the greatest amount of happiness altogether." A moral agent is supposed to judge the merits of the case impartially (pp. 903, 908).

There are at least two implications for education of the qualitative differences between pleasures. Mill (1863/1939b) claims that, after selfishness, the greatest impediment to happiness is the lack of mental cultivation:

> A cultivated mind . . . finds sources of inexhaustible interest in all that surrounds it; in the objects of nature, the achievements of art, the imaginations of poetry, the incidents of history, the ways of mankind, past and present, and their prospects for the future. . . .
>
> Now there is absolutely no reason in the nature of things why an amount of mental culture to give an intelligent interest in these objects of contemplation, should not be the inheritance of everyone born in a civilized country. (p. 906)

Perhaps a common, general education involving these things can enable everyone to choose the qualitatively superior pleasures.

The other educational implication arises from the shift from act to rule utilitarianism already presaged in Bentham's (1789/1939) application of the principle of utility to legislation. If laws are enacted to obtain the greatest good for the greatest number, the individual no longer has to figure out if each action satisfies this criterion. One can obey the laws instead. Not everyone needs to be free to judge their acts by the principle of the greatest happiness of the greatest number. Because the test for quality is the preference of people who have the experience needed to make comparisons among pleasures, it requires "their habits of self-consciousness and self-observation" (p. 904). The goal of life, moreover, in Mill's (1863/1939b) words,

> is necessarily also the standard of morality; which may accordingly be defined, the rules and precepts for human conduct, by the observance of which an existence such as has been described might be, to the greatest extent possible, secured to all mankind; and not to them only, but, so far as the nature of things admits, to the whole sentient creation. (p. 904)

That is to say that moral precepts and rules should be established by those who are able to distinguish adequately the qualitative differences among pleasures, especially by those with a strong sense of human dignity. Then acts are right if they are in accordance with these rules and precepts, for they are thereby in accord with human dignity and "the greatest amount of happiness altogether" (p. 903). In Mill's utilitarianism, one knows an act is right if one obeys the precepts and rules laid down by the connoisseurs, and they know it is right if it is compatible with their sense of human dignity.

Teachers should be such connoisseurs and establish classroom rules that allow students to secure what they might not otherwise choose—the higher pleasures. These differ from Kant's imperatives by shaping the students' conduct by rules "which all rational beings might adopt *with benefit to their collective interest*" (Mill, 1863/1939b, p. 938). Furthermore, although the rules spell out the students' duties, there is no special reason to insure they are obeyed out of a sense of duty (p. 909). To achieve the result, it suffices that they are followed.

Two points of criticism will lead to the theory of John Dewey. First, Mill's inability to specify the factors that distinguish pleasures qualitatively, other than to say who prefers which, is unsatisfactory. The omission is disastrous for the theory. For example, one can appreciate the value of both popular and classical music and sometimes prefer to listen to the former without any loss of dignity whatsoever. It is not only a sense of dignity that is related to the preference for classical music by those who can enjoy both kinds. Popular music yields pleasure because melody predominates and the lyrics often deal with elemental human themes, whereas classical music yields a more refined, delicately nuanced, abiding pleasure because of its more complicated structure and absence of lyrics. One can like both "lower" and "higher" pleasures and choose according to mood and circumstances without having any absolute preference and without any loss of dignity whatsoever. There is mediocrity and excellence, furthermore, in both popular and classical music. Shifting genres for illustrative purposes, a poor performance of *Lear*, for example, gives less pleasure than an excellent production of *Death of a Salesman*, especially to a connoisseur. Mill is correct to make qualitative distinctions among pleasures, but he erred by accepting an elitist interpretation of quality when he might have analyzed the situation more deeply.

Second, as a criterion of the rightness of acts or rules, the greatest happiness of the greatest number is good, but it is not good enough. Nor is it the only good. It is not good enough for a teacher, for example, to make curriculum decisions or classroom rules for the good of the majority of the class. Nor is it good enough to amend this as Mill did to secure the greatest happiness altogether. To retain the happiness principle, the criterion of rightness has to be amended to promote the greatest happiness of the greatest number, excluding no one. Mill (1859/1939a) is quite aware of the "tyranny of the majority" (p. 951), but the point is more fundamental. The teacher ought to be equally concerned for the welfare and learning of each student, without exception. As Mill (1863/1939b) himself recognized, the greatest happiness principle "is a mere form of words without rational signification, unless one's person's happiness . . . is counted for exactly as much as another's" (p. 946). This seems to assume a respect for persons that both considers people as ends in themselves and recognizes the universal moral rules Kant was seeking.

Such is the logic of hedonism. It begins with an individual's pleasure as the only criterion of rightness, but then has to become social and qualitative to become adequate for actual moral life. It loses its primary thrust when martyrdom is justified by the happiness principle. It also has to become applicable to everyone, excluding the happiness of no one. It ends in rule-utilitarianism, wherein it becomes right to do what is conducive to the greatest happiness as it has become codified into specific rules that define rightness. Then everyone incurs the same obligations, just as in deontology. This progression is also found in the substantive criticism of hedonism. If one argues that an act may in fact be right if it promotes the happiness of the majority, providing it does no harm to anyone and takes into account the happiness of the minority, the desire to protect the minority shifts it all back into deontology and universal moral principles that apply to each person alike, regardless of whether they make the majority happier. This places elemental justice, fairness, and human rights ahead of happiness and abandons the nonmoral good as the criterion of the rightness of an act. It becomes more concerned with the right and the obligations to each person than with the good or interest of the majority.

Similarly, teachers who adopt the principle of utility to insure that the rules benefit the majority of students will most likely soon find out that they cannot simply ignore the quiet, shy student or the ones sitting in the back corners of the room and that the rules should benefit every student alike, that is, that some form of community under law should reign in the classroom.

Another similarity to Kant is that neither Bentham nor Mill indicates how the judgment of whether a particular act or rule promotes the happiness of the greatest number can be based on empirical data, although they are about states of affairs that exist in the world. This is why they have been examined as rationalistic exemplars of teleological ethics. The difference between higher and lower pleasures and the means for distinguishing among them in Mill come directly from Plato and his claim that the philosopher whose reason is highly developed is the only one who can distinguish the pleasures most compatible with human dignity. For knowing how to make teleological judgments of value based upon observation, we will have to turn to the theory of John Dewey.

PRAGMATISM AND EDUCATION

Dewey also accepts both psychological and ethical hedonism but in a more sophisticated way. The good is still pleasure, defined as immediate enjoyments, but he comes to grips with qualitative differences between enjoyments by distinguishing between the enjoyed and the enjoyable, the desired and the desirable, the satisfying and the satisfactory, the valued and the valuable, and so forth. He also claims that scientific method and knowledge can be brought to bear upon the judgment and realization of value (Dewey, 1929/1960, pp. 258–263). When an activity is hindered because of a noticeable lack in the situation, a desire emerges into consciousness, prompting one to go through the problem-solving route of finding out the relevant facts and modifying the desire to fit the goal that is formulated as one sees what is possible and desirable in the situation (Dewey, 1939, pp. 33–35; see also 1916, pp. 120–124, 279–280). Statements about the desirable are then warranted by the validity of the knowledge regarding its means of achievement (1939, p. 25).

Dewey's model is praxis in the arts, crafts, trades, and professions, particularly medicine and engineering, which are dependent upon "scientifically warranted physical generalizations" in the way that all judgments of desirable, satisfactory goals should be (1939, pp. 21–22, 52, 62; see also 1929/1960, p. 258). Because the good is enjoyment resulting from the satisfaction of desires,

> ends-in-view are appraised or valued as *good* or *bad* on the ground of their serviceability in the direction of behavior dealing with states of affairs found to be objectionable because of some lack or conflict in them. They are appraised as fit or unfit, proper or improper, *right* or *wrong*, on the grounds of their *requiredness* in accomplishing this end. (1939, p. 47)

Thus all knowledge of rightness is limited to the intellectual judgments made in the course of activities and pertains to the reciprocal adaptation of means and ends to each other in conjunction with the observed facts of the situation. One knows what is right, for Dewey, by judging if it helps achieve one's goal. One knows the goal is right if it is attainable, satisfies one's desire, and is compatible with other goals one may have.

When Dewey's inquiry process is applied to the value domain in education, it is socialized through student/teacher planning of the curriculum. The class as a whole, guided by the teacher, should decide collectively upon group projects to be undertaken. The desire of each student should be expressed and modified somewhat by the consultative process. This enables a conscious evaluation of one's own desires in the formation of a consensus on a desirable project. The process can promote the greatest happiness of the greatest number, excluding no one, if the teacher insures that the group project is sufficiently complex to enable all students to make contributions to it according to their own interests and abilities. In this process of learning to work together, the students are learning right and wrong by learning what is compatible with the group project. More important, perhaps, is that they learn how to evaluate their own desires and convert them into wanting the desirable, guided by the desires of other students and the means of fulfillment.

Although Dewey (1938) refers to the classroom as a social process in terms of his social interpretation of the political concept of democracy, several assumptions are made regarding the classroom application that are not involved in his political or ethical theory. His ethics have to do with the evaluation of one's own desires. In situations of moral choice, one can only compare the present objectives with the enabling conditions and one's own long-range goals. In the school process, however, the teacher is to insure that group projects are productive educationally in terms of cognitive learning. This aim is tactfully, gently, and graciously imposed upon the group planning process. Student/teacher planning, in other words, assumes the children's desires are already shaped so that they want to engage in cognitively productive projects. What they learn as the right are the actions needed to accomplish a group project that is educationally productive.

Ethics in the adult world do not work that way. Group projects among adults are rarely chosen by educative criteria. Nor does democracy work that way: There is always the uncooperative minority party. A vocal opposition is needed to maintain a healthy democracy, and so is the secret ballot. Both of these are absent from Dewey's (1938) application of democracy to the classroom (pp. 77–85). In other words, the claim that an act is right if it is conducive to cooperative, collective achievement of projects is simplistic and naïve. It begs the question of what makes a project worthwhile and why any given person should want to cooperate in a project the group decides to undertake. It is not undemocratic if some students do not want to cooperate, but it is to force them to against their will. Students might also want to do something that is not worthy of being desired. Without the intervention of an objective criterion of desirability, there is no assurance that any student's desires are superior to any other's.

Just as hedonism cannot say that one pleasure is better than another, although we know some are, neither can pragmatism say that the satisfaction of some desires is better than that of others. It holds that only a group of people in their collective wisdom can decide upon what is desirable—for themselves. This may promote the maximization of satisfaction, but it hardly shows what is satisfactory or that the criterion of the rightness of an action is conformity to group decisions. If a given group merely practices collective gluttony, Mill's claim can be amended to say that it is better to be a dissatisfied dissenter than an agreeable pig.

This criticism should not obscure the important truth in Dewey's view. It is very good to learn how to evaluate one's existing desires, or values, and to modify them in the light of the desires and values of other people. Dewey's is a good model for learning some aspects of moral conduct. It probably would develop the social sympathy claimed for it. It needs supplementing by criteria of desirability that can be learned independently of what any particular group of students decides is desirable. Even then, however, it is not a model that can be used everywhere in schools.

Dewey's view should also be supplemented by explicit claims that the student has the duty and obligation to join in the group project. His perspective forbids the use of the words *duty* and *obligation*, but it assumes that everyone in the class is morally obliged to participate in the group planning and group project. It also assumes it is one's duty to let one's desires be modified by them. It is therefore a deontology that is ashamed to state the moral obligations it strenuously advocates. Once explicated, it becomes apparent that their justification is far from obvious.

AN IMMANENT CRITIQUE OF TELEOLOGICAL ETHICS

It is an internal criticism to claim that the logic inherent in hedonism leads to the deontology of Mill's eudaemonism. Another immanent criticism results from G. E. Moore's (1903/1966) claim in *Principia Ethica* that defining the good as "the greatest happiness altogether" commits the *naturalistic fallacy*. Moore replaces the word *happiness* with the word *good* in this phrase because he believes the criterion of right action is to provide "the greatest possible amount of good in the Universe" (p. 147) or to do that "which will cause more good to exist in the Universe than any possible alternative" (p. 148). He is a utilitarian inasmuch as he claims actions should be useful in producing this nonmoral good and should be judged by their consequences (p. 106). He merely objects, correctly, to defining good in more determinant, naturalistic terms such as pleasure, happiness, and the desirable, for these natural properties are not the only good (pp. 58–62). Moore holds that good is a simple idea that refers to intrinsic value that cannot be defined by other terms, no more than *yellow* can be defined. Attempts to define it in naturalistic terms result in ethics that promote the corresponding natural properties instead of good as such. The field of ethics, however, is supposed to be concerned with things that ought to exist for their own sake, that is, for their inherent goodness (pp. viii, 3, 5).

Because he claims ethics are primarily concerned with things that are good in themselves, Moore (1903/1966) regards himself (and is generally so regarded) as an intuitionist. He claims statements about intrinsic value "are incapable of proof or disproof" (pp. x, 143–144). The philosopher who cites evidence for assertions made about what is good is confused (p. ix). After formulating what ought to be, one can consider questions of what ought to be done. Statements about right action, duty, and obligation therefore admit of proof and should be substantiated. Moore's reasoning is as amazing as it is overlooked. Referring to the third and last kind of ethical question (about what we ought to do), he says,

> It introduces into Ethics . . . an entirely new question—the question of what things are related as *causes* to that which is good in itself; and this question can only be answered by an entirely new method—the method of empirical investigation; by means of which causes are discovered in the other sciences. To ask what kinds of actions we ought to perform, or what kind of conduct is right, is to ask what kinds of effects such action and conduct will produce. Not a single question in practical Ethics can be answered except by a causal generalization. All such questions do, indeed, *also* involve an ethical judgment proper—the judgment that certain effects are better, in themselves, than others. . . .
>
> All moral laws, I wish to shew, are merely statements that certain kinds of actions will have good effects. . . . What I wish first to point out is that "right" does and can mean nothing but "cause a good result" and is thus identical with "useful." (pp. 146–147)

The striking thing about this passage is its blatant commission of the naturalistic fallacy by the person who coined the term and accused "almost all ethical writers" of committing it because they "failed to perceive that the notion of intrinsic value is simple and unique" (p. 173). Moore commits it, however, because he fails to perceive that the notion of *rightness* is simple and unique.

Moore (1903/1966) claims the naturalistic fallacy has been as frequently committed in regard to beauty as to good (p. 201). Although he does admit on one occasion that "the emotion excited by rightness as such has some intrinsic value" (p. 179), he does not claim such intrinsic value for right acts themselves. Their rightness is reduced to their natural function as a means for achieving good, that is, to their usefulness. The idea of rightness, however, is as unanalyzable as goodness (*cf.* Ross, 1930). To define rightness as a means of obtaining intrinsic value, as if right actions have no intrinsic value of their own, refers to some of the natural properties of obligations and duties and mistakes them for the moral obligations themselves, just as hedonism mistakes the goodness in pleasure for goodness itself. This is the naturalistic fallacy. Although right actions are followed by good effects, one commits the naturalistic fallacy by reducing them to nothing but their usefulness in producing these effects. Moore even says, "An ethical law has the nature not of a scientific law but of a scientific *prediction*" (p. 155).

This is notably similar to Dewey's (1929/1960) statement that "a moral law, like a law in physics . . . is a formula of the way to respond when specified conditions present themselves" (p. 278) and should always be tested by its consequences. Moore (1903/1966) is remarkably inconsistent when he subsequently accepts the moral rules of common sense regarding industriousness, temperance, and promise keeping, as well as most of the legal rules that are universally enforced (e.g., respect for property) (p. 157), when he claims that one can prove "a definite utility" in most of the moral rules recognized and practiced in society, and when he asserts it is "doubtful whether Ethics can establish the utility of any rules other than those generally practiced" (pp. 160–161). He claims, furthermore, that any rule that is generally useful should always be observed because the probability of its being useful in a particular case is greater than the probability of the correctness of one's judgment that it is not. This is less like Ross's prima facie duties and more like Kant's imperatives. Moore speaks categorically: "Though we may be sure that there are cases where the rule should be broken, we can never know which those cases are, and ought, therefore, never to break it" (pp. 162–163). Moore adds that breaking a rule, even when it should be done, sets a poor precedent for both the agent and others and, to avoid weakening loyalty to the rule, ought not be done. "The individual can therefore be confidently recommended *always* to conform to rules which are generally useful and generally practiced" (p. 164). Whereas for Dewey moral rules are tentative and should be tested by individuals observing their consequences, because they are like scientific hypotheses, for Moore they are not to be tested by individuals because they are like scientific predictions. How they acquired this epistemic status is not explained. We should not think, however, that following such rules is a duty: "We never have any reason to suppose that an action is our duty," because we can never know all of its effects and all the effects of all the alternatives (Moore, 1903/1966, p. 149).

At any rate, although Moore is an intuitionist in regard to knowing value, or good, he is an empiricist in regard to knowing what is right. He does not recommend observation or experience as the means for coming to know rightness, however, for we should simply observe the moral rules recognized and practiced in society and follow them confidently. They are more likely to promote the good than our own judgment. This may be true.

The application to education is for the teacher to design classroom rules to promote the good, using those inherent in the tradition of the school as a basis. These are to promote the realization of things that are intrinsically good, which does not mean that the knowledge in the curriculum has intrinsic value regardless of whether it is valued by students. It means that the processes of acquiring that knowledge should have intrinsic value. Learning it does not have to give pleasure, for Moore (1903/1966) correctly claims that "many complex states of mind are much more valuable than the pleasure they contain" (p. 108). There only has to be conscious appreciation of the intrinsic value of learning what is offered.

Moore (1903/1966) himself believes knowledge has little or no intrinsic value, although it contributes greatly to the value of the "highest goods," of which it is a constitutive element (p. 199). Acceptance of this claim requires that the whole curriculum be chosen for its usefulness for the realization of the "highest goods" in adult life. Then the rules of the hidden curriculum should be instrumental to securing these results. It should be noted, however, that Moore commits the naturalistic fallacy in epistemology, too, by denying that truth is a simple, unanalyzable aspect of knowledge that cannot be defined by its use. Truth is one of those things that has its own intrinsic value.

Moore has pushed teleological ethics to its limit. His error is therefore endemic to all teleological ethics. He is correct to point out the naturalistic fallacy in other versions, but he misidentifies their fallacy and therefore goes on to commit the naturalistic fallacy in his own so-called practical ethics and epistemology. By claiming that the "fundamental question of Ethics" is about goods or ends in themselves (1903/1966, p. 184), Moore continues to commit their most fundamental error, the *axiological fallacy*. He conflates moral good with good, ethics with value theory (i.e., axiology), and then formulates value theory under the impression that he is concerned with ethics. He therefore wrongly concludes it is always our duty to produce the "greatest possible balance of intrinsic value" (p. 222), which he elsewhere denies is possible (see p. 149). To the contrary, it is always our duty to do whatever is morally right, which may or may not achieve the greatest good altogether. For example, it may be right, as Ross claims, to break a promise or conceal the truth, but this is not to achieve the greatest balance of intrinsic value. It is to fulfill a greater duty. It is right to realize the value intrinsic to promise keeping and truth telling, which are moral goods that are qualitatively superior to the nonmoral intrinsic value that may be realized by violating these duties.

To extend the concept of duty to the realization of nonmoral good as teleological ethics does dilutes the distinct sense of moral obligation and causes the moral domain itself to disappear. When Bentham, Mill, and Dewey claim that the only things that have intrinsic value are pleasure, happiness, and satisfactions, respectively, their error is not naturalism. Their error is to create a theory of value instead of ethics. This commission of the axiological fallacy defines away the problems of ethics and morality. It can only occur where there is a previous loss of moral sensibility and therefore embodies moral nihilism. This loss is exemplified in the concluding chapter of *Principia Ethica* when Moore (1903/1966) says, "By far the most valuable things, which we can know or can imagine, are certain states of consciousness, which may be roughly described as the pleasures of human intercourse and the enjoyment of beautiful objects" (p. 188). Whether this narcissistic, hedonistic statement lowers the value of interhuman relations to the esthetic level or raises esthetic experience to the level of the interhuman, it clearly loses the moral domain. The thirteen following pages examine esthetic appreciation as a model for his subsequent two and a half page discussion of the appreciation inherent in personal affection, focused largely on physical and mental qualities.

Moore's "ethics" reduce the ethical to the esthetic. So do the ethics of Bentham, Mill, and Dewey. The tremendous contribution to human welfare of the theory of value masquerading as teleological ethics, however, cannot be gainsaid and should not be overlooked or underestimated. Before this point can be explicated, however, we should glance at a teleological ethic wherein the good to be achieved is allegedly known by revelation.

JESUS AND SELF-REALIZATION

The teleological ethics of self-realization will be extracted from Matthew's account of the sayings of Jesus, which we will regard as recorded natural events that subsequent congregations have memorialized as divine utterances. The most notable saying occurs when a lawyer asks for the greatest commandment and Jesus says, first, to love God and, second, "You should love your neighbor as yourself" (22:39). This is not original with Jesus, for it occurs in the Torah. In Leviticus it is followed by the words, "I am the Lord" (19:28), whereas Jesus follows it with the claim, "On these two commandments depend all the law and the prophets." Just as Moses formulates the Ten Commandments as part of the ethical code supporting the statutory laws partly adapted from the Code of Hammurabi, so, too, does Jesus formulate the moral principle supporting the moral rules adapted from Moses.

Although the principle of brotherly and sisterly love makes the commandments unnecessary, Jesus does not reject the teachings of Moses. He answers the rich young man's questions about which commandments to follow by citing the injunctions against murder, adultery, stealing, and false witness and the obligations to honor one's parents and to love one's neighbor as oneself (19:18–19). The rich young man had asked about how he could have eternal life, a nonmoral goal, and Jesus replies, "If you would enter life . . ." and lists these commandments as the means to this goal, that is, teleologically. When the young man declares he already observes them and wants to know what he still lacks, Jesus says that if he wants to be perfect, he should sell all he has and give the money to the poor. This apparently explains what it means for a rich person to love one's neighbor as oneself. It not only enables self-perfection but allows one to "enter life." The ethics of Jesus are epitomized in the paradox of losing one's life if one tries to save it, as the rich young man was trying, and of finding one's life by "losing" it (10:39, 16:25).

The other mention of the commandments explains this paradox. After saying he wants to fulfill the law and the prophets, rather than abolish them, Jesus admonishes those who violate the smallest commandment or teach others to do so, and he praises those who keep and teach them (5:17–20). Then he refines them in an apparent effort to forestall self-righteous legalism. To not killing anyone, he says one should not be angry at all with one's brother, nor insult him. To avoidance of adultery, he says that to look at a woman lustfully already engages in adultery with her in one's heart, and that one should neither get divorced nor marry a divorced person. To not swearing false witness, he says one should not declare any oaths at all, as if one's word does not otherwise suffice. To the maxim about an eye for an eye, he says one should not resist an evil person but turn the other cheek, give one's cloak, too, when asked for a coat, and give freely to borrowers and beggars. To the saying about loving one's neighbor and hating one's enemies, Jesus says one should love one's enemies and pray for one's persecutors, "so that you may be sons of your Father who is in heaven" (5:21–45). According to the textual Jesus, in other words, rightness in conduct should follow moral rules, but it should be the result of the brotherly and sisterly love that enables one to transcend aggressive self-seeking in a general concern for the welfare of others. It is teleological because the goal is self-realization: "You, therefore, must be perfect, as your heavenly Father is perfect" (5:48).

In neither account does Jesus mention the first four commandments concerning one's relation to deity. This may be related to his reference to the God of Abraham, Isaac, and Jacob (22:32), rather than to the God of Moses, to his attack on the Pharisees, or to the reasons he left the synagogue to teach the people in the fields. At any rate, the textual Jesus abandons the liturgical and ecclesiastical prescriptions of the Torah and might have organized the first reformed church of Judaism had he been concerned with starting a church (Dr. Ruth H. T. Legow, personal communication, December 1982). He is concerned with the inner development of the person that enables a life of non-aggression and concern for others.

We should defer to the existing efforts made in church-related schools by congregations that regard the teachings of Jesus as revealed truth for the educational applications of this ethic of self-realization through self-sacrifice. Our concern here is to include some attention to putative revelation as an alleged source of knowing the right and the good within the framework of teleological ethics. Suffice it to say that the so-called feminist ethic of caring seems to have its origins in the teachings of Jesus and Moses in the statement in Leviticus to love one's neighbor. This is obvious in Nel Noddings's (1984) claims about "the very heart of morality: the sensibility that calls forth caring" (p. 47).

THE HIDDEN CURRICULUM

Three classroom applications of teleological ethics have been made. In a laissez-faire classroom where there is much pleasure because the pupils are doing what they want, the teacher's role is limited to creating choices that will be fun. The students are learning that it is right to do whatever gives them pleasure. They are also learning by experience to choose and plan things to insure their pleasantness. If the teacher thinks that what they learn matters, the choice of individuals can be overruled in favor of the enjoyment of the majority. If the pupil should also learn that very enjoyable results can sometimes require hard work at tasks set by the teacher, this requires the kind of experiences not available in a classroom established on a hedonistic model. The utilitarian principle of self-interest is involved when it is said it is in the students' interest to learn something, such as reading or writing, even if they do not want to at the moment. Similarly, after students choose a vocation or to attend tertiary school, it is in their interest to learn the things necessary to achieve their goals. Doing so should lead to happiness. Teachers, curriculum specialists, and administrators should protect the interest of these students by establishing not only the curriculum but also the rules of behavior necessary to make it effective. Individuals who keep others from learning by violating these rules are subject to restraint. When the teacher enforces these rules to promote the maximum amount of learning for the whole class, the students learn that it is right to do what is in their own best interest and to promote their own long-range happiness. In the application of the pragmatic ethic, pupils should make up the rules themselves, under teacher guidance, as needed to carry out a class project and achieve a collective goal. The rules should be instrumental to that goal, rather than to promoting the welfare of the class. The teacher is justified, however, in stopping to ask if progress toward the common goal can be facilitated by the adoption of some rules of conduct. The students learn what is right by learning to achieve desired goals in a satisfactory manner.

In each of these situations there can be classroom and school rules to define what is right and wrong and to insure that behavior in accordance with the rules is instrumental to achieving something else (pleasure, happiness, or the class project), like the rules on a paint can. In none of them are the rules supposed to have intrinsic value because they define a unique situation that requires its own form as an educational situation. These models involve the consideration of the classroom as something other than a classroom. The school, however, is a social institution. So is the classroom, with its own rules related to its own reason for being the institution of learning. These three models are extremely valuable for their reformative power, but an adequate view considers the classroom as a community of scholars that is structured by the societal roles that have developed with the institution of learning. Of course classrooms should be filled with pleasure, happiness, and satisfactions, but this is not their reason for being. These are not their goals, but by-products of humane, well-conducted classrooms. In the classroom, the good is learning. The rules designed to maximize learning should define the obligations and duties governing the classroom.

There are only two views of how classroom rules can function, teleologically and deontologically. Either they are instrumental to other things, such as pleasure, happiness, and satisfactions, or they define a way of life of intrinsic worth. This is not a psychological concern about the most adequate explanation or manipulation of human conduct. It involves an ethical question about how the young should learn, about what they should learn, and about alternative outcomes. When the rules are justified teleologically, the young learn they are to be followed to obtain certain outcomes. When they function to structure a unique form of activity, the young learn, first, that the rules have intrinsic rightness and are worth following because they define right and wrong conduct as such and, second, that they should focus their attention on the internal content of the form of life they establish, that is, upon learning itself, rather than on some noncognitive outcome. The issue is not how children and youth ought to learn how to make judgments of value in order to guide their conduct with others; it is whether they should learn to make value judgments or moral judgments to guide their conduct.

The result of implementing teleological ethics in education is to insure that students will learn to make value judgments but not moral judgments. Although it is assumed they are learning the latter, the effect is to neglect their moral education. This seems to be a moral negligence and a consequence of moral nihilism. Because much educational literature also psychologizes and sociologizes moral education away, it is worthwhile emphasizing the importance of learning the language of morality in connection with actual moral conduct. We may very well agree that pleasure, happiness, the welfare of the majority, and self-realization are good, but none of these is the equivalent of the morally good.

We can claim that classroom learning ought to provide pleasure and happiness, and promote the student's own interest, without also claiming that learning is good when and only when it is accompanied by these things. This allows us to claim also that learning is good, in and of itself, or intrinsically; and that the good to be promoted in the classroom is the greatest amount of learning by the greatest number of pupils, excluding no one. This avoids the naturalistic fallacy because it does not define the good as learning. It claims that learning is good, too. It ought not be promoted simply as a means to other goods such as pleasure, happiness, or self-realization. If it is seen as having value in its own right, then whatever promotes learning in the classroom is good. The teacher, moreover, is always right to uphold the autonomy of learning. The consequent pedagogical considerations will be investigated in Chapter 5.

CONCLUSION

If there is a moral crisis in Western civilization, it is not because we lack knowledge of the good. We know that pleasure and happiness are good. We know that it is always good to promote the happiness of the greatest number. We do not know that it is the only good, or that promoting it is always right, but we do know it is always good to promote the greatest happiness of the greatest number when it does not occur at the expense of the minority (i.e., when it excludes no one) and when it is compatible with human dignity. It is not always right to promote the greatest happiness of the greatest number, however, regardless of how qualified it may be, because beneficence is at best a conditional duty (Ross). It is an imperfect duty (Kant) that should be foregone when it is in conflict with an actual, greater, or unconditional duty. It would be morally wrong to break a promise to return some borrowed money in order to give it to the poor, even if it did promote the greatest happiness altogether. If it is said that it is always right to give to charity providing circumstances allow it, the qualification manifests the obligation's contingency. It may be wrong to do so even when it is good.

The utilitarianism of Bentham, the Benthamites, and Mill, however, was intended to secure legislation that would promote the social welfare. It is a social and political philosophy, rather than a personal ethic. Focusing too much on the outer horizons of consciousness because of the concern for social reform lets the center drop out, and the ethic disappears. The social concern is quite appropriate, but not at the expense of forgetting the near horizons of personal life and the ethical aspects of one's own existence. To ascertain one's duties, one needs to consider the welfare of others, of course. It is also morally correct to consider their legitimate moral claims upon one when deliberating on one's own obligations. To consider their moral claims, however, is very different from considering their welfare. To listen to their claims upon one is to consider them as persons, as ends in themselves; whereas to calculate the way one's actions affects their happiness and welfare involves a technological, rather than a moral, consciousness. This is why John Caputo can say, "In teleological schemes, people are used to meet ends. Teleological communities are inevitably hierarchical communities" (1987, p. 254). The social welfare program, however, is good. So is the moral community.

We might even wonder if we can have one without the other. Such wonder raises hosts of questions. Is something good because it feels good, or does it yield pleasure because it is good? Is something good because it promotes happiness, or does it promote happiness because it is good? Are pleasure and happiness of intrinsic value, or do they occur when one is realizing intrinsic value? Is it right to do something because its consequences are good, or are the effects good because it is right? Is it right to do things of intrinsic value, or is there also intrinsic value in doing the right thing? Are things right to do because they yield pleasure and happiness, or do they yield these because of their inherent rightness?

These questions, however, seem to accept the opposition between morality and value that occurs in the ideological polemics between deontological and teleological ethics. The issue is not a conflict between morality and value or a conflict between theory of morality (or ethics) and theory of value (or axiology). The issue concerns the relation between the right and the good, or between rightness as such and goodness as such. The relation between rightness and goodness will be the focus of the next chapter's attempt to synthesize the concerns of deontological and teleological ethics.

CHAPTER 4

Value, Ethics, and Education

The synthesis of value and morality will begin with the fact that a choice between qualitatively different pleasures depends upon a criterion other than pleasure. This criterion, not pleasure itself, becomes the criterion of right action. When Mill says it is a sense of dignity, he refutes his psychological and ethical hedonism. He also assumes the sense of dignity is veridical and reliable: We can know right from wrong, and morality itself, by its compatibility with human dignity. This is very basic, and very correct, and very close to Kant's (1797/ 1964) claim that one is obligated to acknowledge the dignity of the humanity in oneself and others by maintaining love and respect for oneself and others (pp. 132, 163). For example, Kant holds that telling a lie destroys one's humanity as a person: "By a lie a man makes himself contemptible—by an outer lie, in the eyes of others, by an inner lie, in his own eyes, which is still worse—and violates the dignity of humanity in his own person" (p. 92f.). The duties to oneself in Kant's theory are often overlooked, but they obligate one to maintain an awareness of one's dignity as a moral being with the correlative self-esteem: "*Self-esteem* is a duty of man to himself" (p. 100). Mill's sense of dignity also involves this awareness of one's own dignity. It is self-esteem and self-respect that oblige one to choose the qualitatively superior pleasures, not because they are superior but because they are more in accord with human dignity.

In both Mill and Kant the sense of dignity is an immediate apprehension of what is and what is not compatible with human dignity. Any interpretation of human dignity, however, is historically relative. Granting Mill's general point does not require an acceptance of his view of higher faculties, for today it seems contrary to human dignity if such a view entails the denigration of people with lower intellectual capacities. Similarly, granting Kant's general point does not require an acceptance of his kind of rationalism. As Gabriel Marcel (1963/1972) claims, it is a legacy of the Kantian correlation with rationality to use the word *dignity* in the decorative sense to refer to the solemnity used on formal occasions that are not without sham and pretense. Today claims about human dignity are made to call attention to the intrinsic value of children, paupers, and old people, who lack dignity in the rationalistic or ostentatious sense (pp. 308–309). The deontology appropriate to human dignity should accordingly be articulated in the presently available language of human rights.

The criticisms of teleological ethics, however, should not obscure the fundamental truth that if one does the right thing it should ordinarily feel good in some sense or another, although Moore (1903/1966) is undoubtedly correct to claim that "self-sacrifice may be a real duty" (p. 170). Performing a duty or fulfilling an obligation should be intrinsically good in the sense of yielding positive feelings of self-respect, self-esteem, contentment, peace of mind, a good conscience, or something else that adds to one's sense of one's own dignity. The result should not only feel good, it should be good. The deontologist seems to be right to claim that at the moment of action the person should act out of duty or in accordance with a rule, without selfish, ulterior motives, but, nevertheless, the objective of morality is to realize value, or good, albeit of a moral kind.

A conceptualization of the phenomenon of human dignity adequate for ethical and educational theory needs to ground a human rights ethic in the characteristics that make human beings worthy of respect. This, according to Herbert Spiegelberg (1970), requires a theory of the essence of the human being, including reference to its constituent elements; its structure; its place in the cosmos; and its values, rights, and responsibilities (pp. 58–61).

VALUES IN THE COSMOS

The approach here will be to consider self-evident axiological and deontological propositions in groups of three. The axioms are synthetic a priori claims in the sense stated by William Blackstone (1970): Human rights propositions "are synthetic in that they hold of all human beings; they are a priori in the sense they are not contingent features of humans but necessary ones" (p. 13). As Moore (1903/1966) suggested, statements about the kinds of things that ought to exist for their own sake do not admit of proof or disproof and all are "synthetic and never analytic" (pp. viii, 7). The statements of values and duties will be very closely related to each other to form something of a syllogism in which the deontological statements follow from the axiological ones.

The first triad is as follows:

1. a. *Existing things have qualities.*
   b. *One ought to value the qualities of things.*
   c. *One ought to care for and preserve existing things.*

Beginning with 1a, things encountered in the natural, social, and cultural worlds on the common-sense level of ordinary experience have qualities that can become known through perceptual consciousness of them. In the natural world these are the qualitative sense data of colors, flavors, sounds, odors, textures, degrees of hardness, and so on. One should value the qualities of things simply because appreciating their value is part of becoming aware of their qualitativeness as such. One cannot become aware of a quality as a quality without responding affectively to its appearance in the world.

This basic truth of hedonism can be shown by returning to the verse from the *Rubaiyat*. A book of verses can contain noble sentiments that elevate one's spirit and contribute to the meaningfulness of one's life; wine has qualities such as sweetness, tang, and bouquet; bread can be even-textured and nutty; and Thou art humorous, joyful, intelligent, affectionate, and comely. Hedonism claims the verses, wine, bread, and Thou are good because they yield pleasure, but this narcissistic interpretation focuses upon the subjective feelings caused by the objective qualities. In the experience itself the qualities of the objects are found to be good. They give pleasure when their intrinsic value is experienced.

The point is similar to Moore's (1903/1966) claim that good is a simple, unanalyzable property of things (pp. 9–10). If, for example, one is eating a fresh pineapple and finds it to be the most delicious one that one can remember eating, one might exclaim, "This is good!" or, "This is delicious!" Goodness, or delightfulness of taste, is ascribed to the pineapple itself because its goodness is experienced out there in the pineapple and because it is the pineapple that is good. The exquisite pleasure does not seem to be merely a subjective experience devoid of contact with reality. It is something about the pineapple itself to which one refers when one says it is good. One refers to its intrinsic goodness, which, according to Moore, is not reducible to its sensible qualities. One gets pleasure because the pineapple is good, and one knows it is good because of the immediate apprehension of its qualities when one bites into it. Where Moore errs is in overlooking the fact that the attribution of goodness is a result of a perceptual evaluation and passive synthesis of the perceived sensible qualities. It is the sweetness, texture, juiciness, coldness, ripeness, and flavor of the pineapple that are said to be good when they please one. These qualities are individually good. In combination they constitute the goodness of the pineapple. Moore is wrong because goodness is not an additional, simple, nonnaturalistic property. Because a lack of sweetness or poor texture or flavor may be the qualities of a poor pineapple, for example, the word *quality* does not itself involve a value judgment when ascribed to things in general. Things said to be of poor qualities still have qualities. They still have some color, shape, odor, taste, texture, and so on, of which one can become perceptually aware. Because of the primacy of perception, moreover, one becomes aware of things first of all through their qualities.

The second sentence of the triad (1b) might seem tautological. If one ought to value the qualities of things and their qualities are their values, it means one ought to value the values of things. This means, however, that one ought to respond positively and affectively to the qualities of things even if at first one fails to appreciate them. One need not have a favorite color, for example, so that other colors look drab. Because it is a much richer perceptual awareness of things that finds all colors valuable, one ought to value all the chromatic values. The same holds true for the other avenues of perceptual awareness of things. If all things have qualities, then one ought to be able to value their qualities when one becomes aware of them. It is part of knowing them, appreciating their existence, and living in harmony with existing things. One ought to know them, furthermore, to avoid autistic self-enclosedness. Because the experience of the value of something is pleasurable, it generates an obligation to conserve things when not consuming them. Why? Simply because they have qualities and are therefore valuable. Anything valuable ought to be prolonged in its being, simply because it has value.

Before going on to 1c, however, it should be noted that 1b corrects the narcissism of hedonism, in which it is forgotten that one's own values are dependent upon the qualities of things. To say "I like pears" calls attention to one's own pleasure in eating pears, but it implies something about pears, too. It is elliptical, in effect declaring, "I find in my own experience that the qualities of pears, such as their juiciness, bland flavor, and soft texture, delight me. They give me pleasure because I find them to be delicious." The qualities are not located in consciousness but in things. As Sandra Rosenthal (1988) says, "Qualities are neither atomic building-block data, nor mental contents, but ontological emergents 'there' within nature" (p. 313). Because one's conscious life becomes richer as one comes to value more things, one ought to value more things for the sake of personal development, which one ought to promote out of respect for the humanity in oneself. One should, of course, also develop a hierarchy of values that keeps the disgusting, ugly, evil, painful, and obscene in their places, but neither the negative nor positive qualities of things can be properly valued without a view of the universe based upon a perceptual awareness of the value of most (an indefinitely large number of) things.

From the first two sentences about value and goodness there follows the third (1c), the obligation to care for and preserve existing things. Someone who values existing things because of their qualities will want to preserve and enhance their existence and will in fact sense the rightness in doing so. It is therefore a prima facie duty to preserve existing things. One might object that obligations cannot be derived from what is in this way. David Hume (1739/1965) called attention to the problem, however, after the modern dissociation of sensibility that occurred with the rise of modern science and the development of the distinction between primary and secondary qualities. After objects in the world were denuded of their so-called secondary properties (i.e., their qualities) because these were erroneously claimed to be subjective, the sciences came to investigate factual states of affairs. Thus Hume's complaint refers to the situation after one accepts the fact/value distinction, when value prescriptions cannot be derived from indicative statements of fact (p. 469). This is true, but the syllogism does not presuppose or accept the fact/value distinction. It is based on a view of the relation of human beings to the cosmos that precedes its adoption. The first sentence claims that existing things in the everyday world have qualities, which is a kind of factual claim about their inherent, nonquantitative values. It parallels factual claims about their quantitative values that can be made after accepting the fact/value distinction, but it involves a different kind of logic, as its explication tries to show. It leads to the conclusion that anyone who becomes aware of the qualities of things will value them, want to care for and preserve them, and will perceive the rightness in doing so. The prima facie duty to care for and preserve things, unless consuming them out of the greater duty to preserve oneself as one of these valuable things, is a respecification of the general duties of nonmaleficence and beneficence applied to the things of the natural world and is equally self-evident (*cf.* Taylor, 1986, pp. 172–173, 197).

HUMAN DIGNITY

Whether the duties of nonmaleficence and beneficence to things in the nonhuman world involve distinctly moral obligations can be considered more adequately after the syllogism is adapted to the class of things called "human beings":

> 2. a. *Each human being has its own value and dignity.*
> b. *One ought to value the unique qualities of human beings.*
> c. *One ought to respect and enhance the dignity of human beings.*

These are the same propositions as before, except the word *things* has been replaced by *human beings* and the general ontological claims are specified on the anthropological level. This requires replacing the word *quality* in 2a by *its own value and dignity* because the distinctly human qualities are the characteristics of inwardness that constitute one as a person. These include one's awareness of one's own feelings, ideas, sentiments, motives, and aspirations as well as the self-conscious dimensions of one's awareness of things in the world. Because these are not visible to external observation, one has to engage in dialogue and cooperative and competitive action, or praxis, with others to be able to encounter their unique qualities. The qualities of the human being's inward sentience, in other words, are manifested outwardly in the person's presence to other people. One's presence appears inwardly as one's own and outwardly as the present manifestation of a life history, or biography, that has its own integrity, its own dignity, and its own value.

The transposition of the obligation to value things to human beings therefore entails the change to valuing the unique qualities of human beings as stated in 2b. To become aware of a particular human being, one has to become aware of the specific qualities manifested in that individual's presence, which results in valuing her as the person she is. It may also involve an awareness of qualities shared with other human beings, but encountering others as the individual people they are requires an awareness of their unique qualities and valuing who they are simply for being who they are.

Someone who becomes aware of the unique dignity of other people wants them to persevere in their being and feels obligated to respect them as individuals and enhance them in their uniqueness. Because each person has his own dignity and value, the duty to respect and enhance their being who they are extends to all (an indefinitely large number of) human beings. Because it is not possible for anyone to enhance the dignity of all human beings, however, this can only be a conditional duty. One ought to respect and enhance the dignity of the people one meets and of unknown others through supporting social legislation, charitable organizations, and so on.

If one ought to respect and enhance the unique value and dignity of all human beings, including one's own, then whatever maintains and enhances human dignity is right. It is always right to maintain and enhance human dignity. Whatever is right by this standard, moreover, will achieve the goals desired by teleological ethics, whether defined as the greatest happiness altogether or as the greatest good possible. These goals are not what makes the action right, however, for the rightness of human conduct inheres in its compatibility with human dignity.

The duty to respect and enhance the dignity of all human beings is similar to Kant's categorical imperative to treat people as ends in themselves, but it is articulated and justified in the phenomenal world of perceptual consciousness. This context makes the "duty" enjoyable and self-enhancing. There is pleasure in valuing the qualities of another human being when becoming aware of them, just as there is pleasure in valuing the qualities of nonhuman objects like pineapples. Moore is correct about the supreme value of the pleasures of affectionate human intercourse, except he gives insufficient notice to the specific values to be realized within dialogue and the way in which these goods are related to the intrinsic rightness of the fundamental obligation to maintain and enhance human dignity (but see 1903/1966, pp. 203–205).

A related point concerns what it means to value people. People who like such things as pineapples might say they are fond of them. Children often say they love some particular food, like chocolate ice cream. These words indicate an affective relation to things that are valued. They are as applicable to human beings as to nonhuman things. To experience another's qualities is endearing. To value another's unique qualities is to like or love him or her. To respect and enhance the dignity of other human beings because one values them, in other words, is to be motivated by positive affectivity, or affection, for them. The upshot of statement 1b is to like all things, or to love the world. The upshot of statement 2b is to like everybody one meets. The upshot of these first two syllogisms is that it is one's duty to love the world and all the things in it, including the people. Whether one refers to this positive affectivity as liking, loving, feeling fond of, or simply valuing, it makes the duties of sentences 1c and 2c a pleasure. One can receive as much pleasure from keeping a promise as from a jug of wine, from speaking the truth to a Thou as in reading verses together, from volunteer work in a hospital as running off into the wilderness with a lover. These are qualitatively different kinds of pleasure. There is no reason why one cannot receive as much pleasure from fulfilling obligations and doing one's duties as from satisfying physical appetites. There is no reason why one cannot generally do both.

This brings hedonism and deontology together. Deontological ethics, or simply morality, does not have to be puritanical, antilife, or burdensome. Someone who is really at home in the universe and who values the qualities of existing things, including the dignity of other human beings, would want to do the right thing simply because it is right and simply for the pleasure in it. Although some deontologists like Kant think that morality is usually in conflict with natural inclinations, which makes doing one's duty a rather austere matter, this may be less a matter of human nature than a sign of an inadequate education. We should ask about how people can be educated to be so much at home in the universe that they enjoy doing their duty and fulfilling their obligations. This is a question of the relation of human beings to the universe, a question of ontology and axiology, as outlined in the first syllogism, and perhaps only secondarily a question of morality and moral education in a restricted sense that would separate the latter from a more general value education. People who love the world take their moral duties lightly, with joy and good cheer, in spite of the fact that they characteristically require some sacrifice from the viewpoint of teleological ethics.

MORAL AGENCY

The pleasure in valuing the unique qualities of people and enhancing their projects of being will be considered within the broadened definition of human dignity enabled by a third triad:

3. a. *The essence of human dignity is moral agency.*
    b. *One ought to respect and enhance the moral agency in all human beings.*
    c. *Moral agency is therefore a human right.*

The logic here may appear to be more Aristotelian, but it is the same as before. It might not be obvious, because sentence 3a is partly a factual claim and 3c is shorthand for saying that everyone is obligated to treat everyone else as a moral agent and everyone can rightfully claim they should be considered as one by everyone else because it is a necessary condition of being treated with human dignity.

A definition of human dignity should be broad enough to include everyone because each human being has its own value and dignity. Kant's claim that dignity lies in one's humanity is a beginning, except *humanity* has to be defined. His idea of rational autonomy is inadequate. H. J. McClosky (1981) inadvertently shows this when he refers to "what is possibly the most important human right: the right to moral autonomy." He adds, "Being morally autonomous is bound up with being fully a person" and then denies personhood—and rights—to infants born without potentiality to develop into persons, brain-damaged people in permanent comas, terminally ill people in great pain, "the insane," and "imbeciles" (pp. 87, 88–89). To the contrary unless a malformed infant is born dying, the question of its potential personhood depends solely on how one defines *person*, and the obligation to terminally ill people suffering great pain is to relieve their pain. Nor is the personhood of people with mental disability or illness in question, for even if they are totally incapacitated but smile or grunt before or after being bathed or fed, for example, they manifest a minimal trace of human dignity and moral agency. Their presence shows in the smallest recognition of help, expression of gratitude, or response to their name. Leonard Nelson (1932/1956) is correct to claim that any human being capable of experiencing pleasure and pain is a person, has dignity, and is a subject of rights (p. 100).

The word *person* is merely the singular form of the word *people*. People with mental disability or illness who require permanent guardianship but are responsible for bathing, dressing, and feeding themselves can be said to live with more dignity than those who are not. They possess a dignity of their own that is not available to the totally incapacitated. They have their own value and dignity that is somehow correlated with the degree to which they exercise moral agency. Moral autonomy admits of no degrees, for it applies only to people capable of self-government, whom McClosky, after Kant, stipulates to be persons. According to Jean Nabert (1943/1969), furthermore, it is defensive, closed, and impoverishing to define oneself by one's rational autonomy because the ethic is nondialogical (p. 148). On the other hand, moral agency is well nigh universal because it is a matter of degree. The small child who can be responsible for getting dressed is to that extent a moral agent. Moral agency can be ascribed to everyone who exhibits any degree of awareness of their conduct and its effect on others. It is also universal in the sense that it is a necessary condition of any moral code in any society. Any moral code presupposes that people can and should be morally aware of and responsible for their conduct.

The claim that moral agency is the essence of human dignity means that human beings are different from other animals because they are moral animals. *Homo sapiens* is that species of *homo* whose members are wise. Wisdom is the capacity for exercising sound judgment and doing the right thing. If what is distinctly human about human beings is that they are moral beings, then one has to develop one's moral agency in order to have any dignity as a human being. Abraham Edel (1969) exemplifies this when he claims that the minimal concept of human dignity is that everyone while still alive "remains a potential source of good and evil—no man is to be 'written off'" (p. 236). In his derivation of human rights as the necessary conditions of action, Alan Gewirth (1984) presupposes a human right to engage in action without justifying it. He ascribes much more importance to human dignity and moral agency than he realizes, for he says, "Agency is both the metaphysical and the moral basis of human dignity" (p. 24). He claims that everyone must affirm the need for human rights "as a person who has dignity or worth by virtue of his agency" (p. 23). He concludes, "Since all humans are actual, prospective or potential agents, the rights in question belong equally to all humans" (p. 18).

The claim that even people with mental disability or illness have their own value and dignity is based on sympathy, for it makes the disclosure of their unique qualities possible and is essential to its truth (Seguin, 1965, p. 55). Sympathy discloses features of what Spiegelberg (1970) calls "the kind of dignity which calls for respect even in cases where there is little, if anything, to admire in a person, e.g., a psychotic patient" (p. 48). The qualities that let one's humanity appear show in one's facial expressions, gestures, words, and actions; in objects created, worn, or owned; and so on. These are given in experience as the outward manifestations of a personally significant interior life. They let us know someone is there. Even when the qualities gathered together in someone's presence are minimal, his or her presence is worthy of respect, if not admiration, because the humanity appearing in that presence is *someone's* humanity.

Human dignity, then, is the appearance of humanity in the specific bodily opening to the world that is recognizable as someone's presence. The paradigm is a wide-awake, speaking presence, but it is nonetheless true for a sleeping or comatose person, who is also given as being someone. The body in the morgue is said to be someone's body, and people go there to identify who it is. It is not said to be a cadaver until it is beyond recognition and identification. Thus the human presence is always someone's presence. The word *humanity* is an abstraction. It is always someone's humanity, given as an individual person with a personal identity and a proper name, inseparably from human agency. Because there is much more to someone's humanity than moral agency, it is not reducible to it, but it can be said that moral agency is the essential characteristic of human dignity.

The previous conclusion to respect and enhance the dignity of all human beings (2c) should therefore be transposed into the imperative to respect and enhance the moral agency of all human beings (3b). This imperative lies implicit in the claim that each person has his own value and dignity. This can be shown in the cases that might be cited as counterexamples. No person who suffers mental disability or illness, and no criminal, should be physically or psychologically abused or terrorized, not even to obtain necessary, conforming behavior. In each case it is a cruelty inflicted upon someone and thus contrary to human dignity. Because the dignity of such persons ought to be respected and enhanced through the use of humane methods of learning morally correct conduct whenever conformity is necessary, they do not count against the universality of the obligation to respect and enhance moral agency. The claim that moral agency is the essence of human dignity and a human right is therefore a terse way of saying that everyone can rightfully claim they ought to be treated as a moral agent by everyone else because it is a necessary condition for becoming an adult human being and living a life of human dignity, and, conversely, that everyone is obligated to treat everyone else as a responsible moral agent.

Just as one ought to value the qualities of things, so, too, ought one to value the moral qualities of human beings. Because it is one's character that defines the contours of the opening to the world expressed in one's unique presence (Ricoeur, 1960/1965, p. 89), moral agency is the main qualitative distinctiveness of the human being. The obligation to value and enhance each other's presence to the world therefore makes moral agency the most fundamental human right. To say moral agency is a human right expresses the universal entitlement to enter into the moral community with other moral beings. The entitlement is to enter into community with other people, or simply to be with other people.

MORAL FREEDOM

Because a human right is a universal obligation, it is always right to treat another person as a moral agent, that is, with the dignity appro-

priate to a fellow human being. The inherent rightness of this obligation coincides with the intrinsic goodness of such moral respect. It is
concretized through the specific human rights that are among the
necessary conditions of moral agency, beginning with this triad:

4. a. *Moral agents attend to right and wrong and are responsible for their
        conduct.*
    b. *Moral responsibility requires freedom of thought, speech, and action.*
    c. *Moral freedom is therefore a human right.*

Because the exercise of moral agency requires one to consider things in
terms of right and wrong, to act upon one's judgment, and to be
answerable for the consequences, it requires personal responsibility.
Unless one holds oneself responsible for one's actions, and subject to
moral, social, and legal sanctions, one can make no claim to moral
agency. To be allowed responsibility for one's actions is therefore necessary to being treated as a moral agent and accorded the dignity
appropriate to a human being.

Acceptance of moral responsibility in turn requires the ability to
contemplate and investigate alternative courses of action, to talk with
others about them, and to act freely upon the results of one's delibera-
tions. Because freedom of thought, speech, and action is necessary for
responsible conduct, which is necessary for moral agency, which is
necessary for human dignity, which is necessary to be a human being as
such, moral freedom is a human right. Not all kinds of freedom are
required to be a moral agent. Freedom of thought, speech, and action
does not require freedom defined as the absence of restraint. Freedom
of speech is bound by the prima facie obligation to tell the truth;
freedom of action, by the duty of nonmaleficence; and so forth. Freedom as a human right is freedom in the moral sense. Moral freedom,
however, does require the traditional civil and political liberties such as
freedom of assembly, the press, religion, and participation in political
affairs through suffrage, accessibility of public office, nonviolent demonstration of dissent, and so on. These civil and political liberties are
therefore *derivative* human rights.

EQUAL FREEDOM

Some contextual determinants will distinguish moral freedom
from psychological and metaphysical freedom, as follows:

5. a. *Moral freedom belongs equally to all human beings.*
   b. *Equal freedom should be established by enacted laws.*
   c. *One ought to do what is right as defined by just laws.*

Arguments for freedom become anarchistic when it is defined as the absence of restraint and it is not explicitly recognized that ethical grounds can be established for freedom only in the moral sense. Moral freedom is the freedom to do the right thing. Freedom to do the wrong thing cannot be ethically justified. This curious twist is not a lapse into authoritarianism, for it merely follows the argument. If freedom is a necessary condition of moral agency, to which everyone has a human right, then everyone has a right to as much freedom as everyone else, or, to equal freedom. The rightful limit to moral freedom is another person's legitimate claim to a similar freedom. Freedom limits freedom. The most that can be ethically justified is equal freedom for everyone.

Because not everyone is equally moral, however, there have to be laws to establish the conditions of equal freedom in society. These laws should repress freedom that is exercised in excess of equal freedom. For example, a speed limit of twenty-five miles an hour might be necessary to establish the equal freedom to drive in residential areas for average drivers under average conditions. If so, it is a just law and repressive only for people who want to do the wrong thing. It constrains their freedom in order to establish freedom equally for all who live and drive in those areas. The enactment and enforcement of just laws is therefore a service to freedom in the moral sense, as was previously discussed in relation to the classroom as a community of scholars under law.

It is consequently a duty to obey just laws. Acting in accordance with them is always right, for it enhances the freedom and dignity of everyone within their purview. If it can give pleasure to protect and enhance the dignity of fellow human beings, it can give pleasure to obey just laws. Doing the right thing when rightness is defined by a just law at least ought to give one pleasure. This pleasure, of course, will be qualitatively distinct from gustatory delight, esthetic rapture, and sexual ecstasy, and it might be available to people only at a Kohlbergian stage three or four (or higher), so to speak. It is nevertheless intrinsically good to do what is intrinsically right. The fact that not everyone feels good about doing the right things as specified by just laws does not mean it is not intrinsically good to do so. That the right to moral freedom is the right to obey just laws should be obvious the moment one transcends the narcissism of wanting to pursue one's own interests and goals and asks in an objective manner about the role of moral freedom in the concurrent maintenance of the dignity of all human beings (see sentence 2c). The community context of a plurality of moral agents, such as one finds in the closed universe of the classroom or a specific society, requires the restriction to equal freedom. It does not require Kant's idea that everyone should be able to conceptualize their actions in universal terms. Perhaps it does not require his idea of respect for law, either, so much as it depends upon self-respect. At any rate, doing the right thing as defined by a just law ought to yield pleasure to someone with an adequate sense of his own personal dignity.

The human right to equal freedom was accepted earlier in the Kantian community of scholars under law. Moral freedom in a context devoted to the maximization of learning can now be claimed to be the student's human right. The rules needed to maintain the equal freedom to learn will vary according to contextual factors, but the goal should be to establish a context of freedom and dignity in education. Learning these rules should be conducive to the development of moral agency, and following them, a pleasure. One response to the moral crisis in society, in other words, is to promote the development of moral agents—that is, people who are responsible for their actions—by establishing in classrooms the rules of equal freedom as they are necessary to maximize learning. There is no guarantee that students who learn moral conduct in the classroom will act that way after school or in adult life, but the moral sensibility it develops falls within the limits of what schools can and should do.

MORAL EQUALITY AND BROTHERLY/SISTERLY LOVE

At least two other human rights are as important to the growth of moral agency as freedom, as shown in this triad:

6.   a.   *Each human being has its own value and dignity.*
     b.   *One ought to value each person, regardless of race, gender, social class, politics, physical characteristics or handicap, and so on.*
     c.   *Moral equality is therefore a human right.*
     d.   *Brotherly/sisterly love is therefore a human right.*

The first two sentences merely repeat 2a and 2b, to show that the logical entailment of the imperative to value the unique qualities of human beings is to forbid discrimination on irrelevant grounds. Valuing the unique qualities of a person occurs independently of external factors such as race, gender, social class, and so forth. Moral obligations incurred by all moral agents, such as keeping promises, telling the truth, repairing damages, and so on, are due to all other people, regardless of race, gender, social class, religion, politics, physical characteristics or handicap, and so forth. Everyone's right to moral agency is everyone's right to equal consideration as a moral subject.

Because valuing the uniqueness of someone arouses feelings of affection for them, appreciating the unique qualities of human beings results in feelings of kinship toward them, regardless of external factors, simply because they are human beings. Conversely, one's right to be valued for one's own dignity and value is the right to receive brotherly/sisterly love from other human beings. It is right to have friendly relations with other moral agents.

Whereas moral freedom is the kind of a right often claimed for oneself, equal consideration and brotherly/sisterly love are usually claimed for oneself only if one is a member of a disadvantaged group. Otherwise they are experienced as obligations to others that arise in response to their rightful moral claims upon one. Cordiality is due other moral agents because the presumption is that they will endeavor to do the right thing and because moral agents do not exist as independent entities. Robinson Crusoe may have had duties toward himself, but he was not much of a moral agent until Friday appeared. One becomes a moral agent through relations with other people that are structured by moral feelings, sentiments, perceptions, concepts, and practices. Morality is simply the regulation of the events between people to minimize the harm they might do each other. This is why Jesus could honestly believe that brotherly/sisterly love sufficed. As Abraham Melden (1977) indicates in his explication of moral agency as a human right, in making a promise one gives the promisee a right to certain expectations that lasts until the promise is fulfilled. A promise is a decision to enter into a moral relation with the promisee for the specified segment of the lives of the two people, who in this way temporarily support each other's moral agency (pp. 62–63). Melden seems correct to claim that promise making is the paradigm instance of moral conduct (if this is understood to include the implicit promise of conversation, truth telling). It shows that all moral relations need to be undergirded by a benevolent good will (p. 145).

A good will without benevolence can enable one to do the right thing out of duty (Kant), but an attitude of benevolence can enable one to overcome, or transcend, self-centeredness and moral negligence. In general, a necessary condition of moral relations with other people is the affection for them that develops as one becomes aware of their unique qualities and appreciates their standing as reciprocally obligated moral agents. Because moral relations with other people are a necessary condition of the development of one's own moral agency and dignity as a human being, the fellow-creature feelings of brotherly/sisterly love are a human right. They support the more specific human rights sometimes classified as welfare rights. A moral agent with fellow-creature feelings will find the isolation of moral obligations from the material conditions of life to be morally intolerable, for to become a moral agent and achieve human dignity (as well as happiness) requires clothing, shelter, a subsistence diet, medical care, and education. Access to the minimal material conditions of human welfare and dignity therefore requires the derivative human rights to food, clothing, shelter, medical care, and education (cf. Benn, 1981; Schneider, 1967).

MARX'S CRITICISM OF HUMAN RIGHTS

These three fundamental human rights—moral freedom, moral equality, and brotherly/sisterly love—are the moral aspects of the democratic ideals of liberty, equality, and fraternity. These ideals prevail in most political parties in most democratic societies, in various interpretations and relative emphases. There is nothing esoteric about them. The transposition to human rights merely contextualizes them as the universal obligations of deontological ethics. The fulfillment of their obligations also fulfills the greatest happiness (or greatest goodness) principle, excluding no one.

When Karl Marx rejects human rights, he actually rejects only some specific passages of certain quoted documents guaranteeing freedom of religion and Article 2 of the 1793 *Declaration of the Rights of Man and of the Citizen*: "These rights (the natural and imprescriptable rights) are: *equality, liberty, security, property*" (Marx, 1843/1967, pp. 235–236). In his analysis, these are reducible to the right to property, which itself is interpreted as "the right of self-interest." Marx is therefore not rejecting human rights as such, but rather the interpretation of the democratic ideals of the eighteenth century, namely, classical liberalism. He believes they justify bourgeois egoism. He is therefore rejecting the ideology of enlightened self-interest of classical, laissez-faire economics (and Bentham).

We can join in this rejection of bourgeois ideology without rejecting the more adequate interpretation of human rights that the Marxist theorist, Ernst Bloch (1961/1986), claims is necessary when he says, "Freedom, equality, fraternity, the orthopedia of the upright carriage, of human pride, and of human dignity point far beyond the horizon of the bourgeois world" (p. 174). Marx's criticism can be transcended by an appropriate emphasis upon equality of consideration, brotherly/ sisterly love, and the derivative, so-called welfare rights (which remain human rights regardless of this categorization). When the democratic ideals of liberty, equality, and fraternity are deontologized as the human rights necessary to sustain the most fundamental right to moral agency and therefore human dignity, it becomes clear that the three have to function in conjunction with each other to protect and enhance the unique qualities of individual human beings. As Bloch says, "The struggle for freedom produces equality; equality as the end of exploitation and dependence preserves freedom; fraternity is rewarded with an equality wherein no one is compelled, or in the position, to be a wolf to others" (p. 169). This may seem like empty schematizing, but it is said within the framework of Bloch's belief that "human dignity is not possible without economic liberation, and this liberation is not possible without the cause of human rights. . . . There can be no true installation of human rights without the end of exploitation, no end of exploitation without the installation of human rights" (p. xxix).

At any rate, we can agree with Marx that, as Jacques Maritain (1943/1960) says, "bourgeois individualism is done for" (p. 89). We can also agree with Maritain's observation concerning the moral crisis of this century:

> The problem is to replace the individualism of the bourgeois era not by totalitarianism or the sheer collectivism of the beehive but by a personalistic and communal civilization, grounded on human rights and satisfying the social aspirations and needs of man. Education must remove the rift between the social claim and the individual claim within man himself. It must therefore develop both the sense of freedom and the sense of responsibility, human rights and human obligations, the courage to take risks and exert authority for the general welfare and the respect for the humanity of each person. (p. 89)

One response to the moral crisis is therefore the application of the human rights to liberty, equality, and fraternity to the hidden curriculum of schooling.

HUMAN RIGHTS IN THE HIDDEN CURRICULUM

The implementation of these democratic ideals in schools results in the democratic classroom as Dewey and his latter-day disciples desire, but the transformation into human rights creates a context of obligations that is not found in these ideals. Ideals express only the good, not the right. The rules necessary to establish the equal freedom to learn, however, are deontological moral rules that express rightness and obligations. They express the students' duties to each other's freedom to learn and establish the community under law, now understood as a synthesis of deontological and teleological ethics, of morality and value. If students engage in classroom activities that encourage them to value each other, building bonds of friendship, then following the rules of equal freedom should enable them to do the right thing with pleasure.

To maintain and enhance human dignity, however, freedom should be proportional to the degree of responsibility students have learned to bear. It is incompatible with human dignity to give a class more—or less—freedom than it can handle responsibly. Once granted that the freedom students deserve as a human right varies according to age, methods of control employed in the community, and so forth, it can be said they should have as much freedom to choose among specified learning tasks and projects as the curriculum allows. One learns responsibility by being responsible. The responsibility exercised in completing a project chosen from several options differs remarkably from that involved in completing an assigned task. Erring on the side of too much freedom encourages students to venture and attempt larger things than they can cope with, but it also enables them to learn to accept difficult challenges and become aware of the limits of their capabilities. Learning to accept the obligations specified by the rules needed to maintain the equal freedom to learn, on the other hand, is part of becoming an adult moral agent who willingly abides by the just laws in society out of recognition and respect for the value and dignity of other people.

Enforcing the rules needed for equal freedom in turn protects the right to equal consideration and insures equal access to education insofar as this falls within the school's power. Equal consideration and equal access require, of course, that there be no discrimination in schools because of race, gender, social class, or other educationally irrelevant factor. Except for explicitly warranted compensation or reparation, discrimination is obviously contrary to human dignity. The right to equal consideration also means that no student should be exposed to a teacher who is a racist, classist, male or female chauvinist, anti–Semite, anti–Catholic, anti–fundamentalist, anti–WASP, or anti–atheist, or who is prejudiced against any category of people whatsoever. Although there has been enough said by others about eliminating biases against the working classes, females, and nonwhites from schools, championing their rights ought not result in prejudice against males, whites, or children from the professional classes. They are not responsible for discriminatory practices in adult society. Discrimination not only violates the dignity of students in the category offended, but prejudices other students and prevents them from becoming aware of the value and dignity of those discriminated against.

Enforcement of the rules of equal freedom, moreover, should allow students to fulfill the obligation that Ross calls the prima facie duty of repairing the damages. The rules have to be enforced, but this can occur with maximum dignity by asking students who have violated a rule to repair whatever damage they have done to property, other students, or the moral atmosphere of the learning climate. Such reparation promotes the development of moral agency because it enables the guilty person to become aware of the moral obligation embodied in the rule violated, replace the bad deed with a good one, and accept responsibility for the misdeed as well as for subsequently acting in accordance with the rule. Reparation enables students to learn that they can and ought to make amends when they have done something wrong and develops moral relations among students. It implements the human right to fraternity by establishing the conditions of friendship. Classroom activities that involve cooperation also help students to value each other, build bonds of friendship, and follow the rules of equal freedom with pleasure.

Enabling students to adopt moral relations with each other in classrooms promotes responsiveness to their obligations as they arise and as actual moral agents, not as the spectators they become when moral obligations are studied in the overt curriculum or as habits of obedience to teachers or schools. Inculcating the rules of equal freedom is more rational than these when it occurs in a friendly, supportive atmosphere that makes it pleasurable to follow them, especially when their enforcement through reparation enables students to acquire and maintain a sense of their own dignity.

Because the three human rights are democratic ideals, their implementation in schools is compatible with, if not mandated by, the cultural ideologies of nominal democracies. To avoid a partisan application of a concept of democracy to furnish a nonauthoritarian model of pedagogy, it suffices to protect the human rights of students in a classroom conducted as a community under law devoted to learning. This does not require a Kantian, abstract respect for law, provided it is founded on the more basic practice of learning to value one's classmates. Students are unlikely to learn to value each other, however, unless the teacher values all individuals for their own value and dignity.

This valuing the worth of each student is not an intellectual matter; rather, it manifests itself affectively in pedagogic love, the equivalent of the bedside manner of medical practice.

Such a community of scholars under law is not undemocratic if it does not include the collective planning of the curriculum. Collective planning does not occur in advanced industrial democracies and is not an essential feature of democracy. It may be more democratic to provide a context in which students respect each other's right to learn within a system of rules that guarantee equal freedom. Moral agents in democracies, *pace* Kant, do not make their own laws. Chaos or tyranny are likely outcomes when democracies are not governments of law. What is essential to promote human dignity in pedagogy is that learning activities occur within a framework of just rules humanely administered, that is, within a community of equal freedom and mutual respect and affection, for these are intrinsically right and good.

THE EXISTENTIAL CONNECTION

Just as a child whose parents hardly ever raise their voices learns to be soft-spoken without ever learning a rule forbidding shouting, so, too, is it not always necessary to formulate and enforce a set of rules to create a community of law in the classroom. A classroom that functions as a community under law, moreover, enables students to become aware of their obligations to each other in conjunction with their own actions. This is a sharp contrast to views that identify moral education with thinking about morality, which, *pace* Kohlberg, can be significant only when it leads to moral conduct and authentic only when it proceeds from one's whole being. A community of scholars under law can involve existential as well as ethical relations of students with each other. These may be as important as the intrusion of rules between students. Friendly, dialogical relations among students are probably as necessary to the development of moral agency as the exercise of responsible freedom and fair, impartial treatment by teachers. They establish the communality of the classroom.

In Kantian terms, the classroom develops as a kingdom of ends insofar as the principle of respect for persons, or treating each person as a moral agent, is developed through such dialogical relations among students. These let them become aware of each other's qualities, enable them to value each other, and foster brotherly/sisterly love. In other words, Kant's categorical imperatives should be seen as coexistential imperatives that are inherent in dialogical relations. For example, one simply cannot lie to someone who is experienced as a Thou, as a unique presence to the world, because of the perceived inviolability of the relation with that person. Someone who experiences deep, extensive, dialogical relations with other people will perceive certain characteristics of dialogical relations as obligations coming from the relations themselves, that, when raised into awareness, seem to be known intuitively. They are sedimentations of meanings deposited in perceptual consciousness. To raise them into explicit consciousness conceptually is to explicate the prima facie duties of morality. For example, a dialogical relation with another person that includes what Buber (1926/1965a) calls experiencing that person "from the other side" (pp. 96, 100) convinces one very thoroughly that one ought to keep any promises made to him or her. Breaking a promise in this case would involve such a deep betrayal of the other person and such a profound loss of self-respect it is simply beyond contemplation.

When a classroom is communalized, the characteristics of the dialogical relations will sediment themselves in the perceptual awareness of the students in the development of moral sensibility. Then students can become conceptually aware of the conditions of dialogical relations with other students if the rules needed to establish the equal freedom to learn are explained in moral language. This should involve words such as *right, wrong, obligation, duty, obligations to others, respect for others, self-respect*; and questions such as "What would happen if we all did that?" "How would you like it if X did that to you?" and "How can they read if you are doing that?"

The compatibility of deontology with "existentialism" was shown earlier by indicating that Kierkegaard's admonition to become oneself through the teleological suspension of the ethical requires a continuous dialectic with principles or rules in order to go beyond them. In the first place, his paradigm case did not suspend the ethical at all, for Abraham did not kill Isaac. Second, as Kierkegaard freely admits, it is a paradox to say that one becomes an individual through maintaining a dialectical relation to the universal, but Kierkegaard did not try to resolve the paradox by a neat but empty sophism. It is an existential paradox that logic cannot unravel.

The analogous paradox of establishing the classroom as a community under law in order to promote authentic, individual existence, however, might be unraveled. When the classroom governed by moral law is seen as providing the conditions of dialogical relations or genuine coexistence among students, it is not the rules themselves with which students should remain in dialectical relations. It is other students, mediated by the universal rules of equal freedom and the cognizable objects of the overt curriculum. It is not paradoxical to claim that moral, dialogical relations with other people are necessary to becoming a particular moral agent. On the other hand, no valid claim can be made for a right to become oneself if that self is prescinded from moral agency. In Nabert's (1943/1969) words, "At no time is a consciousness capable of growth in being without being initially beholden to its dialogue with another consciousness" (p. 139).

To be sure, the reification of rules can render them inapplicable to some unique situations and dehumanize some interhuman relations. It does not follow that there can be dialogue without the mediation of moral rules. To eliminate the universal, as some existentialism does, empties human reality of all that is existential, according to Nabert (1943/1969), who claims, "A disarmed reason would no longer allow one to recognize the advance of existence through the mediation of duty" (p. 138). Whereas Kant wants people to be guided by the pure will to do the right thing, as expressed in a moral rule, in order to overcome natural inclinations, Nabert (1943/1969) holds that the violation of a rule that gives rise to a feeling of fault also gives rise to an aspiration to be that utilizes the motivational force of the natural inclination to fulfill the duty specified by the rule (pp. 5, 120–121). Enforcement of rules in schools through having students repair whatever damage they have done should waken the desire to be in a recovery of being. The deepening of moral consciousness that occurs in such reparation is identical with the deepening of self-conscious existence. A similar fulfillment of one's being occurs when one performs one's duties because of their perceived rightness. This is why doing so can give one pleasure. Kant (1788/1949) recognizes the existence of "the person who is delighted by the consciousness of doing dutiful acts" (p. 150), but he rightly claims that the sense of self-worth gained in doing one's duty cannot be the reason for the action. Its rightness has to be perceived independently for the fulfillment of one's being to occur (p. 150).

In his book, *Purity of Heart Is to Will One Thing*, Kierkegaard (1847/ 1956) claims that the unity of the self can be achieved only by willing one thing, the good: *"Each one who in truth would will one thing must be led to will the Good"* (p. 66). In schools the good is the maximal learning of each student. To will the good requires students to will the maximum learning for themselves and other students. This can establish the unity of their individual projects of being. It coincides with Kant's and Ross's duties of beneficence, which include helping to improve the virtue and intelligence of oneself and others. It also coincides with Mill's claims about choosing qualitatively superior pleasures and the higher order of existence and with the duty to maintain and enhance the dignity of other human beings. To will the maximization of learning for oneself and other students, excluding no one, is therefore not merely willing the educational good. It involves a sense of fairness and acting justly because it is only right. Thus the explicit attention to classroom praxis as moral praxis, in a context of the promotion of dialogue among students in order to establish their awareness of each other's rights, lays the existential, perceptual foundation of moral feelings for the conceptual operations usually associated with moral education.

RESPONSE TO THE MORAL CRISIS

We have not considered the pedagogy of value and moral education yet, but it is implied that the idea of the classroom as the community under law, guided by the human rights to equal freedom, equal consideration, and mutual affection, responds to the moral crisis in a way that schools and individual teachers can implement without further ado. A few historical considerations will substantiate this contention. The criticism that progressive educators have made of teacher-dominated classrooms have been moralistic attacks on the use of moralistic means for maintaining classroom control. Their battle has been won. Defenders of conventional, didactic instruction generally reject the practice of subjecting students to moral judgment and moral exhortation. The continued development of educational psychology and the social sciences in the study of education has led to the understanding of human development, motivation, and social processes in education that has been expressed in a quasi-scientific language that has virtually replaced moralistic language in discussion and thought about educational problems. This use of a quasi-technical language, however, can go too far. Students still ought to learn to conduct themselves in classrooms, and elsewhere, within a moral perspective structured by moral insights, language, and concepts if they are to gain a sense of their obligations and develop as moral agents. The solution is to emphasize dialogical relations among students, to avoid oppression; and the classroom as a community under law, to retain a moral framework.

The recommendation is open ended, for it is compatible with various kinds of progressive and conventional classrooms. In either kind the teacher should take the time to teach the rules, on an ad hoc basis when necessary, so they are seen to define the obligations and duties students have to each other. Such a prosaic proposal is a response to the moral crisis, because this crisis is partly caused by the lack of moral education due to the widespread efforts to eliminate moralistic theory and practice from education in the general demoralization of education. In this respect the schools merely reflect the demoralization of the twentieth century.

Part of the demoralization, or dehumanization, of Western civilization occurred through the widespread influence of hedonism, pragmatism, utilitarianism, and other teleological ethics on a broad, cultural level, accompanied by their sweeping moral relativism. These theories of value, mistaken by philosophers and laypersons alike for theories of obligation and duty, have been thought to be pertinent to morality and moral values, but they have not included specific attention to rightness as such. The point is a logical one. Theories of value and good are not theories of the right, obligation, duty, or morality. The attempt to explain the latter in terms of the former explains morality away. This axiological fallacy is nihilistic because it removes morality from the scene. It is demoralizing in the psychological sense, too, because much of the significance of life depends upon understanding oneself as a moral agent who can and does answer the call of conscience to fulfill obligations purely out of duty, in the process of which one finds one's self.

The teleological theories, including existentialism, cannot be used as first-person moral codes. They cannot generate the struggle with moral problems that is necessary to develop a feeling for the worth of one's existence that emerges only in the obligations one fulfills and the duties one performs in the search for one's own being. It is not wrong to be concerned with pleasure, happiness, satisfactions, or self-realization, but these are nonmoral goods. Their pursuit does not let one cross over the threshold of morality.

This was indicated in the distinction given in Chapter 1 in the use of the words *good* and *right* by a mature adult in the socially responsible position of a teacher within the context of personal advice giving. When talking with children or youth, the teacher is not under an obligation to speak objectively about the matter, as adults might talk about it among themselves; rather, one is morally obliged to tell the young person she or he is always right to choose heterosexual adjustment, premarital chastity, monogamous and lifelong marriage, and marital fidelity. After all, the young person's life is at stake. Although that discussion was compatible with hedonism because it acknowledged other things are good in the sense of giving pleasure, the use of the word *right* crossed over the threshold to morality by invoking moral obligations. Although it is compatible with Reich's countercultural "Consciousness III"— because it does not say other things are wrong, or rule out de facto relationships, or invoke mystical terms about the sanctity of marriage—

it is also compatible with the belief in absolute values supported by a putatively revealed religion and the moral teachings of a church-related school. Regardless of what it is compatible with, it is not hedonistic, nor pragmatic, nor deontologic, nor absolutistic. It is merely the most reasonable advice a teacher can give, when asked for it in a confidential situation, by other people's children.

This is the spirit in which the classroom should function as a community of scholars under law as a response to the alleged moral crisis. Some things are as central to classroom conduct as they are to deontological ethics. Teachers and students in the pedagogic relation are always right to tell the truth. This claim does not oblige one to accept Kant's view that truth telling is a universally binding obligation and that it is wrong to tell lies, even from benevolent motives. The principle of the maximization of learning simply assumes students are learning the truth. Although they do learn even when learning falsehoods, this is not the kind of learning implied in the claim that classrooms should promote as much learning about things as possible. With this principle, in other words, there is no real distinction between the morality of classroom management and the content of instruction. If one presumes that teachers speak the truth all the time, it is even redundant to say they are always right to do so.

A similar principle applies to students, except for three considerations. The pupil may have some difficulty in learning the truth, and the difficulties may be cognitive rather than moral. For example, when people said the earth was flat centuries ago, they were not lying or being untruthful in the moral sense. They were not trying to deceive anyone. It can be said they spoke truthfully in the moral sense, even though they said something that was untrue in the epistemic sense. Second, learning to speak truthfully is the same thing as learning to speak. It is lying that is learned in addition to learning how to speak. A teacher confronted with lying should diagnose the situation to discover why it was learned and practiced. Third, sometimes a student has to be enabled to tell the truth analogously to the way patients and clients tell the truth to doctors, lawyers, therapists, and the like. Learning difficulties cannot be diagnosed without the pupil's frank and candid responses, yet the presence of a learning difficulty may make it hard for the student to speak the truth. In other words, regardless of its status as a moral principle in other domains of life, truth telling is a necessary condition of the pedagogic relation itself.

Promise keeping is similarly close to the objectives of the classroom. It is how students should learn to undertake voluntary, binding obligations regarding schoolwork. To say it is always right to keep a promise does not mean it is never right to break one. When asked for advice, however, it is always right to suggest that one should be careful to make only those promises one intends to keep. Everyone's education accordingly should involve actual practice in making promises and keeping them, for this is the basis of all agreements and contracts. Perhaps more use of the contract method would help students learn how to make promises in good faith, so the question of keeping them might not arise.

Finally, one can say categorically that children should not hurt each other in classrooms. Even if the duties of nonmaleficence were not universally valid, they are unexceptionable in classrooms. The teacher is morally responsible if the children or youths hurt each other.

Truth telling, making and keeping promises, not hurting anyone, and repairing the damage done when violating a rule needed to establish equal freedom are the core of any moral education. They are right for a community dedicated to learning the truth about the world. They already include most of deontological ethics. Students who develop deep in their being the attitudes of nonviolence, honesty, and a willingness to undertake obligations voluntarily, and who assume responsibility for making reparations for damages done, are very far along the road to the authentic, moral life.

CONCLUSION

The theory of value and the human rights ethic synthesized in this chapter attempt to furnish the background for showing how the classroom as a community under law can enable students to learn how to do the right thing and enjoy it, too. The answer to the question of what is good is, everything that exists. The answer to the question of what is right is, to maintain and enhance the existence of everything. The apparent tension between the good and the right is resolved through the observation that existing things are valuable because they have their own qualities and that one ought to learn to value all things by becoming aware of their qualities. The resulting at-homeness in the universe enables one to value other people for their own value and dignity, which makes it a pleasure to do the right thing. The right thing is to maintain and enhance the human dignity in oneself and others, guided by the fundamental human rights to moral agency, moral freedom, equal consideration, and brotherly/sisterly love; the derivative civil, political, and welfare rights; and the moral rules and statutory laws necessary to maintain the conditions of equal freedom. This love of the things in the world will be considered again, in Chapter 5 on the pedagogy of learning to value things, and in Chapters 9 and 10, in the consideration of the role of knowledge in education and pedagogy.

In order to avoid side-tracking the investigation into a historical thesis, the discussion of the lack of consensus and credibility of moral values in modern societies in Chapter 1 did not mention the increasing concern for human rights since World War II. Quite independently of this trend, the present chapter has elaborated a human rights ethic by attempting to show how the basic moral obligation to maintain and enhance human dignity results in the human rights to equal freedom, equal consideration, and brotherly/sisterly love. Each of these human rights is a universal obligation, or categorical imperative, as in Kant's theory. They morally require statutory laws to establish a community under law, as in Moses's moral practice. The derivative welfare rights (to clothing, shelter, a subsistence diet, medical care, and education) have their own correlative, conditional obligations, as in Ross's prima facie duties of benevolence. These welfare rights concern the well-being of everyone, as in Bentham's idea of the greatest happiness of the greatest number, but excluding no one. Human dignity is a greater good than happiness, as in Mill's qualitative distinction between pleasures, in his claim that it is better to be Socrates than a fool, and in Moore's rejection of the naturalistic fallacy. The emphasis on brotherly/sisterly love as a human right is not unlike Moore's claim that one of the most valuable things we can know are the pleasures of human intercourse, and Dewey's concern for the number and variety of interests shared with others; except that brotherly and sisterly love are moral obligations, as in the teachings of the Torah and Jesus.

The classroom as a community of scholars under law dedicated to maximizing the learning of each student should be structured by the human rights to freedom, equal consideration, and brotherly and sisterly love to establish dialogical relations among students in an atmosphere of affection, so students obey the rules of equal freedom out of love, trust, and a sense of fairness and find some pleasure in doing so, as in hedonism. When these fundamental rights inform the social life of the classroom, students will develop the moral sensibility that is necessary to confront the moral problems of adult life in a morally competent manner. This issue will be investigated more deeply in the next chapter on the pedagogy of value and moral education.

CHAPTER 5

Learning to Value Things in Classrooms

The dehumanization in Western civilization includes the decontextualization and reification of values as if these are things one might or might not have. We speak of a person's values, of their learning values in schools, or of their learning moral and spiritual values, as if values are a set of more or less articulated, intellectualized beliefs. We can overcome this alienation from the things in the world by emphasizing the valuing of the qualities of things and appreciating them as a basis for a fundamental morality of the relation of human beings to the universe. Because of the great importance of learning to value things concomitantly with the knowledge and skills of the overt curriculum, the interpretation herein of the main ethical theories of the modern world has inserted the reified, abstract values back into the lived world. As Jean-Paul Sartre (1943/1956) says, in the world of ordinary life, values "spring up like partridges. . . . Values are sown on my path as thousands of little real demands, like the signs which order us to keep off the grass" (p. 38). They appear as the qualitative aspects of existing things because "quality is nothing other than the being of the *this* when it is considered apart from all external relations with the world and with other *thises*" (p. 186). The synthesis of the ethical theories thus establishes an ontological foundation for learning about the good and the right that should occur in schools.

There is more to say about learning to value things and other students through classroom procedures, but their significance will be first highlighted by an elucidation of the teacher as a value exemplar. After the question of learning values from teachers, classroom procedures will be discussed again, before interpreting various suggestions for the explicit study of values in the overt curriculum. The aim is to formulate the general principles for teaching and learning to value things.

LEARNING VALUES FROM THE TEACHER

The concept of the teacher as an example for students to imitate, or as a role model, says nothing about which values should be exemplified by the teacher. It encourages the reification of values, for its advocates often begin with a particular ideology and want the teacher to embody it by being a good Nazi, a good Communist, a good Christian, or a good American, so schoolchildren are not exposed to unorthodox views. Regardless of its value or efficacy in totalitarian societies, this approach requires the selection of teachers on partisan, political grounds, which is contrary to their human rights and virtually useless in pluralistic, liberal democracies. Much more can be said in favor of the teacher exemplifying the constellation of values called *conventional morality*, but it is unlikely that teachers will depart from this standard any more than other educated adults in the community. In any case, this will not be our focus, which will be on the way the teacher appears to the child.

Because the significance of the teacher is greater the smaller the child, we will begin with the baby's relation to the mother, as illustrated by the phenomenologically grounded theory of Otto Bollnow (1968/ 1989, pp. 12–14). According to him, the baby gains access to the world through the mother's presence. If the child is normal and healthy and the mother gives it adequate care, the consciousness of the baby expands to the mother. This first consciousness is corporeal, emotional, and visual as the child is drawn toward the mother through her loving warmth, that is, through her perceived qualities. Then as the child sees the mother handle things, it becomes aware of whatever she draws within her radiance. She opens the world for the child as it becomes aware of the objects she uses. She draws them into its familiar world and extends its familiar world to include them within its lived space. The first access to the world thus occurs across the presence of the trusted mother. Because the child trusts the mother, it trusts what she trusts, fears what she fears, and hates what she hates. Its own feelings toward things become shaped by her feelings, moods, and attitudes toward things. It is aware of what she values and learns to value things as she does. This occurs on the level of perceptual consciousness, before the child can talk, and then is accelerated through the mother's talk.

The child's feelings toward things are subsequently shaped by the attitudes of all the people it encounters. The more the child loves and trusts them, the more it gains access to the world through their presence and learns to value what they value. By the time the child comes to school, it values many things according to their perceived qualities, as its perceptions have been formed through interactions with siblings, toys, other things encountered in the immediate neighborhood, and other adults as well as the parents. Then in school it learns to value things within three distinct spheres: the relation with the teacher, the operation of the classroom, and the explicit study of so-called values. There is no need to ascertain which of these is more influential. How much is learned in the home or peer group and how much is learned from the teacher and explicit study will vary, depending on the trust in the world developed in the home. Although some teachers are more influential than others, the elementary school child who spends most of its working day in the classroom in the presence of a single adult will be influenced by that adult, especially in the way the very presence of the teacher enables the child's exploration of things in the world.

The child is aware of the teacher on three levels: who the teacher is, what the teacher does, and what the teacher says. Who the teacher is—the teacher's being—includes abilities, competencies, abnormalities, personality and character traits, and everything else involved in the makeup of a unique human being. Although the child is not aware of all these features, it is very much aware of the presence of the concrete reality of the particular person. If the teacher is a very different kind of person from previous teachers, the child will be quite aware of it. Even very small children comment on who their teachers are.

The significance of the presence of the teacher might be seen from an adult perspective more readily with the help of images of three television personalities. The first is a naturalist, Harry Wildman, an obviously university trained biologist and conservationist who has "gone native." Wildman has become so immersed in his work in nature that he has become a blood brother in one of the native tribes and can track down animals in front of the television camera. The second example is the Overland Brothers, who travel over the countryside in their motorized camper, taping natural attractions, human interest stories, and other things requested by their viewers. The third is Jane Towers, who has a daily, two-minute spot after the news to comment on a current issue. Judged by their vocabulary, diction, and pronunciation, the Overland Brothers have had no tertiary schooling. Although Towers seems to, her area of specialization is indeterminate. She might be self-educated and seems to have competed in Toastmasters' activities. It is not quite correct to consider these three as teachers using the television as their medium, although Wildman and the Overland Brothers are trying to show us things we do not know, and Towers certainly tries to teach people a thing or two. We are not concerned with the real people or their intentions, however, but with their images as teaching phenomena.

The major difference is not in their teaching styles, although these are different enough. Harry is bearded and wears old clothes and states why an animal might be up a hollow tree, under a log, or down a burrow while he captures it with his bare hands on camera. He speaks directly to us all the while, varying the tone of his voice from a whisper to grunting exertion to normal speech as he goes through the process and explains the animal's habit while holding it. The Overlands never depart from a neutral, disengaged monotone as they stand off and point out features of their current exhibit; whereas Towers never departs from her exasperated, exhortative, often humorous, but always moralistic harangue. The main differences are not in these matters but in who they are. The Overlands are only very superficially interested in and acquainted with what they televise, in strong contrast to the deeply committed Wildman, whose commitment to fauna also differs strongly from Towers' argumentative, self-righteous commitment to the cause of the day. Jane and Harry would certainly agree they are very different kinds of people. It is likely the Overlands would agree, too. In addition to whatever else is learned watching their programs, we become very much aware of who these people are. This is most obvious in the cases of Wildman and Towers, whose personalities are strikingly unique, but it is equally true of the Overlands. Part of who they are is that they have chosen the flat, self-effacing, reportorial style for their work. Wildman and Towers are so fully engaged in their teachings they disclose more of themselves, whereas the relative lack of engagement of the Overlands discloses they are nonentities. They appropriately choose to remove themselves from the center of attention as they show us their strange and wonderful things. Jane would not, and Harry could not.

Wildman loves his "lovely little creatures." His love is obvious when he handles them, firmly but gently, without alarming them. What the Overlands feel toward what they show is hidden. They give an objective treatment suitable for their touristy travelogue. They do not settle anywhere, but hover at a distance from what they exhibit, whereas Wildman obviously belongs in nature, right where he is viewed. There is no separation between him and his world. He is at one with the wildlife he presents. When Wildman discloses things about his lovely creatures, he also bares his soul and reveals precisely who he is. As a result, his presence forms a bridge to the things in the world he discloses, much as the mother draws out the child's consciousness to the things in the world across her presence. The lizard Harry shows us, beloved and valued by him, is not like the lizard we would have seen in the wild without him. His presence enables us to see its qualities and arouses our desire to protect its existence. It becomes important because of the tone of respect in his voice as he talks to it. It belongs in Harry's world, and he in its. Because he is able to disclose aspects of the lizard—or whatever creature—that would not be visible without his presence, we are able to value it more as we become aware of its valuable features, its qualities. He can do this, of course, only because he values it. In other words, as we watch his show, our learning what he is teaching us is accompanied by our learning to value what he values. It is really beside the point that we come to share his values. We do, but what matters is that we come to value the things in the world that he values. They are, after all, valuable.

One of the main points made by Romano Guardini (1959), the source of the distinction between who the teacher is and what the teacher says and does, is that who the teacher is has more effect on the child than what the teacher does or says. The younger the child, the more this is the case (p. 30). The strongest effect of a teacher like Wildman on younger children is therefore his love of the animals in the wild, or his values. This is true because the younger the child, the more it learns with its whole being. As Guardini says, the child takes it all in atmospherically, that is, perceptually. It undoubtedly learns values from its teachers, particularly if they teach with their whole being, as Wildman does because he himself is highly unified in his being. Who he is, what he does, and what he says are completely integrated. He is at one with himself, just as he is at home in the world about which he "teaches." We do not have to praise the content of his values to value him as an example of a teacher who enables students to value the things in the world they are learning about. Wildman simply has a dialogical relation with the things he knows. This is the basis of his dialogical relation with his audience. He is a dedicated teacher because he is dedicated before he is a teacher.

By way of contrast, the Overlands always seem to be reading their script or reciting memorized words. Towers obviously reads from the teleprompter. Neither has a dialogical relation with what their talk is about or with their audience. Their kind of teaching does not involve them existentially and cannot affect their "pupils" existentially. Because Wildman's knowledge does effect him existentially, he humanizes it and its effects on his students' values. He merely has to speak about the things in the world of which he is so highly aware to disclose their truth. Because of his wide-awake presence to the world during teaching episodes, his viewers come to value the things he values.

Learning values from the teacher, then, does not oblige the teacher to exemplify an ideological, moral, or political code. Teachers ought to value very highly the things they are teaching about, so students become aware of how valuable they are. In this way the teacher's values should become the student's values. The point, moreover, is not isolated to the value domain. To come to value the things in a region of the world makes them accessible. This access to them makes knowledge about them possible and desirable. This has nothing to do with moralizing about their importance, as Towers might do, or with remaining objective and disinterested about the things, as the Overlands might do. The frequent recommendations for teachers to have enthusiasm for their subject is close to the point. It reifies the subject, however, as if it were not about things in some region of the world that have their own qualities. Such enthusiasm emerges naturally when the teacher is engaged in the disciplined study of the things in the region of the world that he or she finds sufficiently valuable to want to know more about and teach more about. If something is not visibly important to the teacher as a human being, the students will not feel like learning about it. This means that it is necessary for students to come to value those things in the world that the engaged teacher values in order to find them important enough to learn more about them. The important value to be learned from the teacher, in other words, is that what the teacher is teaching about is indeed worth learning more about.

LEARNING VALUES FROM CLASSROOM PROCEDURES

The maxim that the value one should learn from the teacher is the human significance of what is being learned has its corollary in the moral domain in the idea of the classroom as a place where right and wrong are defined by the way conduct fulfills the obligations to maximize learning. Because the problem is not learning values but learning to value other people, the emphasis has been on the classroom as a community of scholars, as a cooperating group of people committed for the most part to the goal of maximizing their learning while they are together. The more interesting theories of learning, however, do not begin with people learning the kinds of things teachers ordinarily teach, and the more interesting theories of classroom management do not begin with the kinds of learning that should be promoted in the classroom, either. It is therefore important to call attention, first, to the fact that one of the main motivational forces available to promote school learning is the teacher's own valuing what he or she is teaching about and, second, to the fact that one of the main things to learn to value in schools is the classroom itself as a place of learning about the rest of the world.

Similarly, the more interesting theories of learning values in schools do not begin by noting that the knowledge and skills that the teacher knows are of value, or that the learning promoted in classrooms is itself of value. It is therefore important to call attention to the fundamental value of the pupils' coming to value what they are supposed to be learning about. Theories of teaching values actually embody a perversion of values if they divert attention away from the pupils' learning to value the things teachers attempt to disclose in the place established primarily to enable such disclosures. It is therefore worth belaboring the obvious, which is that the most fundamental value that can be learned in schools is that there are things in the world worth learning about through deliberate, disciplined study in classrooms designed expressly for that purpose, taught under the guidance and supervision of a qualified and responsible teacher.

The view of the classroom as a community of scholars under law can be usefully contrasted with other views. It is similar to Dewey's proposal in regard to the promotion of cooperative attitudes. Cooperative activities can be incorporated in classrooms, however, without student/teacher planning of the curriculum and without infringing upon a student's right to learn important things the rest of the class may not want to study. Then, too, within the context of a prespecified curriculum, children can learn that some things are worth learning about because the teacher values them and thereby learn to value what the teacher values. The phenomenon of Wildman cannot occur within student/teacher planning procedures conducted in good faith. Learning to value what the teacher values does not involve authoritarianism; to the contrary, it requires a teacher who has thoroughly incorporated the content of instruction into his or her being and is manifestly enthusiastic about it. Choking off such enthusiasm because of an ideology of student/teacher planning is counterproductive to the achievement of the fundamental objectives of the classroom.

The idea of the classroom as a community under law may seem to resemble Peters' (1966) recommendation to establish the minimal conditions of order, but his conceptualization represents a much more traditional practice (p. 174). He insists upon the teacher's imposing the rule of law to prevent bullies from taking over. We ought not disagree with the factual part of the claim about the bullies in British public (boys') schools, Peters' apparent referent, but his conceptualization assumes a Hobbesian view of human nature. It assumes people are basically selfish, egoistical, and aggressive if uncontrolled by law. If it is true for some people, or some neighborhoods, there are ways to overcome it other than by imposing the rule of law. The teacher can appeal to the students' desires to be friends with one another, give them opportunities to respond to affection and genuine concern, and trust their growing desire to want to do the right thing. It is not the minimal conditions of order but a minimal degree of mutual respect and obligatedness that is desirable in the classroom. This insures the observance of elemental human rights for the right reason.

When one justifies the rule of law by claiming that the minimal conditions of order are needed if anyone is to learn anything, the next thing one says, is that good teachers frequently give commands, as Peters (1966) does (p. 264). This is not the issue, for a teacher cannot tell if obedience to a command is accompanied by insight. *Pace* Peters, commands violate the dignity of the student because something more clearly educative can be used. If some schools require the imposition of the minimal conditions of order in fairly authoritative ways, others do not. The control needed in one place is overcontrol and dehumanizing in another. Both situations, however, are encompassed by the vision of the classroom as a community of scholars under law in which the fundamental human rights to equal freedom, equal consideration, and mutual affection are operative.

There may be deeply seated factors in a specific teacher's being, however, that make it feasible to establish a community under law through a direct and candid approach in precisely the way Peters (1966) recommends. This seems as legitimate as another teacher governing through student/teacher planning. Whether a teacher obtains the minimal conditions of order by imposing the rule of law, or through planning sessions that result in cooperative involvement, or through a laissez-faire approach in which the teacher functions chiefly as a catalyst and helps the pupil unfold from within, the outcome should be the same. Either the classroom becomes a place devoted to serious learning, or it does not; either the students learn to value learning, or they do not. If they do, they can then learn right and wrong conduct in the appropriate way when following the rules needed to maintain the equal freedom to learn. There is no more important moral lesson they can learn in school, for learning that learning is itself valuable makes all the rest possible.

DIGRESSION ON METHOD: UTILITARIANISM

The form of the argument just made might seem to be a version of rule utilitarianism. It claims the rules of the classroom should be formulated to secure the greatest good defined as the maximal learning for each student. Then individual actions are right if they conform to these rules. We might consider why rule utilitarianism is often said to be deontological and then elaborate why the argument is not utilitarian in order to contrast it with an important utilitarian approach not yet considered. One understanding of deontology is that an act is right if one obeys a preexisting rule or principle, rather than to obtain certain kinds of consequences. This can include rule utilitarianism because, even if the rules (or laws) are formulated to promote the greatest happiness, individual actions are right if they are in accordance with the rules. This, however, is a misunderstanding of deontology, which holds that the mind of the agent should be focused upon the rightness, duty, or obligation of the correct action when doing it, rather than on its results. The claim is that rightness acquires a kind of independence in perception. This might be most easily understood through a rule model, but perceived obligations and their rightness are not reducible to rules. A mother who hears her child crying in the middle of the night feels obligated to see what is wrong, for example, because of the perceived rightness in alleviating its distress, and without necessarily being aware of any rule specifying the obligation. The obligation is perceived as coming from the lived world.

Kant's (1788/1949) distinction between categorical and hypothetical imperatives leads to the point. Rules either promote justice or some chosen good. The form of the hypothetical imperative is, If you want X, then do Y. Rules that promote justice are not utilitarian because one should obey them out of respect for the law. Such respect for the law is not a means of achieving morality because it is morality itself (p. 183). The same thing is true for human dignity and the rules needed in classrooms to maintain the equal freedom to learn required by such dignity. Rules that support human rights or human dignity are not a means to something else, for following them is identical with human dignity itself. Keeping a promise does not result in the realization of a subsequent goal, such as dignity; rather, the very act of keeping the promise embodies human dignity. If the justification of those classroom rules that are in fact necessary to promote learning appears to be cast in the logical form of utilitarianism, it is because of an ellipsis in the argument. Because it is simply unfair for one student to disturb the learning of another, the rules needed to promote the equal freedom to learn provide the conditions of justice, or mutual respect, in which learning can occur. The rules establish the classroom as a moral community in which learning occurs because of the enveloping teleology of the school. This moral community is a distinctly moral good. The rules therefore define a way of life by instituting a moral community and are not directly justified by the nonmoral goal of learning. It is the institution of learning in the school that is teleological and that functions as an atmospheric goal-boundedness within which the classroom can come into being as a community of scholars under law. Any rules that are necessary to conduct the classroom with human dignity do not serve a goal extrinsic to the establishment of the moral community itself.

To apply utilitarianism to the classroom requires a conception of the rules as instrumental to the achievement of nonlearning-related goals such as happiness, pleasure, enjoyment, or the satisfaction of desires. The classroom should, of course, be a happy place that gives students pleasure so they enjoy learning, but the ultimate criterion of a good classroom is not their feeling but their learning. Positive feelings are only an important by-product of the more important end, learning. If they do not show that students have come to value learning, they pervert the educational atmosphere of the classroom.

Nor does the argument commit the naturalistic fallacy. It accepts that the good in the classroom is the greatest learning by each student, but this claim that learning is good is not a claim that the only thing that is good is learning. It does not define the good for life outside of the classroom. It merely observes that a dedication to learning is a necessary condition for a classroom to be a classroom, a school to be a school, a university to be a university. The use of deontological language such as rightness, obligation, and duty avoids inconsistency with the institution of learning in schools and insures that the child's fundamental moral education occurs.

The most basic way to apply utilitarianism to education can be considered by way of contrast. It is utilitarian to believe that all laws and institutions should promote the general welfare. Within this framework one can consider the health of the economic system to be of the highest priority, for the interest in the general welfare includes a concern for maintaining and improving the material conditions of life. Then the common good can be said to be best served by schools if they focus on preparing the young for the economic system through vocational education, including university education for some jobs. The classroom as well as the curriculum should then be patterned after the success routes in society. If the society is competitive, so should classrooms be, for in this way students learn right and wrong conduct as it is actually practiced in society. The real utilitarianism is the educational development of personalities suitable for employment in the economic system, complete with salable skills, and so forth. It is not obvious that this pattern can promote the maximization of learning for every student, or even for most. The competitive classroom is nevertheless an alternative to the proposal for a community of scholars under law. Many people believe it can promote learning and moral development, too. Satisfactory longitudinal studies probably cannot be conducted. If it is a moot point, one can ask if both competitive and cooperative classrooms are morally good classrooms, assuming that they do in fact both maximize learning.

VALUE CLARIFICATION

Although learning to value and evaluate things through the explicit study of values are distinct classroom undertakings, their effects cannot be separated from those of the school context and from who the teacher is. It can, moreover, be counterproductive to concentrate on learning values intellectually. What is valued can become confused with statements about valuable things. To learn to speak truthfully, for example, is very different from learning the sentence, "One should speak the truth," regardless of how fully the latter is explicated. The warning of the existentialist is worth heeding: "If he sits back and makes abstract judgments . . . he is in danger of 'bad faith'" (Greene, 1973, p. 256). An abstract intellectual discussion can easily lead students into accepting the noble and sublime words of moral language for their rhetorical properties or for ulterior psychological and social motives. It can result in ideology, the lie to oneself of bad faith, or hypocrisy.

Recognition of this point may have led to some of the popularity of the values-clarification approach in which students' beliefs about values are raised into explicit awareness. Then, too, as originally formulated by Raths, Harmin, and Simon (1966), the strategies of values clarification were highly compatible with the antiauthoritarianism of the Vietnam War era. To help students clarify their values (i.e., beliefs), the teacher, for Raths et al., should be nondirective and never tell them what they ought to value, what society expects them to value, or what the teacher personally values, unless it is stated as a purely personal opinion. The teacher should instead assume a quasi–Socratic stance and merely ask questions that require students to think and become clearer on beliefs they already have. Typical questions are, What do you mean by that? Have you thought about the consequences of that? How strongly are you committed to that? What will you do about your belief in that? Is that consistent with what you said yesterday? Have you considered any alternatives? Is this something you yourself chose? Was it a free choice? Is it a personal preference, or do you think everyone would agree with that?

Raths et al. (1966) claim there is a definable process of valuing that involves the three so-called processes of choosing, prizing, and acting. The "value" should be freely chosen after consideration of the consequences of the various alternatives. The prizing should involve cherishing or being happy with the "value," being willing to affirm it publicly, and acting on it repeatedly (pp. 28–30). These are seven criteria of a value, by which they mean an intellectual belief or rule. It is

1. Freely chosen
2. Selected from among alternatives
3. Chosen after consideration of the consequences of each choice
4. Personally prized
5. Publicly affirmed
6. Acted on
7. Acted on repeatedly

These criteria are also understood by Simon, Howe, and Kirschenbaum (1972) as the seven subprocesses of valuing: "The goal of the values-clarification approach is to help students utilize the above seven processes of valuing in their own lives; to apply these valuing processes to already formed beliefs and behavior patterns and to those still emerging" (pp. 19–20). Strategies are specified in the form of verbal or paper-and-pencil exercises for classroom use, "to help students build the seven valuing processes into their lives" (p. 21). One of the more obviously valid examples is to begin an ecology unit in a science class by discussing current local environmental issues in order to clarify existing beliefs, then return to these issues after the subject matter is studied to see if the new knowledge can be used in an environmental project (p. 22). Most of the strategies, however, are not connected with curriculum content. Hardly any involve the acquisition of new knowledge or new values (i.e., beliefs). The students do the exercise and the teacher asks the quasi–Socratic questions, carefully avoiding interpretation or evaluation of the students' comments.

There is no reason to doubt that this approach is a consciousness-raising process that can help students sort out the meanings of their feelings about things by aligning and refining their perceptual awareness of them with the conceptual processes involved in explicit verbalization. There seems to be cognitive benefit from the exercises. To avoid the reification of values as things one has, as identical with beliefs about values, and the impression that all that is necessary educationally is to clarify the old ones, it should be modified to enable it to become a preparatory phase to learning to value things differently and to learning to value new things.

Three examples will show the difficulty. In the first, the classroom is broken up into groups of five or six students and a controversial issue is given to each group. Each student writes a paragraph about the issue to represent a distinct point on the political continuum, not necessarily one's own. Then they reveal their own views, discuss the issue, and each member selects the paragraph closest to her own view and amends or supplements it properly. Then all paragraphs are given to everyone. The issues cited for this exercise include legalized abortion, population control, welfare, premarital sex, legalization of marijuana, the distribution of wealth, the Vietnam War, and corporate marriage (Simon et al., 1972, pp. 127–128). There is no suggestion that students should do any reading or research to develop an informed opinion based on a deeper understanding of the issues, the relevant facts, or criteria of value or morality. Although they might clarify their values, they might also become prematurely fixated in their opinions and confuse the ethical right to have their own opinion with the cognitive warrant for having one. Although the approach emphasizes processes, it neglects inquiry and reinforces the belief that investigation is unnecessary at the very moment students might be most curious to learn more about the issue.

As a second example, in an exercise designed to strengthen their feelings, students are asked to indicate whether they agree or disagree, somewhat or strongly, with a series of items including, "I am racially prejudiced," "I would encourage premarital sex for my son," "I would encourage premarital sex for my daughter," and "Marijuana should be legalized." The students are not allowed to have neutral or middle-of-the-road responses. They can interpret the statements as they wish, for the teacher should "indicate there is no correct way to interpret them. They are to be used simply as thought and discussion starters" (Simon et al., 1972, pp. 253–254). Because the objective is merely to strengthen the values the students already have, the teacher is obliged to remain nondirective in the discussion, although such a discussion would not clarify existing beliefs at all. Many people who are racially prejudiced think they are not, very few high school students would have views regarding the lives of their unborn children before being asked, and the basis for their views on marijuana is questionable. In these situations the teacher is morally negligent not to introduce moral considerations.

The third example deals with publicly affirming one's values "under the appropriate circumstances" (Simon et al., 1972, p. 183). This is allegedly an important aspect of the valuing process, but apparently it need not require any moral courage or integrity: "It is often difficult to determine when circumstances are appropriate" (p. 183). To give students clarification about when they should *not* have the courage of their convictions, there is an exercise that asks to whom (i.e., to no one, intimates, friends, acquaintances, or strangers) one would tell the following items: that one has had premarital or extramarital sexual experience, the amount of one's salary, the amount of income tax paid, that one has cheated on income tax, for whom one voted, that one uses marijuana or illegal drugs (listed separately), what one's personal racist tendencies are, and so on (pp. 186–187). Although these, too, are beyond the experience of high school students, they learn not only to keep some things appropriately private (one's abortion, means of birth control, feelings of jealousy, etc.), but also to keep illegal acts private, as if it is all right to do them *sub rosa*. The very use of the exercise involves the school in condoning the actions, although some of them are illegal and the morality of others is not beyond question.

This failure to distinguish between value and moral matters is confronted by Raths et al. (1966) when they recognize a student can use the seven processes (or criteria) and decide to value intolerance or thievery. We are told we have to "respect his right to decide upon that value, . . . but we must often deny him the right to carry the value to action" (p. 227). This is the kind of inconsistency Marxists like to claim indicates the presence of bourgeois ideology. The reason for not allowing action upon a student's values is that "some behavior can't be permitted because it interferes too much with the freedom or rights of others" (p. 227).

This should mean that the clarification process itself should involve the consideration of the freedom and rights of others. That it does not indicates that it is all verbal, unrelated to action except verbally, where everything is permitted, verbally. When it comes to real action in the real world, students have to take the freedom and rights of others into account, as deontologists claim. That is to say that Raths et al. (1966) recognize the amorality of their proposal but do nothing about it because they apparently do not recognize its narcissistic, nihilistic solipsism. The model can at best serve as a first part of a two-phase model. It is only truthful and fair to students to insure that, after they have clarified the values they already have, they confront the moral aspects of their beliefs in order to enable them to value things differently and more in accord with the freedom and rights of others. The issue is not over the values they already have, clear or unclear. It concerns the things and conduct they ought to value and how they can become lucidly aware of the moral and legal realities of life with other people.

To enable students to become aware of qualities of things of which they are presently unaware requires the introduction of new concepts that further disclose such qualities of things in the world or other people. As a first phase, value clarification can orient the students' attention to things in their perceptual world, after which there should be further inquiry into the themes that have emerged. This inquiry should involve the use of instructional materials containing conceptual schemata that make it possible to learn something new about valuable things or valuable conduct, and perhaps about rightness, too. Perhaps the least controversial supplement would be civil and criminal law. After students are very clear about their own beliefs, their juxtaposition to existing laws can let them confront the societal means that prevent people from doing what they want when it interferes with the freedom and rights of others. What is legal and illegal within a community, furthermore, is not a matter of opinion. At the very least, when a student values doing illegal things, the teacher ought to ask if he has thought about the consequences if apprehended. For the teacher to remain silent on the laws when students believe it is all right to do something illegal is pedagogically negligent. If the illegal act is subsequently committed, the teacher is an accessory before the fact.

There are such things as poor taste, moral mistakes, and illegal actions. A methodology that intimates to students that they are entitled to have any values they want, so long as they are clear about them, is extremely naïve. Fortunately, when the advocates of values clarification claim it should occur in "a classroom atmosphere of openness, honesty, acceptance and respect" (Simon et al., 1972, p. 25), they do not mean this is merely their personal opinion. In all honesty, they ought to claim explicitly that such honesty and respect for students are prima facie duties or categorical imperatives or morally required by the students' human rights. They ought to clarify their own values. The moral features required by the self-styled "dialogical strategy" of the approach ought to be brought out into explicit consciousness and entered into the explicit content of the processes, as they are in Buber's idea of a moral struggle for the truth in dialogue with students (1939/ 1965b, p. 107; 1957/1965c, p. 83). These characteristics are none other than the obligations and duties of deontological ethics. This will be discussed further after consideration of the moral-dilemmas approach to developing ethical awareness.

DISCUSSING MORAL DILEMMAS

Values clarification probably works well under ideal conditions. With students from stable, middle-class homes, the gap created by the nondirective teacher is filled by the more mature students, whose basic moral education occurs elsewhere. The morally advanced students might not be the opinion makers of the peer group, however; and the least mature can be the most articulate. A step beyond values clarification that retains some of its better features is the discussion of moral dilemmas as it has evolved out of Kohlberg's work. Laurie Brady (1975a, 1975b), for example, has prepared two volumes for the Australian culture that contain series of graded, one- or two-page stories of children and youth who become caught up in moral predicaments. Their discussion in personal and moral terms is supposed to enhance cognitive development in the moral domain. Depending upon the teacher's contribution after the students express their thoughts about the moral predicament and what they would do in it, this approach embodies the conditions Kohlberg (1976) says are needed for moral development:

1. Exposure to the next higher stage of moral reasoning.
2. Exposure to situations posing problems and contradictions for the child's current moral structure, leading to dissatisfaction with his current level.
3. An atmosphere of interchange and dialogue combining the first two conditions, in which conflicting moral views are compared in an open manner. (p. 190)

Beginning with one of Brady's stories insures that the discussion involves a predicament in the students' perceptual world as well as in their current stage of moral, conceptual development. It also lets students become aware of the qualities of conduct between people as they might occur in the lived world, from which the values-clarification approach is curiously abstracted.

More generally speaking, a teacher presents a moral dilemma to the class (e.g., euthanasia, violating authority to maintain trust in a family, stealing an expensive drug to save one's dying wife, p. 187). As the students discuss the dilemma, they develop their cognitive abilities to reason about third-person moral problems, providing there is exposure to the next higher stage of development. This implies that if the more mature students are to benefit, the teacher has to discuss the predicament at a stage higher than theirs. This competence to reason at a stage higher than theirs is also required if the teacher is to insure that the least conceptually able students do not dominate the discussion. It is also necessary in the values-clarification approach.

A criticism can make the value of the teacher's contribution more obvious. To conduct his empirical research, Kohlberg (1984) presented moral dilemmas to the subjects to elicit verbal responses as the basis for inferring the nature of their cognitive processes. After massive data collection, he formulated his six-stage theory from the responses, as if their logic was isomorphic with the logic of the cognitive processes. This is probably not true. In any case, just as Kohlberg was not interested in influencing the moral development of his subjects or in teaching them, so is the teacher not interested in researching the students' moral development. The moral dilemma is a diagnostic tool for Kohlberg. It is fallacious to assume it can be a teaching or learning tool. The teacher who simply presents a dilemma for discussion assumes the role of a scientific researcher rather than a teacher. If the dilemma, through its discussion in class, serves as a diagnostic tool, the teacher's diagnostic purpose differs from the researcher's. The information gained should be used to formulate a prognosis and prescription for a lesson designed to enable the students to become aware of some aspects of morality of which they were previously unaware.

Becoming aware of new things in the moral domain, moreover, can occur horizontally across the same Kohlbergian stage as well as "up" the conceptual ladder. A student might know it is right to keep promises and tell the truth, for example, at the fourth stage of understanding, without knowing it is right to repair damages done and return services received. In other words, the standard dilemmas approach, like the values-clarification approach, is only the first part of what should be a two-phase process. It is also a consciousness-raising process that can result in the actual learning of moral values only if it is supplemented with instructional content that discloses new values.

This is implied in the third of Kohlberg's conditions concerning free and open discussion. The comparison of two or more conflicting views on a controversial issue goes beyond the mere examination of the dilemma. Before controversial issues will be considered as the proper vehicle for value and moral education, however, it should be noted that the moral-dilemmas approach is primarily cognitive. The development of moral feelings and sentiments, however, may be more significant to one's actual moral growth than the development of moral reasoning, as the feminist critique of Kohlberg intimates (see Gilligan, 1982). This is why learning to value what the teacher values (e.g., Wildman) and learning to value other students (i.e., fraternity) are so important.

If the emergence in the 1960s and 1970s of the values-clarification and moral-dilemmas approaches was largely due to their casting the teacher into a nondirective, quasi-dialogical role, it was not unlike the emergence of the Sophists. Those teachers of virtue of classical antiquity were unable to answer Socrates' question when he asked them, What is virtue? Like the Sophists, advocates of values clarification and the discussion of dilemmas focus on processes because they do not know what virtue is. They are anti-intellectual and anticonceptual, in spite of their restriction to the verbal, cognitive domain, although they are right in attempting to ground the discussion of value in classrooms in the student's perceptual reality. It is vital to retain this grounding in perceptual consciousness in any attempt to introduce valid moral concepts to enable students to learn to value things and conduct they have not previously valued. It is equally necessary to supplement their emphasis upon processes with content, that is, with substantive moral knowledge of the kind discussed in the previous chapters.

LEARNING HUMAN RIGHTS AND OBLIGATIONS

Unlike most values-clarification exercises, the moral-dilemmas approach at least presents students with something outside themselves about which they can begin to reason impartially, objectively, and in the third person. Discussing the dilemma of the man confronted with the choice of stealing the expensive drug or letting his wife die encourages reflection upon morality and the legality of stealing, ownership of property, the value of life, the prima facie duty of benevolence, love as a moral motive, and so on—before the matter is existentialized by asking the students what they think they themselves would be obligated to do, were they in the situation. Such objectivity is highly desirable, not for the reasons given by moral rationalists but because Kierkegaard is correct about becoming a particular individual through the mediation of the universal.

On the other hand, such objectivity is spurious. The specific example is a false dilemma because no loving husband would hesitate to steal the drug to save his spouse after other efforts to secure it had failed. The action would not be guided by reasoning processes, furthermore, but by immediate apprehension of what is right. A dilemma, on the other hand, is a situation in which one is presented with two alternatives, both of which are morally unacceptable. Because the dilemmas are fictional, they will probably not be encountered in real life by most students. They can create the misleading impression that morality is about rare and exceptional, spectacular situations, rather than about the ordinary, everyday conditions of human interactions, where one's duties are obvious. They can also suggest it is difficult to know what is right and that hardly anyone knows what is right, not even teachers.

The requisite objectivity and contact with real life can be obtained through the study of issues that are controversial in society. They are moral dilemmas writ large. Kohlberg (1976) himself claims to have found the same patterns of reasoning used in moral and political dilemmas when he queried university students on political issues such as open housing laws; civil disobedience; the rights of a critical, free press; and the redistribution of wealth through taxation (p. 187). Strictly speaking, they are not dilemmas with two morally unacceptable alternatives, for a controversy is legitimate when two or more views on an issue each have some valid claims, all of which cannot be satisfied.

In addition to those mentioned earlier, the controversial issues listed with the values-clarification approach include individual initiative versus governmental control, capitalism versus socialism, independence versus dependence, wealth versus a pleasant life, the role of advertising, democracy versus anarchy versus autocracy, poverty on an Indian reservation, U.S. foreign policy in supporting unpopular governments, loyalty oaths, and civil disobedience (Raths et al., 1966, pp. 95–100). Another listing of issues so common "they could be considered as 'required' subject matter" (p. 187) includes the relationships between men and women, work and leisure, change and stability in life and society, science and humanism, self-interest and social welfare, individual and social planning, and the meaning of love and friendship.

Part of the purpose of studying controversial issues in school is to enable students to engage in genuine learning in the area of their moral and civic education, that is, to let them learn to value things differently by becoming aware of new qualities of things. The issues should be selected on the criterion that they are both contemporary (current events) and perennial, the latter in the sense that the major political parties will most likely disagree about them in the future. Then the students' concern will continue into their adult lives. These kinds of issues will probably include the status of women, handicapped people, and minority groups in society; problems of the economy such as unemployment, inflation, the distribution of goods and wealth, and the depletion of natural resources; the control of international relations by nonviolent means; the freedom of speech, thought, expression, and assembly necessary to debate these things in multipartisan contexts; problems of law, crime, and punishment; and matters connected to the right to life, such as abortion, euthanasia, socialized medicine, political executions, terrorism, and the ecological crisis in the context of the necessity of maintaining a livable environment.

The disciplined study of controversial issues of this kind requires well-prepared units that include relevant information, well-expressed viewpoints representing the major options, and some criteria of judgment by which to evaluate them. These criteria can be the democratic ideals of society, their more sophisticated conceptualization as human rights, human rights in general, and/or prima facie moral obligations. The use of these materials can begin with a value-clarification exercise, even as recommended before the unit on race relations or ecology (Simon et al., 1972, p. 39). Race relations, of course, cannot be studied in a responsible manner without giving moral reasons for nondiscriminatory policies, expressed in the language of human rights such as equal rights, equal access, equal opportunity, and equal consideration irrespective of race. Because the same thing is true of other controversial issues, the language of human rights and/or prima facie duties should be involved in the study of controversial issues in schools. It should also become implicated wherever the clarification of value and discussion of moral dilemmas occurs to provide the conceptual means for acquiring new insights in the value and moral domains.

Students need to study and discuss the alternative perspectives in an impartial manner in order to fulfill Kohlberg's third condition, but only the introduction of human rights principles and/or prima facie duties can enable them to ascertain which view is compatible with human rights and moral obligations. Instead of discovering what they already believe, students should be trying to discover what they should believe about the issue at hand. This can be done in dialogical, nondoctrinating ways in a multipartisan classroom without the use of group pressure to develop the consensus advocated by the earlier reconstructionists (Smith, 1945).

To state it the other way around, because fundamental human rights and the more specific human rights derived from them are the contemporary heirs of deontological ethics, the main content of value, moral, and civic education should be these universal obligations. There are various sources of the language of human rights: the bill of rights attached to a nation's constitution, the Universal Declaration of Human Rights adopted by the General Assembly of the United Nations in 1948, and the International Covenants based upon this declaration and ratified by a nation's federal government. These, of course, should be paraphrased to the level of abstraction appropriate to a given grade in the same way the background knowledge about the issue should be constructed (UNESCO, 1959, pp. 106–108). This policy needs accompaniment with a pedagogy that insures that human rights concepts are grounded in the students' perceptual world. The first phase of their introduction should therefore be a process of value clarification, discussion of a moral dilemma or predicament, or the study of a controversial issue, even as their advocates propose, so long as it is recognized that these activities merely bring students to the threshold of learning to value something. They should motivate students to want to investigate the themes that emerge. Then the thematic investigation should lead them to come to terms with whatever facts and human rights (or prima facie duties) are involved when the matter is viewed in terms of the rightness of what should be done. After consciousness is raised, the conceptual schema of human rights language can help students learn to value the qualities of human beings by disclosing new aspects of their value and dignity. If the matter concerns personal morality, this may occur more readily with the concepts of the prima facie moral obligations.

The goal should not be to learn human rights or moral duties as deontological principles that spell out their own rights and duties as if moral rationalism were tenable. It is to learn through the conceptual schemata of human rights and moral language to value other people and become aware of what their dignity requires of one. It is to let this appreciation deepen into respect for others, for oneself, and for the rule or policy that expresses the right or duty implicated (cf. Hahn, 1987; Shafer, 1987; Vandenberg, 1983, 1984b).

The goal is to unite the conceptual learning with the perceptual learning that has been occurring in the hidden curriculum, for when the learning of value and moral concepts is based on a developed moral sensibility, it can also be a learning to value other people. It is an optional matter whether learning to value things differently begins with what students already value, as in values clarification; or with things people their age and experience might value, as in the discussion of moral dilemmas; or with things that adults in their society already value, as in the study of controversial issues. Any of these allows a lesson to begin with the qualities students are aware of perceptually. With this beginning, the introduction of moral and human rights concepts will not be merely free floating and verbal, but will enable students to learn to value other people and become aware of the rightness of correct conduct. There can be no more universal source of moral concepts for this purpose than the language of human rights, and universality is needed for the transpersonal standard.

THE TRANSPERSONAL STANDARD

Whether students are learning to value things through any of these proposals or through direct, didactic instruction, they need what Greene (1973, p. 285), following William Frankena (1966, p. 236), calls a *transpersonal standard* for morality and public life. It has been the goal of these chapters to elaborate such a standard through the investigation of the ethical theories of the Enlightenment and their subsequent refinements. The question remaining is whether their synthesis in fundamental human rights is the most valid formulation for their use in schooling. As indicated, all democracies, liberal and socialist alike, give allegiance to the democratic ideals of liberty, equality, and fraternity. Although these are variously interpreted, the differences lie mostly in which of the three is considered paramount. To the extent they are balanced in their formulation as the fundamental human rights to equal freedom, equal consideration, and brotherly/sisterly love, their synthesis transcends the narrower perspectives of political ideologies. Any shortcomings might not matter after they are paraphrased to the levels of abstraction necessary for pedagogical purposes.

If the broader question is which formulation of human rights is the most valid, the reply is that the Universal Declaration of 1948 has preempted the field. It is not only transpersonal. It is, according to Alwin Diemar, transcultural, transnational, transhistorical, and transideological (UNESCO, 1986, p. 97). The human rights language of this declaration belongs in all lessons in moral and civic values in schools in nations that do not have their own bill of rights but have ratified one or more of the covenants based upon the Declaration. Just as the 1948 Declaration preempts other international documents until it is revised, superceded, or abandoned, so, too, a national bill of rights preempts the field within a nation, at least in elementary and secondary schools. Its basic criteria of justice, or rightness, apply to all of its citizens, regardless of their political or religious affiliations, and therefore legitimately belong in the study of controversial issues in the schools.

The case is a bit different for the prima facie obligations in the moral realm, but it has been made earlier. Insofar as the synthesis of the two kinds of ethics has successfully established the basis for ethics in human dignity, the transpersonal standard sought is whether a so-called value, moral belief, rule, or principle is compatible with human dignity. Human dignity itself is the transpersonal standard, whether it is applied to the intellectual construction of a philosopher or the behavior of schoolchildren, whether it is a matter of intellectual beliefs or actual moral conduct. Either is right to the extent that it maintains and enhances human dignity.

CONCLUSION

This study of the epistemology of the good and right has found that existing things have qualities that make them valuable. The qualities are disclosed perceptually through personal exploration and manifest appreciation by others, including teachers who value highly the things in the world about which they are teaching. When these things are human beings, the disclosure of their qualities occurs through dialogical relations that manifest the value and dignity of the unique people involved. This awareness of the personal agency and identity of each other calls forth the reciprocal moral obligations of human rights. Whether human rights are unalienable and indefeasible depends less on rational argument than upon personal encounters that disclose their unconditionality within particular moral situations (Buber).

The study has also found that human rights and prima facie moral obligations should structure the organization of schooling, that is, the hidden curriculum. Their conceptualized expressions should enter into the explicit study of values in schools whenever thematically relevant, whether in one of the more formal proposals discussed or in the impromptu asides that occur in the contexts of any subject matter in the curriculum. The moral predicaments in literature or history, for example, can be discussed in terms of human rights and human dignity. Many areas of the social studies and natural sciences have a significance for social life that can be articulated with the language of human rights, thereby disclosing their ethical contexts.

Is such a pervasive attention to moral obligations in an effort to transcend nihilism merely reactionary? It depends partly on whether the study of the historically great ethical theories has been an ideological defense of traditional values or a genuine attempt to reinterpret and repossess the Enlightenment heritage in the confrontation with the moral crisis. Bloom (1987) seems essentially correct when he claims, "The rule of philosophy is recognized in the insistence that regimes be constructed to protect the rights of man" (p. 166). A concern for human rights characteristically emerges when justice cannot be obtained within the existing legal context. The appeal to a natural or human right distinguishes the moral right from legal rights to supplement the latter with progressive reform.

There is also an important difference between traditional and perennial values. In Bloom's (1987) words,

> There is a perennial and unobtrusive view that morality consists in such things as telling the truth, paying one's debts, respecting one's parents and doing no voluntary harm to anyone. Those are all things easy to say and hard to do; they do not attract much attention, and win little honor in the world. The good will, as described by Kant, is a humble notion, accessible to every child, but its fulfillment is the activity of a lifetime of performing the simple duties prescribed by it. This morality always requires sacrifice. . . . Such morality, in order to be itself, must be for itself and not for some result beyond it. (p. 325)

Although Bloom goes on to make some intemperate remarks about how this morality does not necessarily involve the public heroics found in protest movements, he seems to have been misled by street theater. There is more of this morality in the counterculture than can be shown on television—enough, in fact, to have led to the formation of the counterculture.

The failure to distinguish perennial values, which are progressive or conservative depending on the context, from traditional values is partly due to the permeation of the culture by what Bloom (1987) calls "liberalism without natural rights, the kind we knew from John Stuart Mill and John Dewey" (p. 29), which advocates openness to the new and emergent as if newness itself insures that something is good. This liberalism is found among the progressive educationists who attack "absolutes" and universal principles, following Dewey (1929/1960), who holds that such principles are at best hypotheses (pp. 277–278). Clearly, one cannot protest against injustice on the basis of a hypothesis. To claim there is a justice greater than statutory laws, in terms of which they should be reformed, requires a concept of natural or human rights by which to defend elemental human dignity. Because progressive educators have always supported human dignity in the classroom, their protest against so-called absolutes is woefully misplaced. The question is not whether a given obligation is unconditional but whether it is perceived as obligatory regardless of whether fulfilling it gives one pleasure, satisfies desires, or promotes happiness. The abandonment of this sense of obligatoriness does not merely abandon the moral and civic education of the working classes; it gives away their right to complain about the injustices in the world.

The difference between progressive and traditional education is on a wholly different plane from the distinction between teleological and deontological ethics. The latter distinction is as old as Plato, for the entire argument of the *Republic* is devoted to demonstrating that the moral person will be happy, despite appearances to the contrary. One should pursue the truth and justice, not happiness, but one deserves and receives happiness as a consequence. This is so far from obvious that Plato had to invent the myth of Er and the concept of immortality to support his belief. Kant also had to resort to immortality to show that people who fulfill their obligations receive the happiness they deserve. Mill's reliance upon Plato's idea that the person educated to distinguish those pleasures that are qualitatively superior and most compatible with human dignity will live the pleasantest life is tantamount to the abandonment of utilitarianism. Be this as it may, this study has confirmed there are human rights to sustenance, clothing, shelter, medical care, and education, among other things. The existence of the correlative obligations is not contingent upon any subsequent increase in happiness in the world. The obligations stand even if their fulfillment decreases the happiness of the more privileged members of society and lengthens the lifespan of underprivileged people who are destined to wretched lives. The obligations stand simply because the underprivileged are human beings.

Stating this more generally, human rights are not justified by the contribution their fulfillment makes to the general welfare. The general welfare is improved and the common good enhanced by the observance of human rights, but their justification in the final analysis is that they are deserved simply because their possessors are human. Instead of being traditional, then, the recommended implementation in the covert and overt curriculum of the relevant human rights and prima facie duties stands in the same relation to the progressivism of values clarification, nondirective discussion of moral dilemmas, and the objective study of controversial issues that Theodore Brameld's (1965) reconstructionism stands in regard to progressive education in general. It lacks, however, his kind of reconstructive "goal of a planet-wide democratic order" (p. 1) and his "defensible partiality" (pp. 154–155). When Brameld criticizes progressive education for the indefiniteness of its goals, he might have criticized its moral nihilism. The suggestion also parallels the relation of Boyd Bode to progressive education when he said in his 1938 *Progressive Education at the Crossroads*, "The attitude of superstitious reverence for childhood is still with us" (p. 70).

It is not a disservice to children and youth to help them become aware of their moral obligations and their own and everyone else's human rights. The conceptual supplementation of their own musings with the language of moral and human rights merely gives them the wherewithal to think with as they grapple with the important aspects of life. It is "superstitious reverence" to assume they can think about moral and value issues without the conceptual apparatus and schemata for doing so, or to suppose they can invent it for themselves. Because the right to education includes the right as well as the duty to develop virtue and intelligence (Ross), or to develop one's talents and abilities, or all of one's "faculties" (Kant), students have a right to have access to the conceptual schemata of prima facie duties and human rights during every examination of value and morality in schools.

Whether this becomes moralistic in the pejorative sense may depend in the end on the curriculum time and space devoted to value and moral education. The moral education necessary to develop moral agency should be grounded in the value education that occurs when one becomes aware of the qualities of the things in the regions of the world studied in the cognitive curriculum. In the course of this, one should slowly acquire the "cultivated mind" that has an "inexhaustible interest in all that surrounds it" (Mill) and that eventuates in the general love of the world that moves one to care for and preserve existing things. Just as moral education should be grounded in this value education, moreover, so should this value education be grounded in the overall framework of common, general education. The right to moral knowledge is merely a special case of the more general right to have access to the knowledge and skills of general education. The right to education is unalienable and indefeasible if it means the right to develop one's talents and abilities; to develop morally and cognitively; in short, to develop the humanity in oneself so one can assume adult existence in society. The obligation to provide resources for this development, however, falls within the conditional duties of beneficence (Ross, Kant).

Although the hidden curriculum is present all the time, nothing has been said so far about the relative importance of value and moral education in the whole of schooling. This would require an estimation of the extent and depth of the moral crisis in Western society, of the actual presence of nihilism, and of the probability of the schools making an appreciable difference. These issues are beyond the scope of this book, which has been limited so far to the search for the kind of knowledge of value and morality that deserves to be in the school curriculum because of its epistemic characteristics. The place of moral education within the whole of common general education cannot be considered adequately, furthermore, in isolation from the much larger question of the role of knowledge in the curriculum of general education. This question, however, could not have been considered without this preliminary study of ethical theories. The proper question is not, strictly speaking, one of epistemology, theory of knowledge, or philosophy of science. It concerns the knowledge and skills that should be available in common general education if education is a human right. If education is the moral and cognitive development necessary for one to assume the responsibilities of adult moral agency in an advanced industrial society, and if this education is a human right, then we have to ask, What knowledge and skills should comprise the curriculum available to everyone?

The question can be rephrased through the terms of Michel Foucault (1969/1972). He says, "Education may well be, as of right, the instrument whereby every individual, in a society like ours, can gain access to any kind of discourse" (p. 227). Then our question becomes, Which kinds of discourse should be available to everyone through the school curriculum? If the purpose of gaining access to the various kinds of discourse is to gain access to the worlds they disclose, then our question is, How should the curriculum of general education be selected, structured, and taught to enable everyone to have access to the world? To which regions of the world should everyone have access as their human right? We will investigate this question in Part II.

Part II
COGNITIVE EDUCATION

CHAPTER 6

Education and the Intellectual Crisis

Given that education is a human right, the question of the role and content of knowledge in the curriculum is epistemological, but not a question of epistemology, theory of knowledge, or the philosophy of science. It concerns the epistemic characteristics and the cognitive content of education in the development of the humanity of the human being in the midst of widespread disbelief in the value of knowledge and the existence of truth. Nihilism in the cognitive domain is related to the moral crisis because cognitive relativism is frequently associated with moral relativism. In fact, the moral crisis of Western civilization may be fundamentally an intellectual crisis. This is evident in the critique of science first elaborated in the counterculture of the late 1960s and subsequently continued in neo–Marxist critical theory, deconstructionism, and postmodernism.

THE CRITIQUE OF SCIENCE

The educational reform movement of the early 1960s in the United States placed emphasis on the natural sciences and mathematics in the secondary school curriculum for the sake of national defense. This teleology apparently generated its own antithesis in the subsequent reform movement toward humanistic, open education, when the students who had been nurtured on the new physics, chemistry, biology, and mathematics reached the universities. The dominance of the curriculum by the natural sciences was criticized for their lack of relevance, their dehumanization of consciousness, and their role in capitalistic aggrandizement. These charges were often made by students who had studied them assiduously, with the superior achievement necessary for matriculation in tertiary schools. They were also made by students who had memorized more than they understood and who wanted insight and understanding. Their criticism of the use of science in war, however, merely repeated earlier complaints. Even while they had hoped for the sudden end to the war initiated by Japan, for example, not many Americans were happy with the destruction of civilian life that occurred at Hiroshima and Nagasaki. The Society Against Nuclear Energy (SANE) was active on college campuses as early as the mid-1950s. And of course people all over the world were horrified when they finally heard of the use of science to exterminate Jews in the Holocaust.

The critique of science for the uses to which it is put in society sometimes appears to be directed against science itself. Sometimes it is propaganda for partisan politics. One can criticize the amoral or immoral use of science, however, without criticizing scientific knowledge or method itself, and without having ulterior political goals. It is not always easy to maintain these distinctions. The use of science in the development of nuclear deterrent forces, an activity that looks like preparation for war, requires vast numbers of scientists and technologists who have been educated to conduct the research associated with defense and the arms and space races. This makes it very difficult to distinguish learning science in secondary schools in order to learn about the natural world from the preparation for careers as scientists, technologists, and engineers who will be directly or indirectly concerned with using science for ends that may be morally questionable.

The critique of science itself, however, is made by people who identify with the counterculture for this very reason. Their basic claim is that learning science is inherently dehumanizing because its conceptual structures tend to develop a mechanized, intellectualized consciousness that is alienated from its own spontaneous and creative feelings, intuitions, and sensibilities. It is consequently alienated from the qualities of things in the natural world and the inward life of other people. The claim is that science uses intellectual processes that rigorously isolate phenomena from real objects in the perceived world. This reductionism involves a highly technical, abstract language that does not seem to refer to things in the perceived world. People who are not adept with abstract concepts find it irrelevant to their everyday world. Those who do well in science, it is alleged, only become desensitized to the nuances of value and beauty apparent in the world to those not schooled in their abstractions.

The validity of this critique is not at issue. It is certainly easy to find very talented engineers who are morons in esthetic, moral, and cultural pursuits, and male chauvinists to boot. This sort of evidence illustrates without proving the point. What matters is that a great many students in the reform movement of the late 1960s and 1970s thought it was true and went into countercultural things like astrology, transcendental meditation, spiritualism, magic, Eastern religions, mysticism, psychedelic drugs, and a variety of therapies to find a source of knowledge that seemed relevant to the world given to their perceptions. This represents the crisis in reason to the extent that science is the century's prime embodiment of reason and its principal arena of intellectual achievement. It is not clear, of course, that the claim about science being inherently dehumanizing can be maintained. It may be true when science is poorly taught, but anything poorly taught can be dehumanizing. Perhaps the belief that learning science is inherently dehumanizing results from conflating the belief about its use in society for militaristic or exploitative goals with the way individual people pursue and use science for nonscientific goals. If it is true of them, the fault lies not in science but in the technological consciousness that will use anything to achieve its goals.

THE TECHNOLOGICAL CONSCIOUSNESS

In 1620 Francis Bacon said, "The roads to human power and to human knowledge lie close together, and are nearly the same" (1620/1939b, p. 89). Although his *Great Instauration* (1605/1939a) is renowned as a major manifesto of modern science, Bacon's slogan, "Knowledge is power" is a perfect expression of the technological consciousness. In other words, at the very beginning of the modern world it was thought that one should pursue science in order to possess power over nature and people. Propaganda has been used to sell science for its technological usefulness ever since.

The strong connection of the new scientific knowledge with the exploration of the world in the Enlightenment of the seventeenth and eighteenth centuries became an almost complete yoking of science and technology in the late nineteenth century progressive era in American politics, as epitomized in the educational theory of Dewey. Facing an open, expansive world and a growth economy, it was easy to believe that great progress could be made simply by using science to conquer nature for the good of humankind. Imposing these aspirations upon science, however, resulted in the "fusion" of science and technology, that can be called the "technological consciousness" because it sweeps up scientific knowledge in the pursuit of nonscientific goals. In the last chapter of *Toward a Rational Society* (1968/1971), Jurgen Habermas claims there is no necessary connection between science and technology but they tend to become fused because certain characteristics of scientific knowledge make it easy to use in technology. For example, many scientists find full-time employment in industrial research. Those who maintain appointments at universities often devote research efforts to industrial or defense research. They consult with industry or engage in research that shows immediate returns and is readily funded by industry or government. The fusion of science and technology has consequently become the norm. People have come to believe that science should have a technological payoff. The wonders of science are mostly visible through its applications to defense, medical practice, and the electronic world of high technology.

The best evidence for this fusion is the frequent use of the two words together, "science and technology," as if they were one thing. A blessing seems to be laid upon anything called "science," regardless of its scientific or social worth. Scientists become too highly respected and are consulted on matters outside their area of expertise. It becomes assumed that every human problem can receive a scientific or technological solution; in fact, one looks for the technological fix. Habermas (1968/1971) correctly claims that the fusion of science and technology can result in the development of an amoral consciousness that uses a cognitive frame of reference to solve social and moral problems. When doctors, for example, speak of terminating a pregnancy as dilation and curettage, or as medical evacuation of the gravidoid uterus, the bit of scientific-sounding jargon removes the moral aspects of the act from consciousness. Euthanasia can be referred to as terminating a life, as if it were not killing. Most macabre is one doctor's advocacy of the use of the bodies of brain-dead women on life-support systems as surrogate mothers. His reference to these women as machines is only a step away from the use of one's own body as a machine, such as using performance-enhancing drugs to excel in sports. Thus the widespread diffusion of the objective knowledge of the natural sciences can result in the societal dominance of a kind of consciousness that does not consider the validity of its goals or the means of achieving them, that is, the technological consciousness.

Even if heavily technologized societies are beset by the technological consciousness in general, however, it is wrong to attribute this to science as such. The deficiency is more likely due to amorality, or to nihilism, than to knowledge or truth. The defensible claim seems to be that advanced industrial societies are likely to develop people who lack consciousness of the esthetic, moral, and religious dimensions of life and that this is partly due to the great prestige of science. The technological consciousness is not necessarily a negative thing. It is positive, or humanized, as far as it goes, but it needs supplementation by value and moral education, and perhaps by religious education, to complete its humanization. If so, the critique of science merely manifests a lack of credibility in scientific reason: One index of an intellectual crisis is the reduction of reason to technologized science.

THE REPRODUCTION OF THE SOCIAL STRUCTURE

Some of the critics of the role of science in society claim the school's main function is to enable society to reproduce its existing patterns of social stratification. Science and mathematics are central to the matriculation track of the secondary school, not because they are good knowledge but because they enable the technological and managerial elites to maintain their existence as a social class. This criticism is made by egalitarians who prefer a more equitable distribution of wealth and by Marxists who believe this use of the school by the ruling class to reproduce itself involves the exploitation of the working class. In either case it is claimed that the knowledge taught in schools promotes a technocracy rather than truth. All knowledge is said to be socially constructed, which is taken to imply that science does not deserve its high status on its epistemic merits.

The egalitarian goals are defensible on grounds of fraternity, but if tertiary schooling is necessary to maintain society, it is irrelevant to point out that this means that stratification patterns are reproduced through the schools. Of course they are, but the schools do not do it on purpose. It is a latent function of educating people for admission to tertiary schools, necessarily a selective process. This is not done on the schools' own initiative, furthermore, because the basic decisions are made by the governing bodies that establish and finance schools. Egalitarians who want to change this should therefore engage in political campaigns in the adult community to persuade society not to have tertiary schools. They condemn themselves to failure when they try to persuade teachers in teacher training institutions to change schools in this respect, for they can do nothing about it. If the patterns of social stratification in a society are unjust, furthermore, it is not the school's fault so long as its awards and certificates are distributed strictly on merit. The remedy cannot be sought in schools, finally, if the reproduction thesis is in fact true.

The nihilism of the reproduction thesis is manifest in the claim that knowledge is not discovered and learned but socially constructed and produced, as if this undermines its epistemic worth and establishes cognitive relativism. To the contrary, it manifests the intellectual crisis. The sense in which it is true is trivial. Of course only human beings have knowledge, and all human beings live in society. This merely brings us to the threshold of the epistemological question: Which socially constructed knowledge belongs in the school curriculum because of its epistemic merits? The intellectual crisis is manifested in a deeper sense when Michael Apple (1988) claims, "The very notion of the educational system as assisting in the production of economically and ideologically useful knowledge points to the fact that schools are *cultural* as well as economic institutions" (p. 194). He might have found this less surprising had he not previously considered schools through a materialistic paradigm. It is this paradigm that is socially constructed and that interprets the transmission and acquisition of knowledge in schools as production, as if knowledge were some kind of manufactured object similar to the artifacts produced by factories. The reification of knowledge in the use of the metaphor of production betrays the presence of the false consciousness that Marxists often claim manifests bourgeois ideology.

That this false consciousness exemplifies the intellectual crisis can be shown by asking it to become reflexive. If Apple believes that the explanation of knowledge as an object of production is satisfactory for schools, this interpretation should be applied to his own prolific writing, for he is a teacher who writes articles and books that are published for use in tertiary schools, which he has called economic institutions in the sentence quoted. If these writings are simply marketable products, it cannot be argued that they also express the truth. If what they say is true, the product is very different from the production of knowledge to which they reduce such things. And, if they are true, there is no reason why high-status knowledge in secondary schools is not also true. It is very tempting to interpret Apple's best-selling work economically, particularly because his profuse citation of his own writings as if they are cultural capital seems, with all due respect, more like the production than the discovery of knowledge and truth. This will not do, however, because of the truth of what he says.

The enigma can be explained by recognizing that the thesis of the production and reproduction of knowledge in schools is only a partial truth. It is an economic explanation of the role of knowledge in schooling that ought not explain it away. It needs to recognize itself as only a partial truth—as Apple (1988) does in the quoted sentence—to have any truth at all attributed to it. It interprets schools *as if* they were economic institutions, but of course they are not. If it is assumed to be the whole truth, then the requirement that it apply to itself destroys it. It becomes merely the ideology that reflects the author's relation to the means of production. That an economic interpretation of schooling is only one perspective among others is indicated in the opening paragraph of this volume. It manifests the intellectual crisis, moreover, because it is a theoretical interpretation of knowledge that cannot account for its own existence as a theory. It exemplifies the claim of Edmund Husserl (1936/1970) that there is a crisis in the Western understanding of reason because the natural sciences are understood to be the exemplary embodiment of human reason, although the methods of science cannot account for the reason that makes their methods possible (p. 295).

Apple (1987) elsewhere recognizes the genetic fallacy, which he says occurs when it is assumed that "all the insights of a position are fundamentally polluted by the social and political tendencies out of which they arose" (p. 599). It is the genetic fallacy to believe one is criticizing the truth of an idea by criticizing its source, for example, to believe one is criticizing the content of the curriculum by pointing out its origin in a particular stratum of society or its hegemonic functions, without giving independent consideration to its epistemic worth. The latter seems to require not a political economy of knowledge but epistemology and philosophy of science.

LIMITATIONS OF PHILOSOPHY OF SCIENCE

An investigation of the appropriate role of knowledge in education and society may seem to require a proper philosophy of science, but to pursue this route would make several mistakes. It would fail to understand that some of the critics are being turned away from science itself and will not be persuaded by an account of the legitimacy and liberating effects of science. A larger mistake is alluded to by Leonard Waks (1988) when he indicates that philosophy of education functions in three contexts: intellectual, institutional, and ideological. Waks claims it is a mistake to structure a course in theory of knowledge for teachers and curriculum specialists around recent articles from philosophy journals that display the state of the art in epistemology or philosophy of science. The students are so deeply concerned with the institutional and normative contexts that they find these subjects irrelevant to their work. Any inquiry into the role of knowledge in education and human existence is concerned with knowledge in individual, institutional, and societal contexts and can only obtain indirect guidance from a philosophy of science or epistemology formulated independently of these contexts.

The most serious mistake, however, is that philosophers of science are not scientists but philosophers. Philosophers have always formulated an epistemology in an effort to ascertain the nature of knowledge and truth. In this century their attention has generally shifted to philosophy of science. The word *science* comes from the Latin *scienta*, from the verb *scrire*, meaning to know. The words *knowledge* and *science* were originally synonymous. Similarly, philosophy formerly included science. The study of nature was called *natural philosophy* as late as the eighteenth century, much as it is called *natural science* today. Some of the great philosophers—Bacon, Descartes, Leibniz—have also been great scientists who formulated theories of scientific method that have served as models for subsequent research as well as propaganda for the genuine virtues of science.

Only with the nineteenth century has the word *science* come to refer exclusively to the natural sciences (physics, biology, chemistry). Modern universities, for example, do not include the social sciences and humanities within their faculties of science. This shift in meaning was enhanced by the unified science movement of the first half of the twentieth century. The ancient ideal of one unified body of knowledge expressed in a universally valid language continues to be sought by philosophers of science, who attempt to isolate and formulate the method of inquiry imputed to the natural sciences and call this *science* or the *scientific method*. The mistake is believing that there is such a thing as science and that a philosopher of science is supposed to identify the essence of scientific investigation. This is a mistake because there are many sciences: physical sciences, life sciences, social sciences, behavioral sciences, logical and mathematical sciences, agricultural sciences, linguistic and hermeneutical sciences, health sciences, and so on. Within each of these, furthermore, there are various ways of conducting research.

Philosophers of science, however, often take the one science of physics and assume it alone is science, thereby committing the fallacy of composition, reasoning from the part to the whole. Then they take some particular aspect of research in physics and call it the essence of scientific method. Classic examples are the analysis of simple ideas, induction of generalizations from observed data, laboratory experimentation, verified propositions, a set of basic concepts, theoretical falsifiability, and an overarching paradigm within the framework of which experiments are conducted. In each case some aspect of science is reified and advertised in an ideological and programmatic attempt to lay down a priori criteria that all scientific investigation should follow. Such reification involves a false consciousness.

It is quite clear, moreover, that the acceptance of physics as the paradigm for all of science entails a physicalistic model of knowledge and of everything in the universe. It is true that all knowledge should be compatible with what we know of the physical universe, which is the only universe there is, but it is also true that physics, chosen as the paradigm case of knowledge because of its precision and exactitude, is also the science most technologically useful to the economic system. A philosophy of science that assumes physics should be the model for all knowledge therefore cannot escape the economic interpretation. The intellectual fusion of philosophy of science and the physical sciences mirrors the cultural fusion of science and technology. The excellence of the knowledge of physics is not denied by claiming that there is valuable knowledge in the social sciences and humanities that is not accessible through physicalistic methods of inquiry.

According to Richard Bernstein (1983), the philosophy of science has gone through four phases in the twentieth century. These are related to the aspect of science reified into the basic epistemological unit. First it was the single term, which had to be defined observationally or operationally. Then it was a statement of fact, or proposition, that was empirically verifiable. Then it was a conceptual scheme that allowed such terms and sentences to be formulated and that made observation of entities and facts possible. The epistemic unit was broadened once again to include the paradigm that made the conceptual scheme possible. With this the unit of epistemological analysis became the historical development of research programs (pp. 75–77). Attention to the historical development was necessary to recontextualize the aspects of science that had been erroneously decontextualized.

The next step is to focus upon the community of investigators to take into account the concept of the social construction of knowledge in epistemically valid ways. To do this, it should be noted that not all philosophers of science have expertise in the sciences for which they attempt to specify the methodology. Anyone would certainly have difficulty in acquiring the necessary expertise in two or more sciences. Without it, however, speculations go astray. Dewey, for example, seems to have lacked the knowledge of physics that his theory of inquiry might have presupposed. His philosophy of science had no room for theoretical physics, although he was at Columbia University, whose physics department subsequently nourished the Manhattan Project. This was the theoretical undertaking that eventuated in the experiment at Los Alamos, which was almost unnecessary because the chances of it not working were infinitessimally small before it could be risked. *Pace* Dewey, much of the research conducted in the natural sciences is theoretical research. If one wants to learn what science is, one joins the community of investigators. One ought not go to a university department of philosophy but to its science departments. If one wants to find out what is scientific, or epistemically valid, about one of the social sciences or humanities, one ought not to go to the physics department but to the respective department in the social sciences or literature, language, philosophy, fine arts, history, or religious studies. Each of the special sciences or disciplines is a community of investigators due to the extensive division of labor in the discovery of knowledge. The significance of these communities of investigators was first brought to attention in the work of Charles Sanders Peirce (1871/ 1958a, pp. 82–83; 1878/1958b, pp. 132–133; 1958c, pp. 54, 55, 87; 1868/ 1958d, pp. 69, 72). Each community of investigators has its own canons of inquiry and its main dwelling place in a university department of learning. To discover empirically how to do scientific research, one should join the relevant community of investigators or consult with members of the already constituted discipline. One should ask the experts. There is no superior court of appeal.

KNOWLEDGE OF THE ACTS AND DISCIPLINES

The university disciplines are not the only communities of qualified investigators in society. Each of the arts, crafts, trades, and sports (ACTS), as well as the professions, is such a community, constituted as a discursive practice (Foucault, 1969/1972) by its own qualified experts. The skepticism aroused by the critique of science in the culture is no cause for despair. There is a great deal of knowledge in society in addition to that of the natural sciences that is quite appropriate for the school curriculum. This is the knowledge that is attested to by the discursive community in each of the ACTS, as well as in the professions and academic disciplines.

The intellectual crisis is, of course, partly a distrust of the experts in these areas and partly a distrust of expertise as such. The right to have one's own opinion has merged with egalitarian assertiveness to create a general acceptance of the belief that all opinions are equal. In this situation there are no experts, or else all expertise is thought to be merely a matter of esoteric jargon. To challenge the knowledge of the experts in the ACTS or disciplines honestly, however, one has to become expert in the activity or domain in question in order to join issue with their knowledge and skills. Then successful criticism becomes a contribution to the knowledge in that domain. Similarly, the theory of the nature of the knowledge in one of the ACTS or disciplines can be adequate only if it is based upon expertise within the specific domain. When Dewey (1948/1961) contrasts the theory of knowledge with the kinds of epistemology and philosophy of science that specify a priori criteria that knowledge should satisfy to be acceptable as knowledge, he claims, "The legitimate subject-matter of a *theory* of knowledge consists of *facts* that are known at a given time, with, of course, the proviso that the procedures by which this body of knowledge has been built up are an integral part of it" (p. 294).

No one, however, knows all the facts that are known at a given time. It requires considerable expertise within a specific ACTS or discipline to know (1) the known facts and procedures by which they have become known and (2) that what one knows are the significant and defining facts of the given domain. A theory of knowledge in general therefore requires a grasp of what is known in representative ACTS and disciplines that is probably beyond human capacity. The quoted stipulation, furthermore, lays down the same kind of a priori criteria that Dewey immediately afterward says occurs in the kinds of epistemology he correctly rejects. Because Dewey's theory cannot account for itself, it, too, embodies the intellectual crisis.

Be that as it may, the knowledge available in society that is good enough as knowledge to be included in the school curriculum is the knowledge of the ACTS and university disciplines. It does not necessarily belong there, but it is eligible for inclusion if it has been attested to by the respective communities of qualified practitioners and investigators. This claim is partly epistemological, for it is based upon Peirce's discovery of the necessity for such a community of critical co-investigators in the discovery of intersubjectively valid knowledge. The claim is partly empirical, for it assumes the actual existence of such communities of critical investigators in each of the ACTS and disciplines. This claim is open to confirmation or disconfirmation vis-à-vis each one of these. It is also a claim in the sociology of good knowledge about the knowledge that appears in the lived world prior to the explanatory interpretations of political science, economics, the sociology of knowledge, and the programmatic interpretations of epistemology and philosophy of science. It is also descriptive of the sources from which schools actually select knowledge for their curricula. If there are other kinds of knowledge in society that are also eligible for inclusion in the school curriculum because of their epistemic characteristics, they require a different kind of justification.

There is no need to claim at this point that either the knowledge of the ACTS or of the disciplines is superior as knowledge. To do so would repeat the mistakes of Dewey and Plato, respectively, and commit what Jane Roland Martin (1981) calls the "epistemological fallacy" by trying to base the whole curriculum on a theory of knowledge without giving adequate attention to the uses of knowledge in the lives of the people being educated (p. 47). Much of the knowledge of the ACTS, however, can be acquired in apprenticeships in the workplace. The kind of knowledge for which schools are needed is the theoretical knowledge of both the ACTS and disciplines. This observation is not necessarily elitist, for when apprentices who spend part of their time in the workplace do attend classes, they say it is for their theory. Children with mild mental handicaps who attend special schools or classes spend a large proportion of their time learning to read, write, and do arithmetic so they acquire mental processes involved in the use of symbols and concepts. These are the elements of theory. The claim that schools are needed to teach the theoretical components of the knowledge of the ACTS and disciplines becomes elitist only when the practical components of the ACTS and disciplines are not also included in the curriculum. This, however, is what seems to be happening in the postindustrial society.

EDUCATION IN ADVANCED INDUSTRIAL SOCIETY

The emphasis upon the academic disciplines in the educational reform movements of the early 1960s and mid-1980s in the United States can be understood through Daniel Bell's thesis of the postindustrial society. According to Bell, societies are preindustrial, industrial, or postindustrial depending upon whether the majority of the workforce is engaged in primary, secondary, or tertiary industries. Primary industries are the extractive industries of agriculture, mining, fishing, hunting, and forestry. With industrialization, many people move into cities and engage in factory work, manufacturing things out of natural resources in processes that use energy in the form of coal, oil, or electricity. A society becomes postindustrial when about half of its workers are involved in tertiary, quaternary, and quinary industries (i.e., in service, banking and finance, and artistic and entertainment industries). Work in preindustrial and industrial societies is labor and capital intensive, respectively, whereas in postindustrial societies it is knowledge intensive (1976, pp. 198–199). When people engage in services performed for other people, much of their work becomes dependent upon information, knowledge, and intellectual skills. Tertiary industries require tertiary schooling. The development of the professional classes changes the social structure, making it less dependent upon wealth, property, and inheritance and more reliant upon length of formal education, personal achievement, and professional competence (Bell, 1974, p. 115).

Bell does not advocate a meritocracy; rather, he describes historical changes from a propertied aristocracy to a meritocracy that have occurred regardless of whether we accept his conceptualization or the more neutral claim that in the last half of the twentieth century, industrial societies have become advanced industrial societies. Regardless of Bell's claim that theoretical knowledge is the axial element about which social stratification turns, it is true that advanced industrial societies (in both capitalistic and socialistic nations) require more graduates from tertiary schools because of the increased specialization of the workforce. It is therefore not only irrelevant but false to claim that the greater emphasis upon academic subjects in the periodic conservative reform movements in education is caused by the ruling classes in capitalistic societies. It is not the form of the economy but the state of industrialization that requires it. An orthodox Marxist should agree. So long as their technology requires technicians and technologists with strong backgrounds in mathematics and the natural sciences, advanced industrial societies will maintain secondary schools with high-status academic tracks that provide the theoretical knowledge Bell (1974) calls "axial" because it supports technology and economic growth as well as social stratification (p. 112). The criticism of the schools for reproducing the social structure is therefore wide of the mark. Of much greater significance for understanding the intellectual crisis is the use of theoretical knowledge to educate the technological elites, along with the concomitant development of the technological consciousness. This is most readily apparent in the destruction of the environment and the logocentrism that is a target of the feminist critique.

THE CONCERN FOR THE ENVIRONMENT

The technological consciousness embodied in the exploitation of the natural resources of the planet for material benefit that has accelerated rapidly since the beginning of the industrial revolution in the seventeenth century has been called the "white male sexist tradition" of "scientism and logocentrism" by the feminist scholar, Gloria Bowles (1984, p. 186), with some justification. She claims, "Throughout male recorded history, men have been 'takers,' while women have assumed (or have been forced to assume) the role of 'caretakers'" (p. 186). The ideal of science, with its rigorous separation of objective knowledge from value judgments and its formation of the objective consciousness, has through its technological applications enabled the takers to exploit the planet without regard for consequences.

The unforeseen consequences are now such common knowledge that it is tedious to list them. The effects include

1. The pollution of the air, earth, and water with industrial waste and sewage, which leads in turn to the predictable changes in climate known as the greenhouse effect
2. The production of toxic wastes that cannot be disposed of, such as those from nuclear fission in the production of electricity
3. The deforestation, erosion, and desertification of huge tracts of land and the consequent loss of oxygen from the atmosphere
4. The use of nonreplenishable resources (minerals as well as fossil fuels) without regard for the needs of future generations
5. The loss of virtually irreplaceable resources, such as tropical rain forests, wilderness areas, and whole species of plants and animals due to the destruction of their habitats
6. The poor quality of life of animals raised in factory farms and the question of whether animals have any rights
7. The diminution of arable land, which, coupled with the continued expansion of the population, raises in a very literal and serious way the question of the minimal survival conditions of the peoples of the earth.

Insofar as technology is merely the use of knowledge and tools in the exploitation of natural resources to produce goods to fulfill the material needs of humankind, it is good. Other things being equal, it is good to fulfill human needs as efficiently as possible. To the extent that the technological consciousness ignores the qualities of things other than their instrumental values, however, it involves people as takers, not as caretakers. The domination of nature, moreover, carries over to the domination of the underclass, the inhabitants of Third World countries that possess important resources, and, according to Bowles, women.

CONCLUSION

Secondary schools in advanced industrial societies, whether capitalist or socialist, will maintain a track comprising academic subjects for students bound for tertiary schooling. The educational problem is to understand the nature of the knowledge involved, how it should be selected and structured in the curriculum, and how it should be dealt with in a concrete pedagogy so that it does not develop attitudes of domination toward nature and fellow human beings. It is to formulate an educational program for caretakers, not for takers, that is accessible to the broad majority of youth so that students not going on to tertiary schools do not receive a second-class education and do find their schooling vital to their quest to learn more about the world. It is to ascertain the relative importance of the practical knowledge of the ACTS in the education of everyone, and how this knowledge should be combined with the theoretical knowledge of the disciplines, to contribute to everyone's humanization in a curriculum to which everyone has access as their human right.

To transcend nihilism in the cognitive domain, it is necessary to investigate the role of knowledge in education from the perspective of the standard epistemological concerns regarding the nature of knowledge and truth. In the following chapters, however, the more significant theories of knowledge will not be consulted in isolation from education. Instead, representative educational theories of modern times will be examined, with particular attention to the theories of knowledge they embody, in order to interpret the prephilosophical understanding of the place of knowledge and truth in educative processes. As before, there will be no attempt to assume an adversarial or advocatory relation to any of the theories. This abjuration of the prerogative of the standard (white male sexist) tradition of philosophy and philosophy of education might assist in an appropriation of the heritage that would be conducive to our being its caretaker. The methodology involved in this retrieval, already utilized in our study of the great ethical theories of the modern world, will be explicitly articulated before considering the central problem of the epistemology of educational practice.

CHAPTER 7

Interpretive, Normative Theory of Education

The overview of knowledge in society raises typical epistemological questions. What is knowledge? What makes it good knowledge? What makes it truthful? What kinds of knowledge are there? Are there epistemic conditions common to all kinds? To resolve these questions and to insure this inquiry serves the goal of overcoming nihilism in education, the literature investigated in Part II will be that of interpretive, normative theories of education. Attending to their epistemological foundations will enable us to deconstruct their nihilism and synthesize them in an interpretive, normative theory that outlines the curriculum and pedagogy that should be available to everyone. The complexity of this task requires our consideration of the various activities involved when doing philosophy of education.

DOING PHILOSOPHY OF EDUCATION

Diverse movements in philosophy in this century have denied that philosophy is the articulation of a world view and have placed importance on the activities of philosophizing. Instead of wisdom, philosophers have claimed to possess competency in various forms of linguistic, phenomenological, conceptual, hermeneutical, and dialectical analysis by which they do philosophy. From this perspective, teachers and other educational professionals should not learn philosophy of education as a body of doctrine about education. They should learn to do philosophy for themselves. When such philosophizing is about the concepts and phenomena of education, however, it requires knowing something about education, just as doing philosophy of art or law obliges one to know something about art or law. Without knowledge of education, the findings will not be contributions to the study of education. Philosophy may be largely conceptual, but education is largely existential, experiential, and normative. Just as the basic theorists in other university disciplines should be concerned with the phenomena peculiar to their regions of the world, so should the theoretical investigation reflect its substantive content.

Because of this context, Jonas Soltis (1985) claims that the study of pedagogy requires

1. Empirical research, using the methods of the natural sciences to discover causes and correlations
2. Interpretation, using the methods of ordinary language philosophy, phenomenology, and hermeneutics to disclose the human significance of educational phenomena and the subjective and intersubjective meanings and happenings of the pedagogic encounter
3. Normative research, to establish the ethical basis of choices regarding subject matter and pedagogical procedures and practices
4. Ideological critique, to demystify educational ideas and show their relation to societal power structures

These functions, often fulfilled by different kinds of researchers, are all involved in the present study, except for empirical research. The ideological critique occurs in the first and sixth chapters and intermittently elsewhere as the occasion calls for it. The interpretive, normative functions are combined as the understandings of the great historical theories of ethics and education are brought to bear on the question of what should be done educationally to transcend nihilism. To show how to include the various functions in an integrated research program, a number of ways of doing philosophy of education will be considered in regard to their interpretive, normative contributions to the study of education.

NORMATIVE EVALUATION

One of the most important modes is to evaluate the innovative, reformist literature in education, for it almost always combines factual and normative claims invalidly. This evaluation can be analytical and objective if one merely distinguishes between the valid and invalid normative claims in this literature or if one uncovers its philosophical presuppositions. Significant experiential or experimental evaluation of innovations can be undertaken only after a normative evaluation discloses the recommendations worthy of such testing in one's own teaching or in experimentation in more highly controlled circumstances. For example, the reference in Chapter 3 to the hedonism presupposed by both *Summerhill* and *Walden Two* to show that hedonism entails neither the laissez-faire approach of the former nor the authoritarianism of the latter also shows their superficiality and lack of grounding in an ethic or epistemology. Similarly, the reference to the contradiction in the values-clarification approach shows that it mistakes values for morality in its own commission of the axiological fallacy, and that it also shows it needs supplementation with deontological language, concepts, and principles (1) to enable students to clarify their values in the explicit context of the rights and freedoms of others and (2) to involve moral as well as value education.

Such normative evaluation should also be carried out on the scientific theories that attempt to describe and explain things in the educational domain. To acquire such explanatory knowledge, the scientific researcher has to isolate from the rest of the universe the things to be explained and interpret them as being those things. When behavioristic researchers, for example, attempt to describe classroom events and processes as behaviors, without reference to whatever occurs within the minds of the people involved, they begin by interpreting the situation as one in which the teacher's and students' conscious efforts to do what they believe themselves to be doing are not important or significant because they are not observable. The teacher who is teaching theorems in geometry to help students understand them, for example, and the students who are studying the theorems because they want to learn them, disappear. This isolation of the object of inquiry from the lived, human world may be necessary to acquire pedagogical knowledge on the cause-and-effect model of the natural sciences. However, the application of theory derived in this way to teaching and learning situations without reference to covert processes can easily become understood as the normative interpretation of the situation—as how it should appear to practicing teachers. It therefore needs to be evaluated normatively before it is applied to practice. Without denying the role of such research in the complete study of education, it nevertheless indicates the need for an interpretation of practice that does involve teachers and students as conscious and self-conscious human beings. Some of them are.

INTERPRETATION OF PRACTICE

Teachers are taken into account as conscious, self-conscious beings in their own reflections on their own practice. Methodical reflection on one's teaching is extremely important, for so long as one's understanding of educational practice results from experience without reflection, it is a pretheoretical understanding that might not be very lucid, logically consistent, or self-conscious. It can also be confused with the memories of one's own schooling. During one's own schooling, one was constantly bombarded with data, the understanding of which yielded an interpretation of schools that reflects personal failures and successes amidst a mélange of teachers and classmates. Although it can be expressed in opinions and beliefs, the mental processes involved are most likely to be nonconceptual and without theoretical refinement. One can similarly teach for years and learn a great deal by experience, simply by noting what one can make work with students, without formulating the accumulated insights into words. If one is wide awake and fully aware of what is going on without conceptualizing things, one acquires a nonthematic, pretheoretical understanding of pedagogy and educational things. This is an intuitive, perceptual understanding, as distinguished from a discursive, conceptualized, theoretical understanding. The interpretation of practice begins when the common-sense language of ordinary teacher talk is used to conceptualize these insights into a "discursive formation" (Foucault, 1969/1972).

Regardless of the sophistication involved, the interpretation of pedagogy that begins with the language of the staff room and makes the implicit understanding explicit by conceptualizing it is a fundamental way of doing philosophy of education. It involves hermeneutical processes when the experiential, prephilosophical insights become articulated in a vocabulary that allows them to be interrelated; to be compared to meanings articulated by other practitioners; to be substantiated by evidence, elaboration, and argument; and to be more truthful. The more refined the conceptual processes are, the more they will resemble academic philosophy of education. The crux is thinking about what one is is doing. Even when the source of one's concepts is ordinary teacher talk, such reflection on practice can help one objectify the meanings of things, gain distance from them, sort them out, change one's mind, and, on the basis of reason, determine what one should do. All of this is very similar to the reflection on moral experience that is embodied in the writings of the moral philosophers discussed in Part I.

Because the interpretation of one's own practice remains the basis of all other ways of doing philosophy of education, it ought to employ methods that enable one to do it as rigorously as one can. Not every staff-room conversation about students or classrooms deserves to be called *philosophizing*. This requires open-minded disinterestedness and genuine reflection on a real problem or question of practice. It requires criteria that help eliminate idle talk, malicious gossip, rationalization of prejudice, blaming the victim, self-glorification, and other discursive but nonrational processes. The interpretation of practice can become intellectually sophisticated by integrating it into the interpretation of texts of educational philosophers that embody the canons of inquiry in the way the texts of moral philosophers are involved in the present inquiry.

INTERPRETATION THROUGH TEXTS

The reading of significant statements of educational theory can deepen and challenge one's understanding of educational practice. The classical formulations by Plato, Rousseau, Pestalozzi, Froebel, Herbart, Dewey, Kilpatrick, Montessori, Whitehead, Maritain, and Spranger, for example, are a rich source of insights, language, concepts, and conceptual schemata, providing the wherewithal for the conceptualization of one's own prephilosophical understanding of education.

After reading the *Republic*, for example, one understands that Plato put the best knowledge of his society into the curriculum of the school he founded for young (male) adults. Called the Academy, its aim was to develop the intellectual and moral characteristics deemed necessary to enable these men to govern themselves. This interpretation does not quite come from the *Republic*, nor from the commentaries, nor from a history book. It comes from all of these, from a general understanding of life, and from reading enough Plato to distinguish him from Platonists. Because the best knowledge of fourth-century B.C.E. Athens is no longer the best knowledge, one also understands that the best knowledge of any society should be found in its tertiary school curriculum, with the same goals of intellectual and moral development to enable the young to govern themselves. Similarly, after reading Dewey's *Democracy and Education* (1916), one can understand that much of one's own schooling, regardless of its excellence, has been abstract and bookish, relatively removed from experience. It can be quite liberating to realize that an important theory of education supports this kind of understanding of schooling. One does not have to read Plato or Dewey to believe them. They can be read along with other theories in order to gain a broader, deeper understanding of what education is all about.

The interpretation of such texts can be at least as cumulative and rigorous as were the interpretations in earlier chapters of the paradigms of modern ethics (Ross, Kant, Kierkegaard, Bentham, Mill, Dewey, and Moore). Just as the interpretation of these texts enabled a conceptualization of the right and the good that subsumes their partial understandings, so, too, can the interpretations of classical educational theories lead to a cumulative understanding and comprehensive conceptualization of education. Because of the magnitude of such undertakings, however, much more should be said about the acquisition of knowledge by such means.

Because the interpretation of texts, or hermeneutics, is now extended to "texts" other than printed ones (Kroll, 1988; Packer, 1985), the explication here will rely upon what may be the most rigorous expression of hermeneutics as a methodology for understanding printed texts, Hans-Georg Gadamer's *Truth and Method* (1960/1975). Gadamer's account begins with the originator of the contemporary concern for hermeneutics, Wilhelm Dilthey. Writing near the end of the nineteenth century, when most of the university disciplines were attempting to adopt the methods of the natural sciences in one form or another, Dilthey claims they are inappropriate for the *Geisteswissenshaften* (humanities). Although he is an empiricist, Dilthey claims the appropriate data for an understanding of human life are not found in immediate observation but in the literary and historical documents that inform us of the historical existence of the human race and preserve the evidence of the understanding that human beings have had of themselves (Gadamer, 1960/1975, pp. 8, 195). Whereas the natural sciences are synchronic and explanatory, the humanities are diachronic and interpretive, attempting to study humanity as a historical, historicizing reality by means of the cultural products of the past. One does not find out what is human about human beings and human life in a test tube but on the printed page where human beings have recorded their understanding of life.

Hermeneutics for Dilthey is simply the interpretation of (1) the experience one has in reading a historically significant text and (2) the text itself, dialectically. The goal is to gain an in-depth understanding of what the text is about in the context of what it means to oneself, an understanding of human life as disclosed by the text, and an understanding of one's own life (pp. 56–60). It is not wrong to think of it as a sophisticated "reading with understanding." In the intensive reading of a work from the past, whether in philosophy, religion, literature, science, art, or state and political documents, one should simultaneously project onself imaginatively into the past and bring that past understanding into the present, creating a historical consciousness. This modification of one's consciousness is not merely a becoming conscious of something historical, for it is a becoming historical oneself through the adoption of the past as one's own. One's own historicity and a sense of the historicality of the human race cannot result from the study of nature or society in the natural or social sciences, yet it is an essential element of human understanding (pp. 195-197). Thus our attempt to repossess the Enlightenment heritage through the examination of the ethics of Kant and Bentham and their subsequent refinements in the ethics of Ross, Mill, Dewey, and Moore, and in the human rights ethic, is an effort to obtain a historical consciousness as well as a historically grounded ethical and educational theory. The same is true in the cognitive domain when we will study Peters, Spencer, Dewey, Broudy, Freire, and Greene.

After Dilthey, hermeneutics became the general theory of human understanding because of Martin Heidegger's articulation of understanding as a fundamental (ontological) characteristic of human existence (Gadamer, 1960/1975, pp. 230-231). Because understanding is in fact always historical, it is always bound within a horizon limited by the understandings acquired in a specific historical milieu and in a particular projection into the future. This is the problem of the hermeneutical circle. The meanings and expectations brought to a text function as prejudgments, or prejudices, that form a closed horizon of understanding. These make it difficult to perceive what is new in the text and to allow the frame of reference of the author to penetrate existing understandings. This raises the question of the truth of an interpretation and the problem of multiple interpretations of a given text. Gadamer suggests that to break out of the hermeneutical circle, one should always be alert for newness in a text: "The important thing is to be aware of one's own bias, so that the text may present itself in all its newness and thus be able to assert its own truth against one's own fore-meanings" or prejudices (p. 238; cf. Gadamer, 1959/1988; Bernstein, 1983, p. 136).

To let a text assert its truth requires working with it until one sees what it is about from the author's perspective, even if this requires poring over difficult passages or rereading the entire text to set the parts into the context of the whole and to understand the whole as constituted by its parts. Just as the scientist observes by seeing, the reader observes by hearing (Gadamer, 1960/1975, p. 420). One has to listen to the author to hear what is being said in the words of the text. The understanding of the text requires the mutuality between reader and author that is characteristic of dialogue elsewhere. One needs to share things in common with the author until agreement about some object in the world is attained (p. 158). Because one has to let the words of the text disclose things, to bring them into being, "hermeneutics . . . is not 'knowledge as domination' . . . but rather a subordination to the text's claim to dominate our minds" (p. 278). One has to place oneself willingly "within a process of tradition, in which past and present are constantly fused" (p. 258). To be able to do this, one has to forget oneself with the disinterestedness that is reputedly characteristic of natural science (p. 299).

Gadamer (1960/1975) explicates this loss of personal subjectivity in the encounter with a text through the analogy with play and art. One plays a game only by taking it seriously, letting the game take over one's attention completely. So long as the game is held off as an object, one is not playing (p. 92). During full engagement in a game, one forgets oneself completely. The same thing is true in watching or reading drama, for example, a Shakespearean comedy or tragedy. One has to let oneself become totally caught up in the action for it to come into being. Otherwise one remains a spectator of the actors playing their roles in ill-fitting costumes, and so on. Gadamer cites Plato's refusal to distinguish the comedy and tragedy of life from that of the stage because there is no difference for one who can "see the meaning of the game that unfolds before one. The pleasure offered in the spectacle is the same in both cases: it is the joy of knowledge" (p. 101). The word *joy* here requires interpretation, for the feeling experienced when witnessing a tragedy in life or on the stage cannot be ordinary joy without an inversion of values. The new insight Gadamer is voicing refers to a highly sublimated sense of the affirmation of the significance of human life and personal endeavor, even in the face of apparent failure (cf. Desmond, 1988, p. 302). It is not unlike the emotion of the tragic hero on the stage who is undergoing the illumination that compels the acceptance of destiny. It is akin to what Hamlet feels when, after setting things right again in Denmark, as he was born to do, he asks Horatio to "tell my story," recognizing the success of the efforts that will cost his life.

According to Gadamer (1960/1975), "what otherwise is constantly hidden and withdrawn" is brought to light in the tragedies and comedies of the stage and life. When one learns through literature to perceive the comedy and tragedy of life, "what is emerges." The joy in the knowledge results from the disclosure of "the game that is played with us" just as through the drama on stage, "everyone recognizes that that is how things are" (pp. 101–102). Reading tragedies and comedies in genuine, hermeneutical experiences, one learns a bit more about human finitude, about the historicity of one's own life. Although one forgets oneself when caught up in the action of the drama, its resolution brings one back to oneself at a deeper level of understanding of how one is projected toward one's own possibilities (pp. 231, 320). One is less alienated from life and from oneself.

The extreme importance to the understanding of life that can be gained through literature such as Shakespearean or Greek tragedy and comedy can be realized by noting that the concepts of the tragic and comic are unscientific. It is completely unscientific to refer to the comedy and tragedy of human life. This is precisely why Dilthey claimed that the methodology of the natural sciences is inappropriate for the study of human beings. Within its neutral objectivity, the tragic and comic aspects of life disappear. Not only drama but a great deal of life remains a struggle between good and evil. The moral struggles of the human race are a central focus of philosophy, religion, history, and art, as well as literature.

The exemplars of modern ethics discussed in Part I are very much concerned with the moral struggles involved in the tragic and comic aspects of human existence. Although their roles are disguised by the abstract language of the right and the good, the interpretation considered them as central players on the stage of modern life, the better to hear what their words manifest about the good and the right. The hermeneutics of these exemplars accordingly set aside the prejudices against intuitionism, rationalism, observation, and revelation as ways of knowing what is right and good in order to engage in dialogue with the authors and let the truth of what they are saying address us. Also set aside was the prejudice against deontology harbored by teleologists, and vice versa, in order to gain an understanding of what is right and good through observing the principle of multiple perspectives (Greene, 1972, 1974). Each paradigm was read for the truth it discloses about the value and moral dimensions of the lived world in order to bring these dimensions into being. It was realized, however, that these truths are only partial truths that need supplementation by the partial truths of other exemplars in order to be both true to the heritage of moral understanding and integrated with the prephilosophical understanding of what is good and right from present life.

The broader idea of interpreting texts when the text is not a written document originated in Heidegger's 1927 *Being and Time*, where he used as his text the prephilosophical understanding of human existence. For instance, we already understand that human existence is "in each case mine"; that is, it does not occur in the abstract but always belongs to someone who knows it from the inside as her own existence. Heidegger's approach is the original source of the idea of doing educational theorizing from the data bank of one's own experience in schools. This kind of elucidation of the pretheoretical understanding is precisely what the great moral philosophers did with their data bank of moral experience.

Similarly, some of the prejudices brought to the reading of the printed texts of moral philosophy are one's own prephilosophical understanding of morality. These should be brought into relation to the truth of what the texts say, either to change one's mind or to challenge the author. Although one should be open minded to the text and respond to its truth receptively when the author discloses things in the lived world, one should not adopt opinions from a text that do not square with one's own understanding after listening to the author as sensitively and sympathetically as possible. Dialogue is a two-way process, and one should assert one's own truth when confronting those parts of a text that are untrue, such as when it slips into empty rhetoric or propaganda.

CRITIQUE OF PROPAGANDA

One can also do philosophy of education by critically examining the reports and statements made by presidential and royal commissions, state and federal departments of education, and select or blue-ribbon committees, as well as the potboilers in the literature of education. A logical analysis of their inconsistencies and an uncovering of their presuppositions regarding the good, the right, knowledge, and reality, carried out in a classroom of preservice or in-service teachers, can be a highly productive means of stimulating their thinking about the normative aspects of education. Because such writings are highly persuasive, even if not propaganda in a strict sense, they often invite an ideological critique. True propaganda is specifically oriented toward persuading people to adopt a body of doctrine representing a specific partisan or sectarian cause. It is ideological in the pejorative sense because it unabashedly builds its case to propagate the faith without regard for truth. It assumes it already possesses the truth and defines it as loyalty to the party or sect.

The success of artful propaganda in the corruption of education warrants doing philosophy of education in the Socratic style, questioning everything. Performing an ideological critique of a piece of propagandistic literature is quite different from the hermeneutic of an honest and significant text. The latter tries to elucidate the experience of the text. The faults it finds are those made by the best minds due to the finitude of one's historical perspective. At best it wants to plead with the author, "Know thyself." To the propagandist, however, one wants to say, "No, thyself." Things are never so bad as the propagandist says they are. The derogatory generalizations about schools made in such propaganda are not true. To believe they are true, one often has to believe without evidence that thousands of teachers are incompetent. The schools are rather like an ink blot. One can say what one likes and find sufficient evidence to make it appear to be true. Many statements made about schools that appear to be true, however, can be refuted by simply saying the opposite, which will often appear to be equally true.

The important criticism of propaganda begins by separating the factual claims, which are probably not true, from the recommendations. This allows the value judgments and recommendations to be evaluated logically by separating them from their rhetoric and assessing them when they are stated in plain English. Then it can be seen if they are supported by a theory of value or knowledge that contributes to the understanding of education and improvement of schooling. A critique of propaganda can become a proper Marxist ideological critique, provided it is based on the evidence in the text. Without such evidence, the critique itself becomes propaganda (Liston, 1988). Paul Ricoeur (1981) seems correct to say, "Nothing is more necessary today than to renounce the arrogance of critique and to carry on with patience the endless work of distancing and renewing our historical substance" (p. 246).

CONCEPTUAL ANALYSIS OF EDUCATIONAL LANGUAGE

Partly to avoid engaging in propaganda, one of the most common ways of doing philosophy of education among English-speaking scholars since Israel Scheffler's *The Language of Education* (1960) and B. Othanel Smith and Robert Ennis's *Language and Concepts in Education* (1961) has been to analyze the concepts used in educational talk as they are embodied in ordinary language. Instead of depending upon teaching experience, it presupposes an understanding of what makes good sense in standard, formal English. It is sort of a hermeneutic of common-sense understanding as it is embodied in the text of standard English. The concepts of knowing, teaching, authority, indoctrination, and education are among those that seemed to lend themselves to the approach in its early days, although it soon ran into anomalies that caused Soltis (1969, 1971) to question if the claim to being nonnormative is defensible and if the scope of the approach is broad enough to encompass the concerns it purports to investigate.

The conceptual analysis of ordinary language may be an essential means of locating an educational inquiry in the lived world. When, for example, the use of the words *good* and *right* is analyzed in Chapter 1, it is shown that these are two very different concepts, related to very different aspects of value and morality. This is discussed at the common-sense level of ordinary linguistic usage to show that the distinction between deontology and teleological ethics originates in the moral predicaments of life. The language game, moreover, merely elucidates the prephilosophical understanding of some of the features of the context. The theories of Ross and Moore, too, are largely confined to ordinary language analysis, and the examination of the other theories uses linguistic analysis whenever it seems heuristically helpful. Conceptual analysis in education can be more sophisticated than linguistic analysis, especially when it is recognized as the explication of the prephilosophical understanding of education, and the analysis is pursued beyond the horizon of language into an elucidation of the normative context of the educational phenomenon that that language discloses.

NORMATIVE EDUCATIONAL QUESTIONS

When the analysis of educational language and concepts confronts questions about what should be done in education, it needs to become substantive theory to resolve the substantive, normative questions. Gadamer (1977/1985) seems correct to claim that "the language of philosophy does not move and have its life in propositional systems," because the use of formal logic "limits the emergence of the world that occurs in our linguistically formulated experience of the world" (p. 191). This is why in his hermeneutical theory he argues that philosophizing has to start "with the language we already possess" (p. 181) and why he accepts Wittgenstein's later effort to refer "all speaking back to the context of praxis" (p. 192). Although ordinary language analysis may be necessary to become clear about the genuineness of educational questions, their resolution depends upon substantive, normative theory. They require normative ethical theory as it is discussed in Chapters 2 through 5 and normative educational theory as it will be examined in the following chapters.

Someone concerned with the question of freedom in education, for example, is not necessarily interested in physiological, psychological, or metaphysical freedom, nor in positive, negative, internal, or external freedom. If one begins with ordinary language expressions of the kind of freedom a student might ask for, it is for freedom to move around the classroom, to talk freely with classmates, to select part of the content of instruction, to print something in the school newspaper, and so on. The question is not a conceptual one, but one of educational practice that, when elucidated, deserves an ethical, normative answer.

Similarly, students who ask why they should study mathematics or physics in high school are not asking about the nature of knowledge or how we use the word *knowing*. The question is not about the difference between "knowing how" and "knowing that," nor if one is really reducible to the other. Nor is the student concerned about whether mathematics or physics in the curriculum serves hegemonic functions. The question is about how high school mathematics will help one live. It is not about whether physics is the most exact of the sciences, or what exactitude means, or why physics deserves a central place in the organization of knowledge, or if the method of experimentation used by the half of the scientists who are experimentalists is the one and only true method of inquiry. It is about how the knowledge of the things in the physical world is going to help one live. In what sense is it educational?

To respond to these kinds of questions, philosophy of education requires a positive, constructive attempt to build a normative theory of educational practice. If it is to furnish substantive answers to the substantive questions, these are not about the nature of knowledge or what makes it truthful. They are questions of what belongs in the curriculum; why, when, where, and for whom; and how it should be taught. They are questions about the sorts of things people should know about.

When individual teachers confront the normative questions of educational practice, their philosophizing responses should concern the knowledge that should be taught to *these* students *this* year. The context of the students' other years cannot be ignored, but it only establishes the framework within which some major options are still open. To ask this question is to ask how and why the students should be educated. This, of course, involves the question of what education should be, which is the central question of philosophy of education. Contextualizing the doing of philosophy of education in this manner makes it relevant and lowers the level of abstraction. It may seem to abandon concern for the universal that is characteristic of philosophy. By returning to the individual teacher's reflection on practice, however, the question of the nature and aim of education is not relativized. It is existentialized.

DOING PHILOSOPHY OF EDUCATION EXISTENTIALLY

Trying to make sense of one's own life by trying to make sense of one's teaching in a society that places conflicting demands and expectations upon teachers is a very existential thing. When it involves the significance of one's life, of one's very being, it is as existential as it can be. This might wrongly suggest that a necessary condition for philosophizing existentially is the experience of the absurd (*cf.* Götz, 1987). A collapse of received definitions of education amidst the apparent meaninglessness of life may very well be a strong impetus, but it is not the only initiator of existential thinking about education. Very well-adjusted, happy teachers can come to realize that, although they have always taught cheerfully what they were employed to teach, and with considerable effectiveness, there is something about it all that does not fully engage them (nor their students). Existential thinking about the nature and aim of education can therefore arise within effective teachers who want to have more than a temporary cognitive effect upon students. It does not require finding fault with one's teaching, only a bit of Socratic dissatisfaction over the "unexamined life" as a teacher and a desire for something that would make it more real, that would involve one's very being and affect the pupil's very being in a genuine effort to become all that one can become as a teacher. Then doing philosophy of education becomes an intellectual quest that is also a quest for being. In Greene's (1973) words, the teacher "may liberate himself for reflective action as someone who knows who he is as a historical being, acting on his freedom, trying each day to be" (p. 7).

A recapitulation of the gist of the argument will reveal a surprising conclusion. It was said that instead of learning philosophy of education, one should do it. This involves philosophical thinking, but this is redundant because philosophical thinking is simply thinking about what one is doing. This contextualizes the matter so much it should be called "existential thinking." Any doing of philosophy of education by experienced teachers ought to involve reflection on their own practice in such depth that it involves their very existence. As soon as this is understood, however, it becomes clear that all valid thinking about education is existential and the qualifier *existential* can be dropped as readily as the word *philosophical*. If the objective of such thinking is to liberate oneself for a more adequate participation in the dialogics of educational practice by enabling one to become oneself, the word *thinking* can also be dropped. If doing philosophy of education by a teacher is not isolated to the cerebral cortex but engages the teacher's whole being, including the cerebral cortex, it is much more than thinking what one is doing. It is thinking what one is being.

Doing philosophy of education thus becomes virtually equated with existing more authentically as a teacher. In other words, thinking what one is doing entails doing what one is thinking. Whether the thinking and doing occur simultaneously or separately is irrelevant to the conceptual point about the nature of praxis. Similarly, thinking what one is being entails being what one is thinking, separately or simultaneously, as the case may be. In its fullest sense, then, doing philosophy of education is trying to make sense of what an existing practitioner is doing in order to do it better. It is an organic unification of thinking, doing, and being. It is an ontological event because the horizon of self-understanding as a historical consciousness is "more being than being conscious" (Gadamer, 1977/1985, p. 178).

An attempt to unify one's thought, action, and being in one's professional life through doing philosophy of education existentially, however, can subjectivize things in deleterious ways. One can come to believe that the way one teaches is the right way simply because one does it. There is still the problem of the hermeneutical circle. Philosophical methods can be used to rationalize poor pedagogy. One can become more involuted and narcissistic than before. One has to forget oneself by referring outside oneself to something that is sufficiently respected that it can help one break out of the hermeneutical circle again and again, enabling one to expand and change one's ideas in the very process of articulating them. Outside referents can include (1) the principles of grammar, syntax, and rhetoric in the analysis of the usage of educational language; (2) the senses in which words are used in standard English; (3) the logic with which factual and value statements are distinguished and tested in the examination of the propaganda of education; (4) the meanings of a text about education through which one comes to understand educational things; and (5) other canons of inquiry found in one or another way of doing philosophy of education. The crucial point is that some canons of thinking are needed to enable one to objectify one's own processes of conceptualization as one turns the intuitive insights of the pretheoretical understanding gained in practice into the substance of thought. The process should probably include the use of the resources of hermeneutical phenomenology (Vandenberg, 1974; Van Manen, 1984).

When the intuitive, implicit understandings of practice are conceptualized with ideas that can be interrelated and refined discursively, the conceptual processes enable one to become a particular individual as a teacher through the mediation of the universal, as explicated by Kierkegaard. To escape solipsism, reflecting existentially requires the mediation of the universal and canons of inquiry appropriate to dialogue with others, as derived from a hermeneutical engagement with the classical texts of philosophy and philosophy of education. These texts are classical because they contribute to the common meanings of our heritage, which enable us to live within the community of a common world. There should be no problem if existential reflection is prompted by the call of conscience in the quest for the truth of one's being, which in this context is no different from the obligation to search for the truth, regardless of the mode of philosophizing about education utilized.

THEORY OF INTELLECTUAL AND MORAL CHARACTERISTICS

A discussion of research methodology in philosophy of education is incomplete without specific consideration of its appropriate content. According to Broudy, Parsons, Snook, and Szoke (1967), the domain of education is constituted by four problem areas: pedagogy, curriculum, school policy, and the nature and aim of education. Any problem or phenomenon of education that exists objectively in classrooms, schools, or society can be classified in one or more of these areas. The conceptual schemes of psychology, sociology, anthropology, economics, and political science can be used to think about limited aspects of problems within these areas of education, but not with philosophical understanding. The contents that are distinctly philosophical and about which one can do philosophy are the problems in these four areas considered from the dimensions of value, knowledge, and reality. These correspond to the branches of philosophy of axiology, epistemology, and metaphysics (ontology), including ethics and esthetics within axiology. These in turn correspond to moral education, cognitive education, and existential education, respectively. Moral education can be considered in regard to pedagogy, curriculum, policy, and aims, although this book has focused on the first two. The same is true of cognitive education, and, again, the focus here is on curriculum and pedagogy.

This content of philosophy of education is exemplified in the paradigms of Plato and Dewey. Dewey (1916) claimed first that "philosophy is an attempt to *comprehend*—that is, to gather together the varied details of the world and of life into a single inclusive whole," in an effort to obtain a "unified, consistent, and complete" outlook on the world (p. 378). He then defined philosophy of education as the "explicit formulation of the problems of the formation of right mental and moral

habitudes in respect to the difficulties of contemporary social life"
(p. 386). Philosophy of education is therefore the attempt to formulate
the educational program in regard to the pedagogy and curriculum
needed to develop in the young the intellectual and moral characteristics that will enable them to cope with life. It is the normative theory of
cognitive and moral education.

CONCLUSION

An interpretive, normative theory of education uses various philosophical methods in coming to understand pedagogy and education as it
occurs in the lived world, prior to the reductionism of the special
sciences. Whatever methods are used, it will have elements in it that
interpret one's own practice; relate to the canonical literature; engage
in linguistic, conceptual, or phenomenological analyses; and respond to
the normative questions of education in order to make personal sense
of them in the existential context. If it lacks some of these elements, it
lacks the richness that the complexity of educational phenomena deserves. If it is not rooted in practice and significant texts as it engages in
both analysis and synthesis in order to theorize about the normative
and existential dimensions of education, it is incomplete. If it does not
attempt to achieve a macrocosmic scope by interrelating problems of
pedagogy, curriculum, policy, and aims; and if it does not grapple with
the problems involved in the educational development of desirable intellectual and moral characteristics (i.e., the problems of cognitive and
moral education), it is incomplete. Finally, if it does not involve multiple
perspectives from a wide variety of existing, incomplete texts, it will be
incomplete. As Dewey (1916) said, however, philosophy is also an
attempt to be complete.

CHAPTER 8

Knowledge in the Curriculum

The general question of the kinds of knowledge available in society and eligible for inclusion in the school curriculum is answered with the claim that each of the ACTS (arts, crafts, trades, and sports), professions, and disciplines has such knowledge if it has a critical, discursive community of qualified practitioners or investigators (guild, union, association, or learned society) that attests to the validity of its knowledge and skills. The epistemological questions, however, have not yet been considered. What is knowledge? What makes it knowledge? What method makes its discovery valid knowledge? What epistemic characteristics are necessary to establish its truth? What is truth? Is it the same for all of the ACTS and disciplines? Nor have the educational questions been considered. What intellectual characteristics should be developed in response to the crisis of reason? How can the academic preparation necessary for an advanced industrial society occur without developing the technological consciousness with its attitudes toward the domination of nature and other people? What knowledge belongs in the curriculum because it should be accessible to everyone as their human right? The investigation of these questions through the hermeneutics of representative educational theories of Western civilization will proceed after a brief glance at the main options in the history of Western philosophy.

HISTORICAL CONCEPTIONS OF SCIENCE

A myth formerly perpetuated in introductory philosophy courses is that science is empirical, that is, that knowledge begins with the senses and all research should begin with the observation and collection of sense data. Empiricism, however, is an ideology of science dominant among Anglo-American philosophers since the Middle Ages and repeatedly formulated by the Bacons, Hobbes, Locke, Berkeley, Hume, Bentham, Mill, Spencer, Russell, and many twentieth-century philosophers of science. Its main error is the elevation of a half-truth into a whole truth. Criticism of its dogmatism does not deny its claim that in the discovery of knowledge a very large and important role is played by the senses and by observational, experimental, or experiential data of one kind or another. It is better, however, to refer to the processes of knowing things through the senses as becoming aware of them perceptually, or through *perceptual consciousness* of them.

These terms will allow for a subsequent synthesis of empiricism with the half-truth of its main competitor as an ideology of science, rationalism. It is more than amusing to note that Skinner (1948) continuously attacked the philosophical and rationalistic tradition, especially that armchair philosopher, Rene Descartes, because this involves the Descartes of the 1642 *Meditations*. The Descartes of the 1628 *Rules for the Direction of the Mind*, however, describes the method he practiced in his own research in physiology and optics and that Skinner also used in his research and implemented in programmed instruction.

Rationalism is the belief that knowing is a matter of intellectual beliefs that have been arranged from simple definitions of elementary terms and axioms that are immediately apprehended as true, through to complex propositions and involved theories. Examples include Euclidian geometry and many a good textbook. Rationalism is an ideology of science dominant among European (Continental) philosophers since the Middle Ages and repeatedly formulated after Descartes by Spinoza, Leibniz, Kant, Fichte, Hegel, and British philosophers such as Bosanquet and Popper. Criticism of its dogmatism in denigrating the role of perceptual consciousness of things in the discovery of knowledge (and in life) does not deny its claim that in the discovery of knowledge a very large and important role is played by concepts and conceptual schemes. As they say, all observation is theory laden.

It is better, however, to refer to rational, deductive, mental processes as the *conceptual consciousness* of things to enable its synthesis with empiricism. A person's knowledge of a particular thing in the world ought to be a combination of becoming aware of it perceptually and conceptually. Methods of collecting the sense data of perceptual awareness and of refining one's conceptual patterning of the data can work together to discipline one's consciousness of the thing, and one need not worry about which is the foundation of the other. One's knowledge of it is most refined, adequate, and truthful when it is most perceptually and conceptually disciplined. Perhaps this oversimplified statement suffices as an initial perspective from which to consider the various educational theories.

Most philosophy throughout the ages has involved competitive polemics between empiricists and rationalists. Although a few philosophers have tried to encompass the half-truths of each, their efforts have not been regarded as adequate by other philosophers. A distinction with considerable import for education is whether emphasis should be placed upon processes of the discovery of new knowledge or upon the systematization of already acquired knowledge. This is close to the teacher's question of whether pedagogy should emphasize things so that students can see, touch, feel, taste, and experience them in an approach that emphasizes inquiry, or if pedagogy should emphasize concept attainment, cognitive development, and a curriculum as a body of organized knowledge to be acquired. We will accordingly examine the works of both a rationalist and an empiricist, as well as their synthesis in Dewey's and Broudy's theories, before moving on to synthesize the four in the next chapter.

CONCEPTUAL DIDACTICS: PETERS AND HIRST

The conceptual content of the academic curriculum taught didactically is the main emphasis of the educational theory of Richard Peters, the most visible philosopher of education in Great Britain in the 1960s and 1970s. According to the received interpretation, Peters analyzes the ordinary usage of the word *education* in his 1964 inaugural address as a professor at the University of London, and in his *Ethics and Education* (1966), to draw implications for educational policy and practice. He claims we do not use the word to refer to a specific process but to encompass a variety of activities and events in which something worthwhile is transmitted in a morally acceptable manner that develops the student's cognitive perspective and elicits commitment to it. Responding to criticisms of this analysis a decade later, Peters (1977) claims, "Obviously enough, the over-all 'aim' of education is the development of educated men and women" (p. 26). This is less tautologous than it may seem, for it enables Peters to characterize the educated person with a variety of intellectual virtues, including the commitment to pursue knowledge for its own sake. This makes it manifest that, in spite of the paraphernalia of linguistic analysis and transcendental arguments, his theory is largely a modernized statement of Aristotle's view that the human being is the rational animal and the aim of education is the development of this rational nature: "For one of the distinguishing features of man is that he alone of all creatures has a variable conceptual framework which determines the aspects under which he acts" (Peters, 1964, p. 9).

There will be more to say about this indebtedness to Aristotle after we consider Peters' (1966) positive contribution, epitomized in his highly original descriptive/normative definition of the nature and aim of education:

> Education consists essentially in the initiation of others into a public world picked out by the language and concepts of a people and in encouraging others to join in exploring realms marked out by more differentiated forms of awareness. (p. 52)
>
> The overall aim of education is to get children *on the inside* of the activities and forms of awareness characterizing what we would call a civilized form of life. (p. 81)

The force of these definitions lies in their grounding in the development of consciousness. Peters (1966) claims that the child comes to perceive the objects in the world around it as objects only through the acquisition of language. Verbal concepts enable the child to impose their order upon the flux of sensory experience. As various specialized languages are acquired in the academic disciplines, there also develop various modes of consciousness. In addition to having its own language, basic concepts, and body of organized, factual knowledge or content, each mode of consciousness or form of knowledge has its own public procedures that have been involved in the validation and accumulation of its content (pp. 49–50).

Peters (1966) developed the thesis about the forms of knowledge as constituting the heart of education with Paul Hirst from 1962 to 1965 (pp. 8–9). It is articulated in Hirst's 1965 "Liberal Education and the Nature of Knowledge." In their coauthored book, *The Logic of Education*, Hirst and Peters (1970) illustrate their thesis by reference to Kohlberg's work. Just as one can advance through the Kohlbergian six stages to develop a highly refined, conceptualized understanding in the moral domain, so, too, can one develop various modes of consciousness through the gradual acquisition of the conceptual schemata of the forms of knowledge (pp. 45–51). They substantiate their claims by citing the sorts of concepts and testing procedures they find in seven areas: mathematics (and formal logic), physical sciences, the language of subjective and intersubjective reality, moral language, the language of esthetic experience (and fine arts), religious thought, and philosophical understanding (pp. 63–65). It is noteworthy that the language of subjective and intersubjective reality replaces the human sciences and history of Hirst's 1965 listing (p. 131). It is in turn replaced by an interpersonal mode of awareness in Peters' 1977 account (p. 29). The forms of knowledge most commonly given in *Ethics and Education*, in addition to "rational moral discourse," are referred to as "theoretical activities" and include science, history, literature, philosophy, and religion.

Peters (1966) gives some attention to practical activities in the curriculum, mentioning briefly politics, social work, business, farming, medicine, cooking, and carpentry, but he also says, "It is a question of how far the individual child can go in developing a theoretical structure for practical activities rather than a question of which children can do this and which children cannot" (p. 177). This distorts the characteristic excellence of these activities in order to foster conceptual growth. Peters also includes sports ("physical prowess, dexterity") in mentioning outcomes of education, as well as "taste in clothes and in the arrangement and decoration of rooms" (p. 177) and other skills needed in homemaking. Hirst (1974) seems to agree later when he claims it is wrong to delimit the arts and practical activities to the students who are less able academically, for they have a central place in the education of everyone (p. 28). The general emphasis of both, however, is on the forms of knowledge associated with theoretical activities, particularly when they view the pedagogic relationship as a form of apprenticeship with a master who is inside the form of thought and obligated to initiate students into it through some form of conceptual didactics, although not necessarily through instruction (Peters, 1966, pp. 260–261; Hirst & Peters, 1970, pp. 77–80). Hirst (1965) speaks for Peters, too, when he says that a liberal education should include "the study of at least paradigm examples of all the various forms of knowledge" (p. 133), thereby referring not to practical activities but to disciplinary studies that involve basic concepts, logic, and criteria and procedures for determining truth or validity (p. 133).

The evaluation of the claims as to which forms of knowledge exist and which belong in the school curriculum will occur after the consideration of the other views on the role of knowledge in schooling. It suffices to say that the claim that there are different forms of knowledge and modes of understanding and awareness of things in the world that should be acquired educationally is a permanent contribution to theory of education. Although Hirst (1986) claims that Peters' view of education as initiation into these forms is based on the development of categories of thought derived from Kant, Hegel, Oakeshott, and Popper (p. 19), it might also have been derived independently from Alfred

Schutz's concept of the various provinces of meaning, each of which has its own cognitive style, accent of reality, and structure of attention and awakeness (Schutz & Luckman, 1974, pp. 22–25). Peters does not cite Husserl or post–Husserlian phenomenologists, but the claim about modes of consciousness becoming structured by the specialized languages and concepts of the various domains (or regions of being) is phenomenologically true. As Schutz claims, the division of labor and specialization of function that causes differentiated provinces of meaning to break off from the everyday lived world also causes the provinces of knowledge to develop with some degree of autonomy from each other, especially when they become institutionalized in universities. Because of the institutionalization of the division of labor, a province of knowledge gains its own inner-meaning structure and develops "its own logic and its own methodology, just as it must have its own 'pedagogy' (because of the requisites of the role-bound transmission of knowledge)" (Schutz & Luckman, 1974, p. 302).

Peters (1966) actually invokes the phenomenological thesis of the intentionality of all acts of consciousness, albeit without acknowledgment. After claiming that consciousness, the hallmark of mind, is related to objects in all its various modes, he says, "The individual wants *something*, is afraid of or angry with *somebody* or *something*, believes or knows that *certain things are the case*" (p. 50). It is unfortunate that this point, so crucial to his insight into education as initiation into the human world, is followed by his largest mistake: "The objects of consciousness are first and foremost objects in a public world that are marked out and differentiated by a public language" (p. 50). The concept of the public world with public objects in it betrays the ideology behind the definition of education as initiation into "public traditions enshrined in language" (p. 49). Peters is using the word *public*, as opposed to *private*, to call attention to an epistemic characteristic of good knowledge. He wants to claim that the things in the world of which one becomes aware through languages are in fact known objects. Truthfulness is gained by the intersubjective refinement of the language used by everyone who already exists inside of the world of common sense or the specialized modes of awareness that he calls forms of knowledge.

To amend the title of his paper about Plato, however, we should ask, "Was Peters nearly right about education?" and answer affirmatively (Peters, 1977, pp. 119ff.). Nearly right, however, is not right at all. The error lies in the influence of Aristotle, who is cited by Peters (1966) in his history of the development of mind when he refers to the Greeks as living "in a public world of public feats and public concerns" (p. 47). A very different understanding of the concept of the publicness of thought and meanings is found in Marilyn French's (1985) history of the development of patriarchy. She claims that matricentric societies changed to patriarchal societies when men separated themselves from nature and family life in order to gain control over nature and society. The development of forms of life by men to aid in the acquisition of power included the Greek distinction between the private and the public. The private became associated with animality, nature, and necessity, and the public became related to the mind, the human being, and freedom. As French notes, Aristotle relegated women, children, technicians, and laborers to the private realm, comprising the necessary conditions of the state. Men were delegated to the life of the free citizen of the *polis*, to the public realm beyond the restrictions of nature and necessity (p. 76). Females and laborers were supposedly born to their lot and did not need education to become women or human. As free citizens, however, males did need to become educated for the public realm. They needed to learn how to be a man (p. 77). In this perspective, Aristotle's concept of liberal education, which lies explicitly behind Peters' (and Hirst's) view, serves as an ideology to justify a patriarchal society. Although most males may in fact be relegated to the private realm, according to French they all share in the power held by the patriarchs who control public life.

It would commit the genetic fallacy to dismiss Peters' theory on the grounds that its prototype served patriarchal functions. There is internal evidence in abundance to show the sexism in the view, however, for throughout *Ethics and Education*, Peters refers to boys but not to girls. He obviously has single-gender schools in mind. The characteristics of the educated person who remains concerned with the pursuit of knowledge for its own sake is not quite the ivory-tower isolate that Martin (1981) imagines him to be (pp. 41–46). He is a graduate of the British public school and Oxbridge and a member of what Thorstein Veblen (1899/1943) called "the leisure class." Textual evidence includes the patronizing treatment of practical activities, of which Peters seems most familiar with cooking, carpentry, and gardening, and also a very remarkable passage about the kinds of students attending the secondary modern schools in Great Britain. After discussing their limitations, Peters (1966) says, "The problem created by mass education . . . is that of providing adequate avenues for self-realization in a way which does not involve a depreciation in the quality of education for those who are gifted enough to benefit from it" (p. 87).

This disbelief in the educability of the "masses," who cannot be initiated into the public world that is supposedly constitutive of a civilized life, would not have arisen had the word *public* been replaced by the word *common* as the epistemic characteristic Peters wants to stress in his definition of education and interpretation of language. As children learn a language, they become aware of the objects in their world as they are in the world of others, that is, as common objects in the common world. Peters' concern for the intersubjectivity or communicability of knowledge is adequately conveyed by the word *common*, especially when the basic epistemic unit is thought to be a discursive community of qualified investigators. The emphasis upon the commonness—or sharing—of meanings that pick out common objects in a common or shared world, moreover, meets one of the criteria of the new paradigm of education Martin (1981) calls for (pp. 56–57). It furnishes the connectedness that may be characteristic of women's ways of knowing (Belenky, Clinchy, Goldberger, & Tarule, 1986).

To join the common world with the realm of necessity and nature, however, requires consideration of educational theories concerned with utilitarian objectives of schooling such as Spencer's and Dewey's. A point of criticism will set Peters' view into perspective and show on substantive grounds why it needs to be complemented by utilitarian considerations. If the so-called forms of knowledge are really modes of consciousness, each with its own bracketing appropriate to its own province of meaning as Schutz suggests, then one has to be inside a form to understand it. It follows that the external evaluation of a form of knowledge is neither possible nor relevant. Hirst (1974), for example, errs when he decides to drop history as a form of knowledge. He does so because it allegedly contains in large part "truths that are matters of empirical observation and experiment . . . of the strictly physical science variety" (p. 86). He came to this conclusion as a result of reading "philosophical work concerned with differences in concepts and logical structures and truth criteria" (p. 85), not from reading history, historiography, or hermeneutical theory. As a matter of fact, the methods of the physical sciences cannot be used to confirm the content of history because historical phenomena do not exist. They cannot be isolated from the rest of the universe or put into a laboratory for controlled observation or experimentation. All we have are written records and monuments about the events. Reading them is not at all like reading fossils or rock strata. Physical scientists do not ordinarily rely solely on secondhand testimony about the object of their inquiry.

Even if one grants that history is not a distinct form of knowledge, it still belongs in the curriculum because its study can in fact develop a mode of consciousness by which one understands events, institutions, and problems in a historical, chronological perspective, that is, diachronically instead of synchronically. We would certainly hesitate to call people educated if they had no understanding of the historical development of their own country in the context of the history of the world.

The idea that the forms of knowledge should be studied to develop one's mind, in other words, correctly emphasizes conceptual schemata as the content of instruction, but in the wrong way and for the wrong reason. Because these conceptual schemata give one a greater access to the common world, it is necessary to decide which regions of the world an educated person should know something about and that should make up the substantive content of the curriculum of common, general education. What the knowledge is about is educationally more important than its "form." An adequate consideration of the regions of the world in the content of the curriculum requires a corresponding change in pedagogy, as we will see in the theory of the nineteenth-century British utilitarian, Herbert Spencer, which may be more "modern" than Peters'.

PERCEPTUAL HEURISTICS: SPENCER

In his 1850s essays about education, Spencer (1860/1963) uses the theory of biological evolution to determine what knowledge should be acquired in education. In the well-known, "What Knowledge Is of Most Worth?" he classifies all human activities into five levels of priority, each the necessary condition of the next, and then specifies the knowledge needed in each category. For personal, physical survival, one needs knowledge of hygiene, health, physiology, nutrition, exercise, and sport (explicitly for both males and females) (pp. 37–44). For individual survival within the economic system—which to Spencer seems to engage most people in the manufacturing, preparation, and distribution of goods—the knowledge needed is (nineteenth-century) mathematics, physics, chemistry, biology, sociology, and economics. Industrial and agricultural processes involve elements of the various natural sciences. Their management involves scientific knowledge of society, that is, sociology and economics (pp. 44–45). After individual survival comes the survival of the family. Spencer wants the knowledge of parenting in the curriculum, primarily developmental psychology, with particular attention to cognitive and moral development, but also including the nutrition and physiology relative to developmental needs (pp. 54–64).

Biological reproduction in the family is of course necessary for the survival of the society. The knowledge needed for the reproduction of society concerns the historical development of the nation's local and national governments, social-class structure and behaviors, and the industrial system, including "an account of the industrial arts techni- cally considered: stating the processes in use, and the quality of the products" (p. 68), so the division of labor is clearly understood. The object is to gain a macrocosmic view of the whole society in regard to its political, social, economic, intellectual, and cultural dimensions in a historical (i.e., evolutionary) perspective. Then one can understand how a consensus is maintained within society throughout changes in its customs, beliefs, and institutions (pp. 64–71).

Because a society does not merely want to survive but also wants to live well, the fifth level of activities includes the cultural pursuits of leisure, such as literature and the fine arts, of which Spencer (1860/ 1963) mentions painting, sculpture, music, poetry, and architecture. Because artists have to be acute observers of the objects they depict and of the properties of their materials, the fine arts are also based on science (pp. 71–81). Spencer claims:

> Science itself is poetic. . . . Science opens up realms of poetry where to the unscientific all is a blank. Those engaged in scientific researches constantly show us that they realize not less vividly, but more vividly, than others, the poetry of their subjects. . . . Science excites poetry rather than extin- guishes it. (p. 82)

This last point is exceedingly important for overcoming nihilism.

Spencer (1860/1963) has worked out the knowledge needed for the five objectives of education: direct individual survival, indirect individ- ual survival, family survival, group survival, and survival with dignity. In each case he reduces it to science. The knowledge of most worth to Spencer includes those aspects of the natural and social sciences that are necessary in an education for health, vocation, parenting, citizen- ship, and leisure, in descending order of importance, but in due propor- tion. Although he calls the last category "ornamental," he does not want it sacrificed for exhaustive preparation in any of the areas of higher priority (p. 35). He does say, however, that the activities that *"occupy the leisure part of life . . . should . . . occupy the leisure part of education"* (p. 75). It is also clear that the actual school curriculum does not have to be divided to achieve these objectives separately, for the knowledge relevant to one may be relevant to others (p. 34). What is important is that the knowledge be "Science," with a capital "s" to indicate a general orientation to the world that includes the poetics of science in pedagogy to maintain and enhance the childlike wonder in the face of the beauty of the world:

Whoever has not in youth collected plants and insects, knows not the halo of interest which lanes and hedge-rows can assume. Whoever has not sought for fossils, has little idea of the poetical associations that surround the places where embedded treasures were found. Whoever at the seaside has not had a microscope and aquarium, has yet to learn what the highest pleasures of the seaside are. Sad, indeed, is it to see how men occupy themselves with trivialities, and are indifferent to the grandest phenomena—care not to understand the architecture of the Heavens. (p. 83)

Before turning to his pedagogics, we should note that the subject Spencer (1860/1963) finds most important and wants to have "occupy the highest and last place in the course of instruction passed through by each man and woman" (p. 162) can integrate all the others and yield the mental maturity to rear one's children. It is the theory and practice of education (p. 163). This subject in turn makes possible the last stage of mental development, which for "each man and woman is to be reached only through the proper discharge of the parental duties" (p. 216). Because he sees education as concerned with the rearing of the young to adulthood, Spencer's pedagogy is progressive in the sense of being established in the natural development of the child. He is not sentimental like Rousseau, for he warns, "Do not expect from a child any great amount of moral goodness" (p. 205). He does believe, however, that the content of the curriculum should be arranged on the natural interests of the child to insure it is appropriate to the child's developmental situation and to let learning be a pleasure (p. 110).

Spencer (1860/1963) believes the child should evolve personally in much the same way as the human race evolved in regard to the complexity of the knowledge acquired. Although this recapitulation theory is untenable, it explains why Spencer explicitly borrows and refines some of Pestalozzi's principles to assist in the evolution of consciousness. For example, he argues that learning should proceed from the particular to the general. Students should be allowed to form the generalization from the particulars, by their own inquiry, and thereby organize their knowledge (pp. 104–105). For Spencer, however, this should be a guided discovery process. The teacher should provide "from day to day the right kind of facts, prepared in the right manner . . . in due abundance at appropriate intervals" (p. 114). The right manner of providing facts, moreover, is not through verbal abstractions but through object lessons. He claims that the powers of observation need to be developed: "Without an accurate acquaintance with the visible and tangible properties of things, our conceptions must be erroneous, our inferences fallacious, and our operations unsuccessful" (p. 106).

He therefore outlines a program whereby the mother can aid in the development of perceptual discrimination by helping the preschool child to become aware of the qualities of household objects. She should not only give the child the vocabulary with which to identify the various aspects of their texture, hardness or softness, color, form, and sounds, but she should also ask questions about the qualities to insure the words are understood and to promote an inquiring attitude. He suggests that this "systematic culture of the perceptions" (Spencer, 1860/1963, p. 138) teaches the "rudiments of science in the concrete instead of in the abstract" (p. 109), particularly when the objects are not limited to the content of the home but include "those of the field and the hedges, the quarry and the seashore" and are continued into youth, when they should become gradually identical to the objects studied by naturalists (p. 136). To assist in this in school, "every study . . . should have a purely experimental introduction; and only after an ample fund of observations has been accumulated, should reasoning begin" (p. 124). What should be learned everywhere through the object lessons is, according to Spencer, the most important knowledge of all: the laws of life. These are everywhere the same, but they cannot be understood abstractly until they have been studied concretely, simply, and perceptually (p. 139). The outdoor education in childhood and the continuous assimilation of similar information through the senses in youth stores up "raw material for future organization—the facts that will one day bring home to it with due force those great generalizations of science by which actions may be rightly guided" (p. 140).

The importance of the cultivation of perception for overcoming nihilism lies in the development of the nonconceptual, prescientific awareness of the qualities of things in the world. This is similar to Harry Wildman's disclosure of his "lovely creatures" (cf. Chapter 5). Although Spencer (1860/1963) combines the terms of faculty psychology with a naïve, inductive view of science, in actual practice there would develop a perceptual consciousness of the qualities of things through the implementation of his proposal. This would supply the needed experiential grounding for the explicit generalizations in the study of the natural world that establishes their perceived truthfulness. If a philosopher of science or science educator would demur and say, as Peters would, that science has become much more conceptual since Spencer's day, the reply is that that is exactly why his concern with object lessons and the development of perceptual consciousness is so important educationally.

The sensibility developed by the extensive use of object lessons, furthermore, involves both their so-called primary and secondary qualities. These became distinguished from each other in British empiricism when John Locke (1689/1939) said that qualities such as bulk (or solidity), figure, extension, number, and motion are primary because they are in things themselves, or are objective. Qualities such as tastes, odors, sounds, colors, and textures are secondary because they allegedly are not in the objects themselves, or are subjective (p. 265). Locke accepts the results of Descartes' analysis of complex things into their simple natures, "the cognition of which is so clear and distinct that they cannot be analysed by the mind into others more distinctly known. Such are figure, extension, motion, etc.; all others we conceived to be in some way compounded out of these" (Descartes, 1628/1931, pp. 40–41). Locke imposes this rationalistic prejudice for mathematics and physical science upon the phenomenology of the case simply by asserting that these are primary qualities. Spencer, however, denies this prejudice. The so-called object lessons are intended to develop awareness of all of the objects' qualities. What Locke mistakenly calls their secondary qualities are their values, but these are as objective as the so-called primary qualities. Spencer's pedagogy therefore promotes the development of a value sensibility that would support the obligation to care for and preserve existing things (*cf.* Chapter 4). It appears to support what French calls the "feminine principle" and therefore serves to balance the so-called masculine principle underlying the heavy emphasis on conceptual learning as advocated by Peters and Hirst, among others, that is alleged to be destroying life on this planet. As French (1985) claims, "It is the quality more than the quantity of things—air, water, color, scent, friendship—that arouses pleasure. Our world, however, is devoted to quantity, to that which can be enumerated on a balance sheet or a poll" (pp. 468, 539, 542) because it is a patriarchal world. Before we will be ready to combine the development of perceptual consciousness with conceptual consciousness in education, however, we need to look at several previous attempts to pattern a curriculum upon a synthesis of the two.

EXPERIMENTAL HEURISTICS: DEWEY

The difference between Spencer and Dewey on curriculum and pedagogy is Yankee ingenuity. Dewey replaced the observation in Spencer's theory with activity and the object lessons with typical social activities. The generalizations formulated to organize the factual particulars, furthermore, are to be tested in action (Dewey, 1916, pp. 166–169, 258–261). The typical social activities comprising the curriculum, moreover, are the great historical occupations, that is, Peters' practical activities (pp. 232–234). Our consideration here will be restricted to Dewey's *Democracy and Education* (1916), because it is his magnum opus. In this work, the knowledge he considers of most worth is that which is used vocationally. An education for a vocation should be an education through vocations (p. 362). A Spencerian scientism also prevails in Dewey, but the interpretation is experimentalist, accompanied by the outrageous claim that the form of intelligence used in vocations is the same as that involved in scientific inquiry. Both allegedly require the definition of a problem arising in activity, collection of data, and formulation and testing of a hypothesis that will resolve the problem, unify the situation, and free one to continue with the activity (pp. 176–177, 235–237).

Related to Dewey's view that intelligence is simply a function of the whole biological organism interacting with the immediate environment—whether in everyday life, a vocation, or in a scientific laboratory—is the claim that the method of experimental natural science is the only form of knowledge. There are, however, three phases of knowledge that should affect the curriculum and pedagogy. The first is the actual handling of materials. The second is communicating with others about these handlings, which changes knowing how to do something with the materials to knowing that they have certain factual characteristics. This second phase of informational or propositional knowledge does not yet yield the generalizations Dewey finds characteristic of the third phase, which is the rationalized knowledge of science, stated with the formal conceptualizations that allow for the interrelation of experimentally tested ideas.

Although the experimental testing of ideas of the third phase has received the most attention by the interpreters of Dewey, it can be argued that what seems most characteristically his, educationally, is the first phase. As he says, "Only by starting out with crude material and subjecting it to purposeful handling will he [the student] gain the intelligence embodied in finished material" (1916, p. 232). To make the point, this principle should be fleshed out with Dewey's own enumeration:

> There is work with paper, cardboard, wood, leather, cloth, yarns, clay and sand, and the metals, with or without tools. Processes employed are folding, cutting, pricking, measuring, molding, modeling, pattern-making, heating and cooling, and the operations characteristic of such tools as the hammer, saw, file, etc. Outdoor excursions, gardening, cooking, sewing, printing, book-binding, weaving, painting, drawing, singing, dramatizations, story-telling, reading and writing as active pursuits with social aims

(not as mere exercises for acquiring skill for future use), in addition to a countless variety of plays and games, designate some of the modes of occupation. (p. 230)

While the children are cooking, gardening, or weaving, for example, they should also be reading and talking about the relevant background in physics or chemistry and the agricultural and textile industries to enlarge their conceptualized awareness of what they are physically involved in with their hands. The engagement with these materials is also supposed to run into snags or obstacles every so often to insure that students have to stop and observe, read, ask questions, get ideas, think them through, and test them experimentally (or instrumentally) in an effort to return to the activity with a greater understanding of it. This raises their acquisition of knowledge to Dewey's third level because it incorporates some of the knowledge of the experts into their own experience.

Dewey (1916) wants teachers to arrange things so students solve larger and larger problems, using what is learned through experimental testing in one as information in the next: "The problem of teaching is to keep the experience of the student moving in the direction of what the expert already knows" (p. 216). The possible routes for moving students from the active occupations to the organized knowledge of the experts are explained in Dewey's profound chapter entitled "The Significance of Geography and History." The occupations have a context in space and time, in nature and society, and in geography and history, the understanding of which adds significance to what may otherwise seem trivial (pp. 244–246). Gardening, for example, can lead to the understanding of the role of agriculture in the history of the human race, or to a grasp of the geographical locations where various crops are grown, and why. Understanding the latter can enrich the meaning of the beans growing in the plastic cup on the classroom windowsill and also elevate the occupation of farming. Or, gardening can lead to an understanding of soil chemistry, types of soil, the virtues of natural and chemical fertilization, climatic conditions favorable to various crops, and the interrelation of plant to animal life (p. 235). It can lead to nature study, considered as the study of the flora and fauna of the local environment and their relation to climatic and geological conditions, and expand outward to the natural geography of one's nation and further.

Similar routes outward can be followed from any of the occupations, *mutatis mutandis*. Thus Dewey believes that students can be led from classroom activities to their place within the local geography, to the study of the natural world as it occurs in the natural sciences and to their place in the development of social life through examining the historical roots of contemporary social problems (pp. 250–251). The resources of industrial, economic, and intellectual history can be joined to the study of geography to develop a macrocosmic understanding of the place of human beings and their occupations on Earth (pp. 252–253, 255).

This expansion of the cognitive perspective of the occupations serves as one's liberal education because it enables a broader grasp of the vocation with which one will earn a living as an adult (1916, pp. 235, 363, 372). Dewey in fact denies that the so-called liberal education that fosters the pursuit of knowledge for its own sake is nonvocational (pp. 301, 364–366). Although he is right, because liberal education is preparation for professional vocations, no one has ever been able to show convincingly that preparation for vocations through vocations can enable students to secure the organized body of knowledge Dewey himself believes they should acquire. One gathers vaguely that activities should predominate in the elementary school and that students should be studying relatively structured, organized subjects and using conceptual schemata from the disciplines by the time they reach adolescence. There is, however, no assurance this can or will happen within the framework of *Democracy and Education*, nor is there any clearly outlined route whereby it might happen. These things are necessary for students planning on attending tertiary schools, for whom some other pedagogy and curriculum is needed, as well as for all other students, none of whom should receive a second-class education while the elite prepare for university matriculation.

A curriculum and pedagogy other than one built upon active occupations would be necessary for adolescents even if Dewey's experimentalism were tenable. His ideology of science tries to articulate the methodology of the natural sciences, then claims that it is scientific method in the fusion of science and technology that results in the technological consciousness. Although his pedagogy enables students to become aware of the qualities of things in the immediate experience of the activities proposed for the classroom, the main goal of the knowledge to be acquired through the problem-solving method is control of the environment, which places the emphasis upon the functional aspects of objects. The suggestion that this fault is not attributable to the mature Dewey is an admission that it is in fact found in his educational theory (*cf.* Burnett, 1988). Furthermore, the testing of an idea by its consequences when acting upon it is a psychological examination of its usefulness, not an epistemic test of its truth, because for

Dewey (after Peirce), inquiry stops when the tested idea frees one for the activity. This makes its instrumental meaning clear but does not guarantee its truth (Dewey, 1916, p. 192). Dewey's theory shows us, however, that the emphasis upon the development of conceptual consciousness at the expense of perceptual awareness, found in ideologies of liberal education like Peters', is as unacceptable as the emphasis upon the development of perceptual consciousness at the expense of conceptualization found in such utilitarian ideologies of education as Spencer's.

Although Peters, Spencer, and Dewey exemplify rationalism, empiricism, and pragmatism, respectively, their epistemologies may be of less importance than their educational aims, understood as the way the knowledge acquired in school should be used in adulthood. Peters (1966) assumes that educated people have become so committed to the intrinsic values in science, history, and literature, for example, that they continue to study science and read history and literature in their adult lives. He is concerned with adults using the forms of knowledge as they were learned in school. To achieve this degree of *replication* in adulthood requires the pedagogy of initiation into the forms of knowledge, as noted earlier, "for those who are gifted enough to benefit from it" (p. 87). His claim that the forms of knowledge give cognitive perspective on what should be done, however, involves the use of knowledge to *interpret* things. For Spencer (1860/1963), the knowledge to be used for personal and familial survival are the habits and skills of personal hygiene, physical exercise, and vocation. These are to be learned for exact replication and for *application* in solving problems. The knowledge required for citizenship and group survival, however, should be used interpretively to understand society. Dewey's (1916) curriculum is concerned with the general education that furnishes a cognitive perspective on one's occupation(s) and is designed to be used interpretively, but the great emphasis upon problem solving in Dewey's pedagogy reflects his attempt to have the knowledge acquired in school applied to the problems arising in adult society. An attempt to steer between these leisure-class and working-class objectives in a program of common, general education is made by our next author.

INTERPRETIVE DIDACTICS: BROUDY

An early scheme for general education to promote the interpretive use of knowledge is made by Broudy, Smith, and Burnett in their 1964 book, *Democracy and Excellence in American Secondary Education*. It is deepened in Harry Broudy's mature statement in *The Uses of Schooling* (1988), upon which the following is based. His thesis is that the school's main task is to provide students with a broad, allusionary base that functions tacitly to help them understand things in adult life. He disagrees with the common expectations regarding the replicative and applicative uses of schooling. The knowledge and skills in the area of basic education, such as penmanship, spelling, number facts, and the multiplication tables, should be used exactly as they are learned, but otherwise the replication of knowledge occurs mostly in one's vocation (pp. 12–13). Some knowledge acquired in vocational education may be applied within the vocation with the emergence of problems for which one's skills do not suffice. It is only professionals, however, who by definition use their knowledge to solve problems, that is, applicatively (pp. 14, 21). The *associative* use of schooling occurs when one supplies the associations or connotations of words heard or read. If one hears about a Promethean task, Procrustean bed, or the Gordian knot, for example, one adds the meanings to the words that were embodied in the original myths. These meanings are not conceptualized but merely associated with whatever is said to be Promethean, Procrustean, or Gordian. The interpretive use of knowledge occurs when the study of academic subjects builds up cognitive maps, or conceptual schemata, through which one perceives things and events and makes sense of them even when solving the manifest problem is out of the question.

To promote the development of the associative and interpretive uses of schooling through common, general education in Grades 7 through 12, Broudy (1988) recommends three strands of curriculum content: basic sciences, developmental studies, and exemplars of value. We will discuss each in turn.

Because Broudy (1988) believes that the content of the sciences should be restricted to the most general concepts that are most widely useful in understanding things in the world, he recommends that only general science, biology, chemistry, and physics should be included (p. 89). To maximize their interpretive value, they "should be taught as science, i.e., as logically organized subject matter, with the precision required for such study" (p. 90). Little heed should be given to descriptions of physical phenomena, technological applications of science, and laboratory experiments unless they contribute directly to the mastery of the basic concepts. Acquiring the basic concepts is necessary to the formation of the patterns or templates that structure consciousness of the world and enable one to locate new phenomena on one's cognitive map of the world (pp. 90–92). The role of science in the education of everyone, in other words, is not primarily for its later replication or application, or to make little scientists of everyone. It is to furnish "the vocabulary and syntax of educated interpretation" (p. 33).

The second strand is concerned with the development of the universe, social institutions, and human culture. The resources for the former include highly selected content from astronomy, geology, climatology, paleontology, biological history up to the emergence of *homo sapiens*, physical anthropology, and ecology. The aim is the same, "to develop cognitive interpretive maps" (Broudy, 1988, pp. 93–94). The second area of developmental studies takes up where the first leaves off by focusing on the social institutions that help distinguish human from animal life, such as "the family, church, economic systems, governmental systems, laws, and other institutions devised by men [sic] to order and nurture their societies" (p. 94). If it is historically correct to claim that these institutions were largely devised by males, however, we should add that their study should occur within a gender-conscious framework to test French's (1985) thesis about men and power. Be that as it may, the resources should be highly selected from anthropology and sociology and from economic, political, and juridical history. This content should replace history, geography, and social studies in the curriculum because the institutions themselves "are among the key social arrangements in our life." Content should be organized around "the role of social institutions in social change, and how social institutions develop under the stress of change in other sectors of human life" (pp. 94–95). Finally, the developmental studies concerning human culture should include "the sciences, technologies, art, literature, systems of ideas, and religions" (p. 97). They should add the historical aspect to the study elsewhere in the curriculum of science, art, literature, philosophy, and religion.

Broudy's (1988) third strand of curriculum content is the value exemplars in art, literature, philosophy, and religion to the extent that these can be selected and adapted to match the cognitive abilities of secondary school students. These exemplars are the classics, by which he means the paradigms of excellence that establish the norms of good judgment (pp. 24, 99–100). Their role in general education is to furnish images for their associative use and evaluative maps for their interpretive use (pp. 65–69, 120–121).

Broudy (1988) accompanies these three strands of substantive content with strands in the study of large-scale, interdisciplinary problems and the symbolic skills (the three R's, including the study of basic concepts in language and mathematics and art education as the fourth R). The symbolic skills largely precede general education, whereas the social problems largely follow it to give students practice in using the

cognitive, developmental, and evaluative schemata acquired in the substantive areas to interpret the predicaments of life (pp. 81–87, 103–
106). Broudy lists only foreign trade and taxation as examples of such
large-scale problems (p. 104). The former, however, implicates all the
problems of international relations, including war and peace and phenomena related to the existence of multinational corporations, relations with Third World nations, and so on. The latter implicates the
various means of taxation and the use of tax revenues for various
purposes such as national defense and social welfare. Both topics mentioned, in other words, are reducible to the issues of conflicting interests and human rights.

To justify the entire proposal, Broudy (1988) lists personal achievement, justice, and compassion as criteria of the good society, ideals that
are apparently achievable through common, general education. Of the
three, only the freedom to realize one's own potential through personal
achievement can "be derived from the struggle for survival in the
animal kingdom. Survival goes to individuals of the species who are
strong, energetic, or cunning" (p. 115). Broudy claims the ideals of
justice (or fairness) and compassion toward the less successful "run
counter to Darwinian natural selection" and are compatible with
human nature as distinguished from animal nature and natural selection (pp. 116–117; cf. Broudy, 1977). That this is tantamount to calling
these three criteria the human rights to liberty, equality, and fraternity
is not the only difference between Broudy and Spencer.

Because the skills used replicatively in regard to health, exercise,
and vocation can be learned outside of school and after general education, they are not, for Broudy (1988), part of the school's obligation to
furnish general education, regardless of how important they may be to
life (p. 5). Knowledge about health and industrial processes is, however,
a part of general education (p. 88). More significantly, Broudy replaces
the object lesson with objects in the visual arts to enable instruction in
art to develop perceptual consciousness and supply imagistic aspects of
the allusionary base, thus complementing the conceptual aspects of the
remainder of the curriculum. He claims, "What art education needs is a
method of perceiving and analyzing aesthetic properties that can be
taught to children in the elementary grades by the classroom teacher"
(p. 61). Then he specifies a means of esthetic scanning to help students
distinguish sensory, formal, technical, and expressive properties in
works of art. He apparently believes that this technique is also applicable to drama and literature, *mutatis mutandis* (pp. 61–64). Practice in
esthetic scanning should enable students to achieve phenomenological
objectivity. It involves looking at the art object to discern its qualities,

rather than projecting one's own feelings and ideas on it, in an attempt to break out of the visual hermeneutical circle (p. 65). The activity should develop perceptual schemata that support the cognitive, developmental, and evaluative schemata that provide the associative, interpretive basis for understanding the predicaments of adult life that cannot be resolved by the replication or application of knowledge.

The way this allusionary basis works as a form of knowing, with these schemata functioning on the tacit level, is illustrated in morality. Broudy (1988) says, "Much of what is called moral education operates by way of maxims learned in youth, which become part of the tacit imago-emotional-noetic store *with* which the rightness of action is judged in mature life" (p. 52). The meanings become sedimented in consciousness during moral education via the maxims, and they later shape the person's actions on the tacit level of moral sensibility, emerging into conceptual awareness only in the rare experience of moral illumination, when fresh insight occurs within the context of a personal moral situation, as Buber claims. Similarly, the cognitive, developmental, and evaluative schemata function tacitly when adults are exposed through the media to political, economic, and international events.

A difference from Peters is noteworthy. Peters expresses considerable concern for the quest for truth in the processes in which the students learn the basic concepts and their relation to propositional knowledge and tests of experimental and other validation within the forms of knowledge. Broudy removes these latter elements from the curriculum to make general education accessible to all students. The basic concepts can be learned at various levels of abstractness and understanding. He also wants to have the contents of the basic sciences, developmental studies, and exemplars selected by experts within the contributing disciplines because the current "consensus of the learned" is as good as one can do in regard to truth. He says, "The educated mind thinks *with* the conceptual and associative resources of this consensus, and the school needs a criterion of truth no less fallible than that which the learned themselves employ" (1988, p. 57). If this is indoctrinative, Broudy says it is preferable to indoctrination into the beliefs and values of a particular social class. Any choice between social classes should be made according to their truth claims, which need to be "tested by the institutions devoted to scholarship" (p. 106). His explication of what he means by the "consensus of the learned" in an earlier work (1976) is invaluable:

> The striving after exactitude in theory and life produced the sciences, the humanities, and the fine arts. Each discipline is the crystallized residue of a

long critical inquiry by specialized persons into a domain of experience. They constitute academic or scholarly guilds sharing problems, modes of inquiry, and criteria of truth. Each discipline, like a stencil, when brought to bear on a segment of existence, discloses a distinctive mode of perception and interpretation. Together they make up the formalized portion of the cultural heritage. To share in that heritage one need only develop the ability and disposition to confront reality with these stencils. (p. 293)

Whereas Peters holds there are only seven (or eight) forms of knowledge and only the gifted can be initiated into them and become educated, Broudy believes there are as many forms of knowledge as there are disciplines and that everyone can acquire their schemata at some level and become educated.

The attempt to develop in everyone the ability and disposition to confront reality with the schemata of the sciences, humanities, and fine arts, however, requires didactic teaching. Because Broudy reserves heuristics for the study of the large-scale social problems after the schemata of the disciplines are acquired, it can be inferred that didactics are preferred when teaching the substantive areas for their subsequent interpretive use. He refers to the earlier work (Broudy et al., 1964), which assumes that teaching is inherently didactic (p. 103). The teacher should be committed to working with an organized body of knowledge in order to help students develop cognitive and valuational structures based upon the concepts, principles, norms, and facts of that body of knowledge. This obliges teachers to require their students to perform the logical operations appropriate to the acquisition of the conceptual apparatus of that body of knowledge (pp. 85–86). Such interpretive didactics should be adapted to the students' intellectual ability in regard to the depth of understanding of the basic concepts essential to the development of the desired schemata.

CONCLUSION

We have now considered the epistemological aspects of four normative theories of education: conceptual didactics, perceptual heuristics, experimental heuristics, and interpretive didactics. They are exemplars, respectively, of liberal education, child-centered progressive education, society-centered progressive education, and general education. Because most of the forms of knowledge Peters recognizes are humanities (history, religion, literature, art, morality, philosophy), his view is a twentieth-century version of the preceding centuries' Platonic education in the classics, designed to develop the mind and character of the guardians. Spencer rebels very strongly against education in the classics, of course, and represents through his use and extension of Pestalozzi's pedagogy the New Education ushered in by Rousseau's *Emile* (1762/1966). Dewey represents the stream of progressive education that has become socially aware of itself by recognizing the sociality of the classroom and of knowledge itself. He is just as much concerned with the development of mind through the acquisition of the forms of knowledge as Peters, except he defines mind as functional intelligence (after Darwin) and claims there is only the one form of knowledge of experimental inquiry (after Peirce). Dewey therefore combines Spencer's concern for the child's learning about things through the senses with his own concern for the child's conceptual development, except the concepts are defined operationally, as instrumental to the achievement of the student's own goals. This enables Dewey to stand liberal education on its head. Whereas for Peters liberal education is strongly opposed to vocational education, for Dewey an adequately conceived vocational education becomes liberal education and education is extended to everyone. The nobility and correctness of this goal disguises the fact that it is gained by the artful sophistry of making the wrong seem the right. Dewey offers a theory of educative experience for use in the schools in flat contradiction to his own statement that societies have schools when the culture becomes too complex to be learned through experience (Dewey, 1916, p. 9; see Vandenberg, 1980).

Broudy undertakes the challenge of formulating a program of formal education to insure that every student acquires the organized body of knowledge that progressive education such as Dewey's is unable to deliver. He cuts the cloth of liberal education to everyone's size by abandoning the ideal of developing the mind through forms of knowledge. Focusing on what the knowledge is about, he outlines a curriculum content that will be generally useful to understanding things in adult life. Whereas Spencer is concerned with the uses of knowledge in achieving biological goals, Broudy's distinctions between acquiring knowledge for replication and application on the one hand and for association and interpretation on the other are epistemic distinctions that transcend the issue between liberal and utilitarian theories. Broudy's view is closer to Aristotle than Plato because of the emphasis upon the basic concepts in the sciences and developmental studies and upon acquiring virtue through the study of role models in the exemplars (rather than through the discursive, reasoning processes of moral education found in Peters and Dewey). Broudy's view is Aristotelian, however, only if the basic concepts in the sciences and developmental studies correspond to actual ontological structures. If these concepts are merely the articulation of current paradigms that are subject to change, then their use to establish schemata falls into a Kantian critical idealism, for these schemata will not suffice to let one know things in themselves. This would be like Peters' liberal education after all, for the forms of knowledge are "ways of understanding experience," not modes of knowing things in the world (Hirst, 1965, p. 122). In this case, both views are truthless.

The truth of Peters' view, however, is that certain subjects should remain central to the academic track of the secondary school to prepare students for tertiary schools. Science, mathematics, literature, and history, for example, should remain in the curriculum, not because of the forms-of-knowledge thesis but because they are important areas of substantive knowledge with which people going to tertiary schools ought to be familiar. This, however, is more like the views of Anthony O'Hear (1981) and Mortimer Adler (1982). These subjects do have different ways of knowing, but this is a consequence of the different kinds of content and of much less importance in regard to their inclusion in general education. The truth of Spencer's view is that the conceptual content of the curriculum ought to be explicitly related to the student's perceptual world and demonstrably contributory to individual or group survival with dignity. What Dewey's view adds to these half truths of Spencer's is that the usefulness ought to be extended to everyone, regardless of their social class and occupational future. From Broudy we obtain the truth that the kind of usefulness that general education should have for everyone is neither utilitarian (replicative) nor pragmatic (applicative), but the associative/interpretive use of a cognitive perspective that renders things in the world intelligible.

These four views represent the main theoretical possibilities, except for the extremes of right-wing fundamentalism and left-wing anarchism and liberationism, the latter of which will be considered in the next chapter. Of the four, only Peters' and Broudy's are compatible with the reality that secondary schools in advanced industrial societies have to prepare students for tertiary schools. Only Broudy offers a way of selecting and organizing the knowledge in the curriculum so the academic track is accessible to everyone. Paradoxically, his view is both the most and the least sensible. The recommendations regarding the symbolic skills, basic concepts, developmental studies, exemplars, and the study of social problems can be readily introduced, without further ado, into existing programs in language arts, science, history, and English and into courses in problems of democracy. As it is expressed, however, Broudy's proposal is least sensible because it is a total curriculum plan, and these are exceedingly difficult to implement in ongoing institutions, even with the will to do so. Broudy's view can escape the criticism Paulo Freire (1968/1970) levels at "banking education" (pp. 58ff.) because of the insistence that pedagogy succeeds only if students perform the logical operations necessary to acquire the conceptual schemata, but this incurs criticism of its logocentrism. It would develop objective consciousness.

Without disagreeing with the importance of art education in the curriculum and the development of perceptual consciousness through esthetic scanning, instruction in this area is not a satisfactory substitute for the object lesson in perceptual cultivation. We cannot smell the rose in a picture, hear the bee buzzing after its nectar, feel the fragility of its petals, nor sense the transitoriness of its beauty. Not even in a painting by Van Gogh can one become aware of what makes a rose a rose because artists do exactly what Descartes does. They reduce things to extension (plus color) and focus on what Locke called their primary qualities while omitting their so-called secondary qualities. Art and art education develop a visual, spectator consciousness that is alienated from the nonvisual qualities of things unless it is supplemented by unreduced object lessons elsewhere.

Broudy's program similarly does not include the history of one's own country, world history, nor the history of the twentieth century. The development of institutions and human culture in these places and times is curiously abstracted from the raw historical contexts and messy details of social life in the creation of a spectator consciousness. To be sure, laboratory experiences and technological applications are included in the sciences to the extent that they are helpful to students in grasping the basic concepts, but this is a peculiar inversion of the practice of the scientist in trying to understand things in the world. The development of an objective, conceptual consciousness so singularly abstracted from perceptual reality expects a great deal of students, not so much in regard to learning abstract, conceptual content, for this is to be simplified as necessary, but in respect to accepting the truth of what is learned without witnessing its confirmation in their perceptual world.

This criticism is not about indoctrination or the use of inquiry methods. It is about the separation of art and science education from the beauties of nature, and the abstraction of the development of institutions and human culture from the grandeur and pathos of the heroic and infamous, sublime, and abominable deeds comprising human history. It is about how this separation can promote the development of a consciousness alienated from its own feelings and sensibilities, from

the qualities of real things in the world, and from the sentient inwardness of other people, because these are omitted from the curriculum.
Broudy's view is not concerned with the factors that make knowledge
humanizing, except for its Aristotelian assumption that the most important human characteristic is rationality, which should be developed
by acquiring the most general concepts in the formation of the Kantian
categories of the mind at the expense of the loss of contact with the
perceived world. The problem of common, general education is to
retain organized subject matter that is selected and arranged for the
interpretive use of knowledge (as Broudy wants) and that also has
intrinsic value not as abstract knowledge but through the truth of its
disclosure of the qualities of things in the world (as Spencer wants). It is
their qualities, after all, that make things worth knowing about.

Broudy's assumption that the most general concepts are the most
generally useful begs the question. The formula $E = mc^2$ may be one of
the most general formulas known to humankind, but it is not very
useful for most people in the understanding of the events of their lives
and societies. Thus, the interpretive value of the most general concepts
is open to question. Although Broudy's addition of "knowing with" to
Ryle's (1949, chap. 2) "knowing that" and "knowing how" is necessary
to include the tacit, preconceptual context of complex skills and propositional knowledge, these senses need to be supplemented by "knowing
about," which is not reducible to "knowing that" because it includes
awareness of the perceptual qualities of things as well as what can be
said about them in factual statements.

General education should enable everyone to know a little about a
lot of things to help them live in an advanced industrial society. The
question is how, in addition to one's specialist education for an occupation, the knowledge of the ACTS and disciplines can help one live a life
of human dignity. Knowing about the world is necessary, for it includes
what Bertrand Russell (1918) had in mind when he said,

> Education destroys the crudity of instinct, and increases through knowl-
> edge the wealth and variety of the individual's contacts with the outside
> world, making him no longer an isolated fighting unit, but a citizen of the
> universe, embracing distant countries, remote regions of space, and vast
> stretches of past and future within the circle of his interests. It is . . . the
> endeavor to make us see and imagine the world in an objective manner, as
> far as possible as it is in itself, and not merely through the distorting
> medium of personal desire. Education . . . is to be judged successful in
> proportion . . . as it gives us a true view of our place in society, of the
> relation of the whole human society to its non-human environment, and of

the non-human world as it is in itself apart from our desires and interests. (p. 39)

General education should give us enough knowledge about ourselves, our society, other societies, the natural world, and the interrelations among these to enable us to be at home with ourselves, our society, with other people of other places and other times, and with the natural world as we and the world truly are. Instead of creating an objective consciousness through an undue emphasis upon conceptual development, as recommended by Peters and Broudy, general education should promote the development of phenomenological objectivity in all the regions of the world, not simply art education. This requires the kind of attention to perceptual cultivation that occurs in Spencer's empiricism and Dewey's experimentalism. Their theories, however, give insufficient attention to conceptual development and the acquisition of organized knowledge.

The examination of the four perspectives shows that Peters correctly emphasizes the acquisition of conceptual schemata as the means for gaining access to the public world. These schemata, however, have to open up the common world in order to accommodate Dewey's and Broudy's concern for common, general education. Spencer correctly restores Locke's so-called secondary properties to primacy in his poetics of science, outdoor education, and perceptual cultivation. Dewey correctly adds (1) the actual physical involvement with material things in order to accommodate the embodiment of consciousness, (2) the involvement of handling in the emergence of knowledge, and (3) a proper respect for the knowledge of the ACTS and their place in the educational development of everyone. Broudy presents an exemplary image of an integrated, coherent curriculum for common, general education and correctly claims it should not include the disciplines but knowledge carefully selected from them to achieve the educational objectives related to the use of knowledge, particularly interpretation.

The problem is to go beyond the nihilism inherent in each of these exemplars due to their exaggerated emphasis upon certain epistemic characteristics at the expense of others and to unite these disparate insights in a coherent theory that responds productively to the intellectual crisis. This is the task to which we now turn.

CHAPTER 9

Knowledge in Education

If the synthesis of the normative theories should show the school's responsibility for providing an organized body of knowledge for the general cognitive development of all students when education is considered a human right, the emphasis upon organized knowledge should not overlook the role of perceptual consciousness in education. To insure the latter is adequately accounted for, the synthesis is preceded by an examination of the theories of Freire and Greene. Then the synthesis, while indebted to them, is oriented toward overcoming their lack of concern for the organization of knowledge in the education of the person.

CO-INTENTIONAL DIALOGICS: FREIRE

The epistemological aspects of Freire's pedagogy have received too little attention because of his more conspicuous and endearing political theory. The context of its development will be recounted briefly to demystify it and separate the pedagogy from the politics.

The story is that, until the military coups in Brazil and Chile in 1964 and 1969, respectively, Freire traveled from one community to another in these countries, staying for several months at a time, working in an adult literacy campaign. When he used the materials he brought with him, the peasants at the teaching sessions would not pay attention. So he abandoned his materials and went around the class, asking each person in turn, "What is your word?" He wrote these on the chalkboard, using them as the experiential vocabulary for the reading program. The shift to working small plots of land cooperatively, after formerly working the land of the owners of very large estates, often left the peasants with the mental habits and attitudes of their former serfdom; they were perhaps more in need of political education to uproot their outdated customs than the literacy training Freire was appointed to give them. Because the words put on the chalkboard reflected their existential and political reality, their acquisition of literacy was accompanied by gains in political literacy in a general consciousness-raising process. Seeing their own words on the board and making sentences from them thickened their meanings and elevated their consciousness from an intransitive to a transitive level, in Freire's terms, or from a concrete, representational to a formal operations stage, in Piaget's (1953/1965) terms. The transitive consciousness, like the transitive verb, always has an object (1967/1973a, p. 17).

Freire relies thus on the phenomenological thesis of the intentionality of consciousness that we saw in Peters but emphasizes the necessity for a kind of praxis in education. Consciousness is not an empty container to be filled with knowledge, but a swift stream of sentience in which there is always an awareness of something in the world. When Freire used his own literacy materials, the peasants merely heard or saw words they did not relate to. Because the words were not about their world, there was no praxis. When he used their own words, he relied on their being in the world, for these words stood for objects in their world. A discussion of the words in a reading lesson therefore became a discussion of the world in a politicizing lesson. Because reading the words was reading their world, it brought the whole world of their former oppression into the classroom as an object lesson. Then using these words to construct sentences about that world distanced them from the object lesson sufficiently to let them discuss its characteristics critically. Through this hermeneutical process of making the implicit explicit, or of becoming aware of what they were conscious of, the peasants came to be with their world as well as in it.

Because this transcendence and the pedagogic relation itself could be maintained only so long as the teacher and (adult) students discussed things together, the pedagogy had to be dialogical. All presentations were therefore brief, ending with a problem-posing question that allowed the consciousness of the adult students to reemerge in interaction with the world. Because the dialogue had to be "mediated by knowable objects," that is, about perceived objects in the peasants' world, it had to be co-intentional. This simultaneous, mutual awareness of something in the world is constitutive of pedagogy. As Freire (1968/ 1970) states it at the end of the first chapter of *Pedagogy of the Oppressed*, "Teachers and students . . . co-intent on reality, are both Subjects, not only in the task of unveiling that reality, and thereby coming to know it critically, but in the task of re-creating that knowledge" (p. 56).

According to Freire (1968/1970), co-intentional dialogue in pedagogy requires that the teacher and student participate in the discussion as equals. This insures that it is about some knowable object (pp. 67, 81). If the teacher engages in a monologue, the words may become separated from the students' perceptual world and no longer show them anything about the world (p. 57). Then the words are memorized, if they are learned at all. Freire does not insist upon an actual, material object in the classroom, as do Spencer and Dewey, although it would make his point. Things in the lived world of the students' lives outside of school will suffice when the teacher and students participate in the dialogue about them as quasi-equals, both learning and both teaching. The ending of short presentations with the teacher's problem-posing questions to stimulate the students' inquiry is supposed to maintain the transitivity (or intentionality) of consciousness and enable students to re-create the knowledge just acquired from the teacher (pp. 71–73). The quotation refers to a two-phase learning process. First there is the unveiling of reality, whereby students become aware of it through the teacher's words. Then this awareness should be re-created within the students' own minds in the inquiry generated by the problem posed (1969/1973b, p. 101). It is very much like William James' (1899/1958) principle, *"No reception without reaction, no impression without correlative expression"* (p. 39). Perceptual consciousness seems to predominate in the first phase, when the new insight occurs as one becomes aware of something in the world. Conceptual consciousness seems to predominate in the second phase, when one conceptualizes the new insight for oneself, re-creating it, as Freire says. Both phases, however, should involve both perceptual and conceptual consciousness, because they should involve "true words" that actually disclose something in the world (1968/1970, p. 75).

To emphasize the kind of pedagogic relationship that belongs in co-intentional dialogics, Freire refers to the teacher/student and the student/teacher. He himself certainly would have learned much about peasant life in the villages as the peasants learned how to read from him. Although the terms are meant to suggest that teachers should always be ready to reconsider their statements in response to students, it is nevertheless clear that the roles are not interchangeable for Freire (1968/1970, p. 68). *Pedagogy of the Oppressed* lends itself to a misunderstanding of this issue. Freire says, for example, "Dialogical theory requires that the world be unveiled. No one can, however, unveil the world *for* another. Although one Subject may initiate the unveiling on behalf of others, the others must also become Subjects of this act" (p. 169). This means the teacher can and should disclose things linguistically ("initiate the unveiling") so long as the disclosures occur within conditions of dialogue, which means the students should use the knowledge immediately in the discussion to insure their conceptual processes are correlated with their perceptual projection to the knowable object.

What is crucial is not who initiates the disclosure but that "the united reflection and action of the dialoguers are addressed to the world" (p. 77) and that both teacher and student "address their acts of cognition to the object by which they are mediated" (p. 81). Without the continuous dialectic between the students and the object in the world in the midst of the pedagogic dialogue, there are for Freire only opinions and beliefs but not truth understood as the disclosure of the thing in the world. For truth to emerge, teacher and students should be co-intent on the object so that both are the subjects of knowledge. To speak metaphorically, they should be looking out the window at the world together in a concerted effort to help the students explore it and fulfill the ontological vocation of becoming more fully human as Freire phrases the quest for being.

The implications of co-intentional dialogics for the curriculum of common, general education cannot be inferred from *Pedagogy of the Oppressed*, where the curriculum is to be built upon the themes embedded in the minds of adult peasants who had grown up dominated by the owners of large estates. Thus Freire's propaganda against a "banking education," which presumes that the student's consciousness is an empty place to be filled with knowledge, erroneously persuaded his interpreters that all didactics, not just poor didactics, should be eliminated from schools and that only an ad hoc, negotiated curriculum will suffice. This misunderstands Freire's work, for whom political literacy was a by-product of reading literacy, not the reverse.

The misinterpretation is incompatible with the actual requirements of a co-intentional pedagogy within an ordinary school with students who have not been reared to adulthood as serfs. Freire (1969/1973b) elsewhere says the classroom should be "a meeting-place where knowledge is sought and not where it is transmitted" (p. 150). To establish this condition requires not the elimination but "the problematization of the world of work, products, ideas, convictions, aspirations, myths, art, science, the world, in short, of culture and history" (p. 154). To problematize these things and develop a critical consciousness in the student, they have to be in the curriculum. Freire's intemperate polemic against didactics itself became problematized for him because he is correct when in his 1987 dialogue with Ira Shor in *A Pedagogy for Liberation* he says, "Not all kinds of lecturing is banking education. . . . The question is the content and dynamism of the lecture, the approach to the object to be known" (p. 40). Instead of merely imposing reading assignments on students as "banking teachers" do, the teacher should "demand that students confront seriously the texts" (p. 11). Working-class students should learn the language of the dominant class for their own survival, to be able to fight the dominant class, and to be able to engage in the kinds of reading required at the university, which they should strive to attend (pp. 73, 83). Teachers should gradually introduce students to academic, theoretical language to get them into more rigorous levels of knowing reality than is possible in their untutored language (p. 150). Oversimplifying things is a form of elitism (p. 153). The student's own goals for vocational training and employment credentials place valid obligations upon teachers and schools (p. 68).

Freire claims it is wrong to expect of education "what it cannot do, transform society" (Freire & Shor, 1987, p. 37). He claims, "Teaching is not a lever for changing or transforming society" (p. 46), and, "Systematic or formal education . . . cannot really be the lever for the transformation of society" (p. 129). These comments do not reflect a change in Freire's view. His earlier work was, after all, formulated to teach people how to read. In the later work he says, "Serious reading is part of the rigor of the dialogical class. Of course, the students *have* to read. You *need* to read, to read the classics in your field. . . . I don't accept a kind of *scientific racism*, where some classics are . . . not considered part of the fundamental literature" (1987, p. 83).

To complete the liberation of Freire's (1985b) co-intentional dialogics from his politics, it should be noted that it is simply untrue to say, "Education is a political act" (p. 188) or, "An educational act has a political nature and a political act has an educational nature" (p. 188) or, "All instances of education become political acts" (p. 188). The middle quotation makes sense only if educational acts are in fact distinguishable from political acts, which cancels out the other two. Although every educational act may have political consequences, most of these are very remote, inconsequential, and unpredictable, like the political consequences of the physician's curing a child of the common cold. Educational acts can look political only if one adopts a political point of view toward education or views everything in the universe within a political perspective. This is only one perspective, and it cannot be adopted without falling into sectarianism (i.e., fanaticism), which Freire elsewhere properly rejects (1967/1973a, p. 11; 1968/1970, pp. 21–23). This politicizing turns all private acts into public, political acts and then views them in terms of power and control (Raywid, 1973). Because it invites a political solution instead of an educational one, it is as patriarchal as Peters' view.

Freire's patriarchal sectarianism shows more strongly in his religious commitments. He says, "The educator must be prepared to die as the exclusive educator of the learners. . . . The educator has to live the profound meaning of Easter" (1985b, p. 105). Writing on another occasion about the apprenticeship necessary to learn how to teach the oppressed, Freire (1973/1985a) says it requires of liberals that "they really experience their own Easter, that they die as elitists so as to be resurrected on the side of the oppressed, that they be born again" (pp. 122–123). This Easter occurs without a proper Calvary. Freire seems to mean the metaphor quite literally, for he goes on to distinguish the old, bourgeois Easter from the genuine Easter as the "death that makes life possible" (p. 138). He claims the church itself must always be reborn, purporting to speak from within the "prophetic position" (p. 138). He can assume his writings are divinely inspired if he wishes, but in the sentence, "Christ was no conservative" (p. 139), his own "language conceals more than reveals" (p. 136). Had he said, "Jesus was no conservative," the statement would not have been an antidialogical communique, for it would have been open to intersubjective co-investigation. Nowhere in the gospels, however, will one find evidence that Jesus was in fact the christ, the messiah the ancient Hebrews were awaiting. Albert Schweitzer (1956) finds evidence to the contrary because Jesus's own statements about his mission cannot be distinguished from messianic delusions. Because Freire's (1973/1985a) statement is itself messianic, it disqualifies itself as educational philosophy, which must meet the criterion Freire establishes for his own prophetic perspective: It "demands a scientific knowledge of the world as it really is" (p. 138).

CONCEPTUAL DIALOGICS: GREENE

Co-intentional dialogics has received independent formulations in English by Vandenberg (1969, 1971) and Scudder and Mickunas (1985). Our investigation is better served, however, if it turns to a theory that applies elements of Freire's theory to the classroom in an advanced industrial society. Our source will be Greene's *Teacher As Stranger* (1973), which explicates the kinds of choices teachers ought to make if they are to act freely in constructing the world as liberated, professional people. This usually involves working within a given curriculum. After her discussion of the intellectual crisis in society and various epistemologies, Greene accepts the standard disciplines in the curriculum as sources of perspectives on the world, each with its own "distinctive methods and protocols in the pursuit of meanings" (p. 173). She mentions history, physics, economics, and literary criticism and later refers to the social and natural sciences and the arts, explicitly including music, literature, dance, and painting (1988, pp. 128–131).

In other words, Greene accepts the academic disciplines Peters and Broudy want, but she wants teachers to be free to organize them according to the existential and heuristic needs of students, as Freire and Dewey want. According to Greene (1973), the teacher should not try to initiate students into public traditions as such or expound the knowledge of a discipline as if it corresponded to reality because these approaches will alienate students (pp. 174–175). Although the students should utilize the materials of a discipline to generate its structure for themselves, this activity should be introduced by a discussion of the students' everyday world that leads them to investigate the discipline for ways of looking critically at the world and transforming it. The aim is not to acquire knowledge but to make sense of the world (pp. 167, 170).

Without an adequate grasp of the phenomenology involved, the idea of using the conceptual schemata of the disciplines this way may seem very subjectivistic and willful. Greene (1973) begins with the principle that consciousness is always of something in the world, but her exposition is based on the primary sources of phenomenology rather than on Freire. All phenomenologists agree on this intentionality. Even in reveries, daydreams, fairy tales, mental arithmetic or chess, reading novels, and hallucinating, the objects of which one is conscious are posited as existing out there in the world. This can be demonstrated with an example. To have a "cognizable object" to mediate our dialogue about this positing, look at Figure 9.1.A and stare at the x until you can see the figure as either a solid cube as in 9.1.B or as an empty box as in 9.1.C. Visualize the cube for about four seconds, then the empty box for the same duration, then the cube again. Seeing the box posits it as the object of consciousness (as the meant object). The same is true for the cube. Try to posit the cube and then the box at two-second intervals and then answer the phenomenological question, What moves?

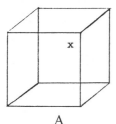
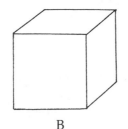
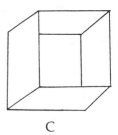

A   B   C

Figure 9.1 The Necker Cube.

Although the x stays the same actual distance from one's eye, one "sees" it as closer to one (on the near corner) when positing the cube than when positing the empty box (where it sits on the bottom). Because the focal distance of the lenses of one's eyes remains the same, the eyes do not move. Any adjustment within the lenses is caused by the freely chosen movement of consciousness and controlled wholly by itself from within itself. Alternating the positings at selected intervals shows this. The movement occurs in the sphere of transcendental subjectivity (Henry, 1975, p. 65). What moves is you. It is your consciousness—you, who are the subject of knowing—that freely constitutes the world as it appears within the horizons of your perceptual awareness of the box or cube. Your action, or praxis, is a free transcending of the resistance of the world, for, not only do you have to posit the cube to visualize it, you also have to hold back the empty box, which threatens to engulf the cube should attention on the cube weaken.

Now comes the ontological question: Where does the movement occur? Try staring at the x once more, alternately positing the cube and the empty box while attending to the location of the movement. Where does it occur? One has to be loyal to the data, to the phenomenon as it appears, regardless of how odd it may seem when articulated in words. As Michel Henry (1975) says, "The internal transcendental experience is always also a transcendent experience" (p. 72). What is given "up here" (in one's head) is given "out there" (in the world). Or, in the words of Alphonso Lingis (1971), "The constitution of objects requires an intentionality that is situated somewhere—within the very space it constitutes" (p. 78). The situatedness or locality of consciousness is "out there" by the cube or in the empty box. This is manifest in the movement, which appears to be located between the eyes and the page. Any lens adjustment is accompanied by the ebbing and flowing of the lines on the page, as they recede or advance in the positing of the other object. Although one might say that the box or cube is projected out there on the page from "in here," this projection is strictly correlated with the phasing in and out of prominence of the lines on the page. The lines that are objectively out there contribute to the phenomenon. Because the movement occurs between the eyes and the page, consciousness does not exist behind the eyeballs but out there in the world. It is pure transcendence (but always given as "mine"). This is what is meant by the claim that human reality is being in the world.

Next is the epistemological question. How do we know whether the composite figure is really a cube or empty box? It is not merely a matter of which perspective one chooses to adopt. The movement to become aware of it "is the very place in which original truth takes place" (Henry, 1975, p. 72). One can look at the figure again and try to see a sphere or dinosaur. It cannot be done because consciousness has to be loyal to what is given by reality, which in this case is simply a number of short lines on a flat, two-dimensional surface that are put together as a figure that lends itself to the phenomena discussed. The three-dimensionality of the box or cube is only partly contributed by consciousness while making sense of the figure through the words of the text. The general claim of phenomenology is that consciousness constitutes its objects as the things that are perceived. This occurs just as the box or cube are constituted from the lines on the flat page. The explication shows this to be a phenomenological constitution whereby one comes to know the object. It is compatible with phenomenological objectivity, for it is a passive, receptive constitution. It is not a material or metaphysical constitution. In other words, phenomenological description, like quantum mechanics, requires a minimal realism and observation-independent entities (Bennett, 1989).

The composite figure is given as existing whether or not it is perceived. The unveiling or disclosure of the box and cube through the prose of the text is truthful to what is given. In the disclosure, both consciousness (or subjectivity) and the thing (or objectivity) contribute to the cognized, or known, object, just as Freire says. Seeing both the box and cube, moreover, involves the multiple perspectives Greene says are furnished by the disciplines. Seeing the one thing—the flat lines— as both box and cube enables us to make more sense out of the cognizable object than seeing it only one way. The several perspectives are not reducible to one of them. They are even mutually exclusive, for one cannot see the box while positing the cube, and vice versa. Thus the object lesson embodies Greene's claim that the conceptual schemata of the disciplines should be learned in such a way that they enable students to use them for personal sense making. The discussion involves conceptual schemata from the discipline of philosophy regarding consciously positing a meant or constituted object in a free act of transcending a resisting world to help make sense of perceived reality.

The force of Greene's (1973) view lies in her claim that the knowledge from the disciplines is existentially significant when their conceptual schemata are used for personal sense making (pp. 16, 169, 173). If constituting a cube or empty box out of flat lines seems to have little existential significance, asking what moves proves the existence and transcendence of consciousness, which is human reality, human dignity—you; Thou, beside me, singing in the wilderness. You are a subject, a transcendence who is not reducible to a material, physical body or brain. The dual perspectives on the composite figure, moreover, are analogous to the sequence of the several perspectives of conceptual didactics, perceptual heuristics, experimental heuristics, interpretive didactics, and co-intentional dialogics (or the sequence of ethical theories). This may have existential significance if the views of Peters, Spencer, Dewey, Broudy, and Freire are now used for personal sense making. This is what Greene means by recommending that the disciplines should be used as sources of multiple perspectives (pp. 8–9, 17, 60). Just like the empty box and the cube, they furnish authentic possibilities to the extent that they disclose part of the truth.

This does not mean one is free to choose which of these various views to adopt, not any more than one is free to choose to say that the composite figure is an empty box. The truth is more complicated than that, for it requires the multiple perspectives. For example, when Greene (1973) considers how the teacher should choose among the alternatives in epistemology, she asks,

> Can he [the teacher] not function on some occasions as a latter-day rationalist, and, on other occasions, as an empiricist? Can he not, while functioning as a pragmatist, pay sufficient heed to the truth of the student's being to integrate a notion of liberation with the Deweyan conception of what is most worthwhile? (p. 168)

These rhetorical questions suggest that within the teaching of any discipline, there are times when it is appropriate to emphasize concept acquisition, as Peters and Broudy want, and there are other times when contact with the perceptual world is imperative, as Spencer wants. There are, similarly, times when the effect of acquired concepts on one's conduct deserves the attention Dewey wants. Some of these times the practical effect ought to have the particular impact of transforming the world that Freire recommends. Greene does not provide an abstract synthesis but turns the matter over to teachers, who should try to achieve a practical synthesis within a lesson or unit of instruction. It is a dramatic synthesis of the major players on the stage, for she claims that regardless of whether the teacher thinks the aim of education is initiation, self-realization, or liberation, the main task is to enable students "to conceptualize, to develop perspectives on their worlds . . . to develop cognitive capacities" (1973, p. 115) with the pedagogy designed to enable them to make sense of the world. She is postmodern in the sense that the quoted passage shows the abandonment of the attempt to secure an epistemological foundation in one perspective, yet she transcends postmodernism in her retention of the

Enlightenment faith in the capacity and desirability of human reason to make sense of the world.

Such a pedagogy is not adequate to overcome nihilism, however, unless it also involves the disclosure of reality Freire emphasizes. Greene's (1973) admonition against presenting "subject matter as a disclosure of 'the real nature of things'" (p. 175) has to be carefully understood. The conceptual apparatus of many disciplines involves hypothetical, postulated entities that are constructed to explain the phenomena perceived in the particular domain. These constructions do not describe anything in the visible world. It is incorrect to teach these fictions as if they disclose reality even if they help make sense of it. Greene's sense-making pedagogy, however, is inadequate unless the students' acquisition of the conceptual schemata of a discipline also provides access to the things in the real world through the disclosure of their characteristics and possibilities. In other words, the unity of perceptual and conceptual consciousness should be maintained peda-gogically through the actual disclosure of things to sustain the inten-tionality of consciousness, as Freire says.

The content of the disciplines selected for the curriculum of general education should therefore be that which in fact does disclose reality when submitted to the appropriate pedagogy. This will enable it to be the knowledge about the things in the world suggested in the statements by Mill and Russell. This includes propositional knowledge, except the customary attribution of truth to the propositions about the world reifies them and reflects the male, logocentric tradition responsi-ble for the calculative, manipulative thought of the technological con-sciousness and the destruction of the earth. Bowles (1984) accepts Heidegger's rejection of this tradition with its claim that truth is a feature of correct assertions made by a subject about an object. She also supports his interpretation of truth for its feminine characteristics: "Truth is disclosure of things through which an openness essentially unfolds" (p. 188, quoting Heidegger, 1977, p. 129).

This unfolding of an openness occurred in the game we played with Figure 9.1 when the space between the eyes and printed page unfolded into the openness of the world in which the empty box and cube existed while the true statements about the phenomena were stated. Hei-degger's (1927/1962) claim is simply that designating truth as a charac-teristic of an assertion, or proposition, is too late. There has to be a genuine disclosure before the true sentence can be formulated. Truth is therefore primarily a characteristic of the disclosure and only second-arily of the proposition formulated to disclose the matter to other people. Heidegger therefore rejects the idea that a proposition is true if it corresponds to reality in favor of an interpretation that it is true when it uncovers reality, disclosing (i.e., dis-closing) it (pp. 56–58, 105, 261). This changes the locus of truth from the reified proposition to the event of the disclosure itself, which, when recontextualized, is a way of being in the world (p. 263). The disclosure of the cube or empty box during the two- or four-second intervals is truthful. The subsequent statements about the disclosure occur at some distance from the known object. Because of this distancing, there may be some loss of the active projection involved in the emergence of the cube or empty box into the clearing. If so, this is the loss of the being of truth.

This loss of the being of truth occurs when truth is ascribed to propositions. It is a loss of the authentic unit of knowledge involved in the disclosure, a loss of the truthful disclosedness. It occurs because, in decontextualizing the proposition, one forgets the matrix of being in the world, isolating the statement from the speaker's existence and losing the being of its truth. The proposition is only a reminder of the original disclosure. When truth is taken to be a property of propositions, it gives rise to the problems of epistemology and the logic of science. The ontology of science (i.e., the relation of the human being to the world), however, is the more basic question (Rochowiak, 1988, p. 243). This is manifest in the general demise of epistemological foundationalism and the emergence of the concern for the conditions of intentionality that make disclosure of things possible (C. Taylor, 1987, pp. 472–476). It is not enough to develop a pedagogy that enables the knowledge in the curriculum to have existential significance unless it also insures the truthful disclosure that creates access to the world through the opening that unfolds in the disclosure. Freire (1985b) is correct to say that students should not be allowed to impose their own meanings on reality, to domesticate it for their own ends: "The critical and careful student . . . wants the truth of reality and not the submission of reality to his own truth" (p. 158). We will return to these issues and the details of Greene's pedagogy after establishing the curriculum needed to give access to the regions of the world that should be explored and disclosed in everyone's general education. The curriculum content has to be decided before its pedagogy can be meaningfully discussed or one offers symptomatic relief while begging the main question.

EDUCATION IN THE COSMOS

To ascertain the regions of the world everyone should know about requires a view of the relation of human beings to the world that is compatible with human dignity. It requires a cosmology. Since Copernicus, Magellan, and Galileo, however, a theory of the relation of human beings to everything that exists has had to be compatible with the knowledge of the universe obtained through scientific investigation. This necessity has augmented modern nihilism, for it makes it no longer possible to believe the universe is itself meaningful or purposeful. Heidegger's (1956/1958) lament over nihilism as the negation or oblivion of being, however, misdiagnoses the problem (1956/1958, pp. 87, 103). His concerted effort to revitalize being-talk leaves him locked within a hermeneutical circle that at best can distinguish between inauthentic and authentic existence in terms of anticipatory resoluteness (1927/1962, pp. 434–439). Regardless of the validity of this distinction or the truthfulness of the disclosure that occurs in its "moment of vision" (p. 463), it is a category mistake to try to overcome nihilism with a kind of being-talk that fosters moral and cognitive relativism, increases normlessness and truthlessness, and contributes to the sense of the meaninglessness of human life. Just as it requires an independent ethic to generate the struggle with moral problems that is necessary to achieve a sense of the integrity and worthiness of oneself as a moral agent and of one's life as significant, so does it also require an independent theory of knowledge to inspire a general confidence in the capacity of reason to know about the world (Vandenberg, 1987b, p. 6). Although nihilism is the loss of morality, knowledge, and truth, it also includes the absence of a religious outlook and a belief in the meaning of life. A consideration of the relation of the human being to the cosmos that can overcome nihilism needs to give attention to the religious dimension of life.

In his effort to emancipate the religious aspect of experience from supernatural religions that he contends isolate the human being from nature, the agnostic Dewey (1934/1966) defines the religious as a harmonizing of the self with the universe that enables one to have "attitudes that lend deep and enduring support to the processes of living" (pp. 15, 19). Religions purport to produce this outcome, but Dewey reverses it. He claims that wherever there are "changes in ourselves in relation to the world in which we live that are much more inclusive and deep seated" because they "pertain to our being in its entirety," there is a religious outlook (pp. 16–17). Dewey thus equates the religious element of experience to a sustaining confidence in life and faith in the natural order of things. It is natural piety, "a just sense of nature as the whole of which we are parts . . . marked by intelligence and purpose" (p. 25). Dewey himself, however, considers human beings in isolation from the cosmos of astronomy and in his enthusiasm to control nature overlooks the limitations nature places on human projects. Because he substitutes inquiry for truth, "which is dependent upon facts largely outside of human control" (Russell, 1946/1984, pp. 781–782), and which compels one to accept a humility before the cosmos that is lacking from his philosophy of power, the agnostic Russell claims Dewey lacks cosmic piety (pp. 781–782).

Dewey is correct to distinguish the religious aspect of life from organized religions, but his view needs deepening to encompass the religious as an element of human existence. Instead of returning to the community of the early Christians to obtain a sense of the religious in human existence, as we might, we will go back earlier, to Abraham, the fountainhead of three great world religions, to retrieve a sense of the religious prior to its institutionalization and the emergence of a priestly class. According to the Revised Standard Version of the *Holy Bible*, Abraham went to Canaan from Ur of the Chaldeans with his wife, nephew, and retinue when he was 75 years old. He briefly visited Egypt and Gerar, where, for his own protection, he let the pharaoh and then the king Abimelech consort with his wife, Sarah, after telling them she was his sister. When they each in turn expelled him after finding this out, he returned to Canaan. At 86, he sired Ishmael by his wife's maid, and at 100 he sired Isaac (when Sarah was 90). After Sarah died at 127 years of age, he took another wife, by whom he had six more children. Dying at 175, he left everything to Isaac, except for presents to the sons of his concubines. Although he acquired riches and had a train of slaves, servants, and herders, he apparently remained an itinerant shepherd, a nomad. When buying land for Sarah's burial, he referred to himself as "a stranger and a sojourner among you" (Genesis, 23:4).

The religious aspects of the textual Abraham's life occur in three forms: alleged encounters with God, altars, and sacrifices. Ten of the eleven alleged conversations with deity are directly or indirectly about the promise that he and his descendants would be allowed to live in Canaan forever. These occur from the time of the original call to go to Canaan until the ram is sacrificed in lieu of Isaac, some thirty to forty years later. In other words, after Abraham settled in Canaan, the deepest recesses of his being opened with a feeling of being at home in the world. The happiness was so great, the response of the ground of his being so resonant, he thought he heard an overpowering voice tell him he was at home, not just temporarily but for all his descendants forever. The textual Abraham believed he had to deserve the homecoming, but it was not to be earned through the rituals associated with organized religions designed to propitiate God. The three altars he built, like the tree he planted, expressed gratitude after he was reminded of the promise (Genesis 12:7,8; 13:18; 21:33). The two sacrifices also expressed gratitude and loyalty (15:9–11; 22:13). The single prayer asked that Abimelech be granted a son (20:17).

On the other hand, after maintaining his integrity by refusing gifts from the king of Sodom, Abraham was allegedly reminded of his heritage and told, "Walk before me and be blameless" (Genesis 17:1). He was said to have done his part, "by doing righteousness and justice" (18:19). Isaac was allegedly told the covenant would continue "because Abraham obeyed my voice and kept my charge, my commandments, my statutes, and my laws" (26:5). Abraham's self-understanding of the obligations was not liturgical but ethical and monotheistical.

There are two aspects of the covenant. One concerns becoming the father of a great nation, having many descendants who will prosper, and so forth. The other is the promise of a homeland, which reflects Abraham's ontological insecurity from living in a homeless world. A depth interpretation is needed to understand Abraham better than he understood himself, particularly since hearing voices is now considered to be a psychotic phenomenon. It would seem that the alleged statements of God were the unacknowledged aspects of Abraham's being that were projected out into the universe. Repressed, they appeared "out there" as God's voice, but they came from the ground of his being and reflected his deepest fears and desires. If so, the religious element in Abraham's existence was the inner victory over cosmic homelessness.

Other things in Genesis corroborate this interpretation. The religious element in the twenty generations of the clan preceding Abraham was related to being at home in the universe. For their disobedience, Adam and Eve were driven out of Eden, made homeless. For his fault, Cain was condemned to wander the earth homelessly. Noah was promised there would not be another flood to make him homeless again. The Tower of Babel, built so people would not be scattered over the earth, allegedly displeased God, who therefore scattered them homelessly over the face of the earth. Condemned to be an outcast, Ishmael was driven out of Canaan with Hagar, to wander homeless in the wilderness. Except for the people supposedly killed by the great flood and the destruction of Sodom, the punishment said to be meted out to people who displeased God in Genesis was homelessness, the apparent equivalent to Hades. This can be understood, without reference to the supernatural, as evidence that the main problem of life for the people depicted in Genesis—and for the people who preserved it as an account of their origins—was cosmic homelessness. Conversely, the reward bestowed upon the people who allegedly pleased God in Genesis was a homecoming of such intensity it seemed it would affect them and their descendants forever.

If the religious is an inner victory over cosmic homelessness, it has to be continuously won anew because of the openness of human existence to the world and future and the consequent homelessness inherent in being in the world. This interpretation is compatible with Dewey's idea of a harmonizing of the self with the universe, but it omits his complacency and includes the existential and phenomenological aspects. The change of names from Abram, Sarai, and Jacob to Abraham, Sarah, and Israel signifies that establishing one's home in the cosmos is correlated with establishing one's identity and the meaningfulness of one's life. It is also compatible with elements foreign to Dewey, such as Abraham's gratitude, reverence, and piety.

The liturgy, ecclesiastical structures, and articulated creeds and cosmologies of the religions built upon Abraham's experience were institutionalized, conceptualized means for coming to feel at home in the universe. These means are contingent shortcuts. The Babylonian cosmology grafted onto the early chapters of Genesis in the creation and flood myths merely gives the earliest members of the clan an auspicious beginning. It embellishes a monotheism that is otherwise functionless until Abraham (Heidel, 1967, pp. 129-139; Sollberger, 1971, p. 10). It shows that the authors of Genesis used whatever was available to articulate a meaningful world in which they themselves may have felt at home, but it says nothing about the universe or deity. Similarly, the cosmology of the early Christian tradition, promising a home in heaven instead of Palestine, is dependent upon Ptolemaic astronomy, which is also largely a historical accident (Toulmin, 1985, p. 221). Similarly, the view that behind the appearance of things there is an underlying reality that is rational, orderly, harmonious, good, and purposeful—that is, the view that there is a divine reason permeating the universe and guiding all events within it—is the Greek cosmology that became joined to the teachings of Jesus, partly through Paul but especially through the grand synthesis of the Middle Ages (Zuurdeeg, 1958, pp. 204-218). The Greek cosmology is as untenable as Ptolemaic astronomy. One can no longer believe that God is working through human history, not so much because God is dead as because Greek cosmology is dead. It is no longer possible to formulate a cosmology of the whole universe. The only way to know the natural world with sufficient validity to construct a cosmology now is through the methods of the natural sciences, but the division of labor corresponding to the increased specialization of knowledge separated physics, chemistry, and biology from each other in the nineteenth century and left no one to do the science of the whole universe (Toulmin, 1985, pp. 228–237). One cannot extrapolate a general principle of entropy from the second law of thermodynamics, and there is no general, unitary process of evolution from which one might extrapolate an ethic or cosmology (Toulmin, 1985, pp. 41, 60).

The importance of the religious for human existence, however, is not about cosmological beliefs. It is about becoming at home in the universe. It is not about beliefs, nor about the universe, but about becoming at home. Knowledge of astronomy and astrophysics informs us about the universe but not about a home in it, except to indicate that Earth is indeed our home. The textual Abraham has no explicit cosmology or theology; as his example shows, they are not essential to the victory over cosmic homelessness. For Abraham it sufficed to become at home on Earth, in Canaan, except his idea of a home was patriarchal and dominated by the will to power. This is the origin of nihilism. As David Levin (1985) claims, "Our metaphysics desperately needs to recollect the ancient maternal power of the earth if it is to see us through the historical danger of total nihilism" (p. 314). We need to imagine how the religious would have been expressed in Abraham's existence had he been a tiller of the soil instead of a cattle baron. Precisely because we now have to recognize that the Earth is not the center of the universe, it has to become the center of our universe. We have to recognize that the religious now has to do with becoming at home on our mother the earth, giver and taker of all that we are and can become. The great historian of religion, Mercia Eliade (1969), claims that the estrangement from the earth attributed to religion by Marx and Engels applies only to the other-worldly religions of post-Vedic India and the Judeo-Christian tradition. For the overwhelming majority of religions throughout history, however, "the religious life consists exactly in exalting the solidarity of man with life and nature" (p. 64, n. 7).

It is compatible with geology and biological evolution to ask about the place of human beings in the natural world, that is, in the larger scheme of things here on Earth, where the lives and destinies of human beings are interwoven with the lives and destinies of all terrestrial things (Toulmin, 1985, pp. 260, 268). This requires us to know about the conditions under which the Earth can continue to be a home for human beings and the kinds of conduct required to maintain these conditions (p. 265). Because these concerns have always been the themes of cosmology, the proper resources for a cosmology limited to the relation of human beings to the Earth is the science and practice of ecology, providing it is accompanied by the attitude of viewing nature as an object of piety, for in the world of nature, "human beings can both *feel*, and also *be*, at home" (p. 272).

Although the study of ecology as a subject in the school curriculum is an indispensable source for learning about some of the conditions under which the Earth can continue to support humanity and be its home, it does not follow that its study will enable the young to feel and be at home in the natural world. This would follow only if knowing what things are good for, ecologically speaking, leads to seeing the good, and if seeing the good leads to right conduct, that is, only if the Greek cosmology is still valid. The word *ecology* comes from the Greek *oikas*, house. Ecology studies things housed in specific environments, which collectively make up the natural world that houses humankind. The house that everyone lives in, however, is more like a hotel, dormitory, or barracks than a home. To know about the natural world as providing a house is different from finding a home in nature.

Things in the world are disclosed within one's general attunement to the world (Heidegger, 1927/1962, pp. 176–177). In the everyday world, things are disclosed primarily in terms of their involvements, as Dewey and Heidegger claim. The adoption of a scientific point of view requires a decentering of consciousness that changes the perceived world from a place in which one dwells to the objective space of the natural world as it exists independently of human involvement, where no one lives. As Russell said, one needs to relate to the world the second way for truth and cosmic piety. If the first world is disclosed as "my world," the second is "everyone's world," or "the world." Ludwig Binswanger has pointed out a third world, which is disclosed as "our world" in the context of love and unselfish participation, when people live together in dialogical, I–Thou relations. When the world is disclosed through I–Thou relatedness to it, it can manifest itself as the common world, as home (Zuurdeeg, 1958, p. 102).

The relation to the first world is one of calculating, technological manipulation; to the second, detached, theoretical observation; and to the third, appreciative participation. The study of ecology by itself cannot enable people to feel and be at home in the natural world because this calls for a deep, affective attunement of one's whole being. This also involves being at home in the human and societal worlds. To become at home in the cosmos, one must become at home in the interhuman, societal, and natural worlds first. This means that the regions of the world that should be explored in everyone's general education, in order to promote the relation to the world that is most compatible with human dignity, include the regions disclosed by the humanities, social sciences, and natural sciences.

Before schematizing the regions of the world that should be explored in general education, however, let us examine once more the adequacy of the idea of the religious drawn from the primordial source and attested to by primitive religions. It can be confirmed and its significance estimated by reference to the thesis of Berger, Berger, and Kellner in *The Homeless Mind* (1973/1981), where they claim, "From a sociological and socio-psychological point of view, religion can be defined as a cognitive and normative structure that makes it possible for man to feel 'at home' in the universe" (p. 75). The modern mind is characteristically homeless because vast, historically profound changes have secularized the modern world. These include the technologizing of production, the bureaucratization of government, social and geographical mobility, mass education, mass media of communication, and the development of a private sphere of life (pp. 94–95). These changes have created a distinctly modern consciousness that is functionally rationalized and adapted to a mobile, migratory existence. Lacking substantive rationality, the individual person is intellectually homeless. The specialization of labor, urbanization, and pluralism make it necessary for individuals to construct a private life, a "do-it-yourself" universe, in order to create a home, but they do not know how to do it (p. 167). The counterculture that developed in the 1960s and 1970s was largely a nostalgic attempt to find ways of being at home (chap. 9). When the homelessness of the modern consciousness becomes self-understood as cosmic homelessness, there is a turn to preexisting religions to find a home in them (p. 77; and Zuurdeeg, 1958, p. 90). Whatever personal value these may seem to have, the resort to a truthless cosmology lacks cosmic piety and constitutes a recidivistic attempt to demodernize consciousness. To make this reaction unnecessary, general education ought to furnish legitimate cognitive means to enable people to feel and be at home on our good Mother Earth.

ELEMENTS OF COMMON, GENERAL EDUCATION

In one sense it has been premature to speak of regions of the world. It is developmentally necessary to explore things in the world that only subsequently become located within regions that differentiate themselves according to the things found within them. It is the things that need to be explored, not the region, to gain the knowledge about the world that enables one to be at home in it. To become at home in an advanced industrial society, children and youth ought to explore fabricated things, playthings, natural things, human things, and societal things. The exploration should be both perceptual and conceptual to include both the things and the previous disclosures of their characteristics to older people. To make these previous disclosures available requires the exploration of written things and quantified things. The regions that should be explored to become at home in the world therefore include the tactile, manipulable world; the play world; nature; society; the lived world; and the worlds of books and numbers. Their curriculum corollaries are the arts, crafts, and trades; sports and the dance; the natural sciences; the social sciences; the humanities; reading; and mathematics.

The Manipulable World

The child's exploration of the things in the manipulable and play worlds is chronologically and phenomenologically prior to any conceptualized exploration of things in the natural or social worlds. Even before it can walk, the infant learns about the tactile characteristics of things through touching, grasping, squeezing, rubbing, tasting, and chewing them. Then the contact with the things in the manipulable world is expanded to include the things it plays with as it learns about things and itself, correlatively, through its motility. These tactile, motile modes of perceptual access to the world are phenomenologically prior to the conceptual understanding of things because of the embodiment of consciousness. Somewhat like Dewey, Henry (1975) says, "Objects are not originally or even ordinarily contemplated objects, they are the objects of our movements" (p. 94). Or, in Ortega y Gasset's (1957) words, "The decisive form of our intercourse with things is touch" (p. 72).

Referring to consciousness as embodied, however, still reifies consciousness. It is, rather, the body that is conscious of the world. As Maurice Merleau-Ponty (1945/1962) says, "To have a body is to possess a universal setting, a schema for all types of perceptual unfolding, and all of those intersensory correspondences which lie beyond the segment of the world we are actually perceiving" (p. 326). One does not, however, *have* a body; one *is* a body (and a *somebody*). The body is not only "our general medium for having a world" (p. 146), it is "our anchorage in a world" (p. 144). Education should therefore enable the young to move from the play world to the natural and social worlds, as perceived by natural and social scientists, without the loss of feeling of being at home in the world that is characteristic of childhood play. The child's participation in the world of play under the aegis of parental love should be retained by adequate curriculum provision for activities that involve playlike participation, that is, that involve the bodily modes of knowing in the arts, crafts, trades, sports and dance (ACTS).

One of the influences in the emergence of the homeless consciousness is the academic development of conceptual processes without due regard for the bodily basis of being in the world. According to Henry (1975), however, "It is only to the extent it is a constituted reality that the body is capable of entertaining with other beings of nature relationships such as those which the sciences would have us conceive" (p. 108). Without the adequate acquisition of bodily knowledge, one develops a mind/body dualism through the acquisition of objective thinking that is at best grounded in the perceptual world visually. If the acquisition of conceptual schemata develops the cognitive processes of objective thought that are not somehow grounded in previously established corporeal schemata, they can close one off from the bodily awareness of oneself and things in the world.

The child, however, is genetically structured for bodily movement and awareness, for tactile and motile perception (Levin, 1985, p. 100). The repetitive movements involved in learning how to use the body in the manipulable and play worlds establish corporeal schemata that disclose things through participation in them. The great significance of these corporeal schemata is expressed by Merleau-Ponty (1960/1964): "To the extent that I can elaborate and extend my corporeal schema, to the extent I acquire a better organized experience of my own body, to that very extent will my consciousness of my own body cease to be a chaos in which I am submerged and lend itself to a transfer to others" (p. 118).

There are two points here. One is that the development of corporeal schemata establishes contact with the objects within the range of one's arm that one can literally grasp, manipulate, and make things with. This bodily knowledge is "a primordial and irreducible ontological knowledge, the foundation and ground of all our knowledge and in particular, of our intellectual and theoretical knowledge" (Henry, 1975, p. 94). It enables us to constitute our body as a reality through which the valid relations between things discovered by the sciences can be perceived and understood. The acquisition of this bodily knowledge occurs first in childhood play and later on in the arts, crafts, and trades. The corporeal schemata also establish contact with the objects within the range of one's running stride in the play world, extending one's lived space several yards into the immediate environment beyond arm's length. This bodily familiarity with things also functions reflexively to promote bodily self-understanding. Without the development of the corporeal schemata, the awareness of one's own body is necessarily chaotic and unorganized. There is no way to become aware of one's body except through its tactile and motile perceptual awareness of things in the world. As Heidegger (1927/1962) says, we understand the "here" in terms of "yonder" (pp. 142, 171).

The second point is that without acquired corporeal schemata, the lack of self-understanding entraps one within one's body, which then cannot serve as a vehicle of transcendence to the world. Without this transcendence, one cannot engage in reciprocal, dialogical relations with other people, for these require co-intentionality. Dialogical relations with other people, however, are a necessary condition for being at home in the world. They are also extremely important if Merleau-Ponty (1960/1964) is correct in saying that "the intellectual elaboration of our experience of the world is constantly supported by the affective elaboration of our interhuman relations" (pp. 112–113).

To summarize, the articulation of the bodily schemata is a necessary condition of self-understanding, which is necessary for dialogical relations with other people, which are necessary to develop a loving attunement to the world, which is necessary for the optimum acquisition of the conceptual schemata of the disciplines and their disclosure of the world as the home of human beings. If one is at home with oneself, one can be at home with others. If one is at home with others, one can be at home in the natural world. If one is at home in nature, one can learn more about it and still be at home on Earth and in the universe. Existential piety precedes natural piety, which precedes cosmic piety.

So children should play jacks and marbles and engage in constructive crafts. In elementary school they should have a broad experience in activities drawn from the arts, crafts, and trades that involve manual, bodily modes of knowing, and then in high school they should continue to study at least one art, craft, or trade to the depth necessary to practice it as a lifelong hobby. This should not be the whole curriculum as Dewey wanted, for it suffices to include his epistemological concern in one strand in the curriculum of general education. It should develop the corporeal schemata that enable one to gain and maintain a firm grasp on the world through one's hands, letting one feel at home and comfortable with things because one knows some of them in their primordial being.

Through constructive manipulations, one learns the values of things as they lend themselves to their fabrication into useful or artistic objects. Levin (1985) claims that if we are to overcome the nihilism of the mind/body dualism that is our legacy from Descartes, we have to acknowledge that we can think with our hands (p. 121). A hobbylike skill enables a primordial awareness of the presencing of things involved in the art or craft. The gentle, intelligent touch of someone with expertise in one of the arts, crafts, or trades lets the things in the activity present themselves in the intimate, delicate qualities manifested only to someone who cares for them, as the grain of the wood reveals itself to the cabinet maker (pp. 128–129), the texture of the stone to the sculptor, the drape of the fabric to the seamstress or tailor, and so on. As one works with things in one of the arts, crafts, or trades, one becomes aware of their qualities, finds them valuable, cares for them, and wants to preserve them. Most important is Jan Jagodzinski's (1988) claim that knowing the texture of things is the route to overcoming alienation from the world and to being at home in it. She says, "When we know the texture of things we feel comfort, security, and belonging as when we see familiarity in the face. We must touch things in order to make them our own, participate in them to see the surfaces and their responses" (p. 125). In other words, the fundamental value education begins in the manipulable world.

The Play World

The games and sports of childhood and youth develop corporeal schemata involving the whole body. After broader participation earlier, high school students should learn at least one sport or the dance in depth sufficient for it to become a lifelong pursuit, because knowing the world through a full, bodily immersion in it creates and maintains confidence in one's bodily undertakings in and with the world. While walking, running, leaping, dancing, and in sport, the rhythm of one's stride restores a primordial relation to the earth that changes the structure of lived space from that of everydayness or detached observation to that of a place in which the earth presences itself as the original ground of being (Levin, 1985, pp. 268–269, 291). The periodic return to the felt sense of one's bodily motility originating from within and on one's own initiative in sport or dance balances the socialization into the public, anonymous, and homeless space that occurs in the conceptual curriculum, school life, and the bureaucratic structures of urbanized life. The return to the home world of one's own motility from everydayness opens up "a space of much greater openness, greater richness, and greater emotional hospitality" (p. 341). It opens a place wherein one can be at home in a primordial awareness of being.

This concern for the development of sensory, bodily awareness of things in the manipulable and play worlds is like Spencer's and Freire's concerns for the object lesson and cognizable object with the added dynamic of Dewey's activity classroom. It is unlike their views, however, because it is not intended as the first phase in the acquisition of conceptual knowledge. Instead of being an application of epistemology to the classroom, it is applied to the curriculum to indicate the importance of two strands that belong in general education to enable the two regions of the world to be explored and known. Enabling students to make things with their own hands and engage in complex movements with their whole bodies in dance and sports enables them to be intimately aware of, and to be at home in, the immediate foreground of the natural world. This foreground should become a place to which they can always return to restore a sense of their own being, much as the child should have a room of its own at home to which it can always withdraw and feel safe and at home, and much as it is necessary for the family itself to have the home as a safe, protective haven to which its members can withdraw and feel completely secure and at home (Bollnow, 1968/1989, p. 18). Just as the young should feel their neighborhood is their home ground when they return to its horizons after sallying forth into the broader, unfamiliar society, so should all adults be able to engage in one or more sport or dance to return periodically to being at home in the play world.

The Natural World

The child's explorations of things in the manipulable and play worlds generally leads to explorations of physical things; living things; growing things; changing things; homemade things; marketed things; manufactured things; human things; economic, social, and political things; historical things; esthetic, written, and musical things; and so on. These are found in the physical world; the animal world; the plant world; the agricultural world; the chemical world; the personal and interpersonal worlds; the worlds of art, literature, and music; and so on. The various regions of the world can be grouped together according to whether the things are found in nature, society, or the lived world of human life. Because each region is studied by one or more university disciplines, their concepts should be used to enrich the common-sense explorations of things. Educational events occur naturally when the exploration of things in the world leads to the investigation of materials from the disciplines to become more deeply aware of things. The theoretical knowledge of the disciplines should therefore be organized to facilitate the child's or youth's becoming aware of things in the perceptual world in more disciplined ways than would occur through ordinary experience.

The developmental and existential priority of the manipulable and play worlds should be extended to the natural world because things in nature are more accessible to a relatively nonconceptualized, visual, and tactile perception than are social or human things such as institutions and moral courage. Nature study as such, where schoolchildren go out into the wilderness to study things nonscholastically, can serve as a transition from the play world to the conceptual knowledge appropriate to school science. Nature study is an essential part of learning to be at home in nature, if Merleau-Ponty (1945/1962) is correct when he says,

> Natural perception is not a science, it does not posit the things with which science deals, it does not hold them at arm's length in order to observe them, but lives with them; it is the "opinion" or "primary faith" which binds us to a world as to our native land, and the being of what is perceived is the antepredicative being towards which our whole existence is magnetically attracted. (pp. 321–322)

The very being of things in the natural world attracts us when we become aware of them on the level of perceptual consciousness because of our awareness of their qualities. These qualities enable us to dwell with them and bind us to them. They enable our being in the world to be a dwelling in the world. The analogy of being bound to the perceptual world as to our native land is not accidental, for the tie that binds us to our country depends upon our attraction to its physical geography. This is manifested in the words of patriotic songs: "I love thy rocks and rills, Thy woods and templed hills, My heart with rapture thrills"; "O beautiful for spacious skies, For amber waves of grain, For purple mountain majesties, Above the fruited plain"; "From the mountains, To the prairies, To the oceans, White with foam"; and in Woody Guthrie's words about redwood forests, diamond deserts, wheat fields, and dust clouds when he heard the voice chanting the title of his song, "This Land Was Made for You and Me." These words are about the beauties of the natural world in which the people of the land have made their home. They celebrate being here in this place, the presencing of the earth, the emergence of being. The words are hymns of praise to Mother Earth.

To enable children and youth to hear their own voices singing hymns of praise, as Abraham and Woody Guthrie did, the school curriculum should include an outdoor education program that incorporates camping in the wilderness and ecology taught on site by a naturalist who loves the wild and can disclose the qualities of wild things in their own habitat as Harry Wildman can (*cf.* Chapter 5). Before participating in such an outdoor program, however, children should acquire manual and bodily schemata from the ACTS to enable them to become at home in the natural world rather than intimidated by it. More formally taught science in the elementary school curriculum should include a preparation for the first and most fundamental science that should be taught at the high school level—biology organized as ecology (or integrated through ecology). Subsequent courses in the natural sciences, such as chemistry and physics, should be about the living and nonliving, terrestrial and celestial things that everyone should know about in order to understand the place of human beings in the larger scheme of things and to feel increasingly at home in the natural world.

To learn how to use the accumulated knowledge of the natural sciences to make sense out of the world around one (Greene) is more important than learning the so-called methods of inquiry reified by philosophers of science through laboratory experience (Dewey), unless the latter serves as the means for maintaining contact with the perceptual world. Then it is extremely important because the abstractness and frequent focus on what is too small, too large, or too distant to see with the unaided eye readily separates the conceptualized knowledge of the sciences from the perceptual world, the only world in which students can feel and be at home.

The suggestion is like Peters' and Broudy's claims that the curriculum should include biology, chemistry, physics, earth science, and astronomy as school subjects, with content basically determined by university experts in the disciplines, but it lacks their emphasis upon structuring them by their basic concepts. That emphasis reflects the elitist tradition, oriented toward the preparation of specialists in the sciences despite their disclaimers. It reflects the mind/body, subject/object dualisms that manifest "a violent, nihilistic rage in the very heart of our metaphysics" that is found in the technological consciousness and that persists in "our patriarchal metaphysics . . . because it has not allowed itself to be *touched* by the truth of the body" (Levin, pp. 48, 56). The sciences should therefore be organized around the basic phenomena, or most important things, in the respective regions of the world, things that everyone should come to know about in their formal education in order to be at home in the world. The emphasis should be on cognizable objects (Spencer, Freire), but they should consist largely of conceptualized knowledge that can be used to make sense of them (Greene). This might involve basic concepts, but only for their ability to disclose things, not for their own sake or for the sake of the schemata they can establish.

Because the natural world contains all the resources that sustain human life in the material sense, much adult activity is dependent upon the epistemically refined knowledge of the things in nature that the unschooled adult knows only as common-sense objects, as Spencer and Dewey recognize. Access to things in the natural world can be greatly increased by the methodology and conceptualized knowledge and schemata of the natural sciences, the educative function of which is to yield a truthful picture of reality. For example, in their general education, students should acquire an image of the vastness and age of the universe, including an exposure to detailed information regarding light years, galaxies, black holes, nebulae, and super nova, aware that neither UFOs nor the constellations of astrology exist; cognizant that living and nonliving things exist in dynamic interplay because they evolved that way, perhaps only on Earth; aware that nutrition is a biochemical process that can be guided by knowledge to promote health and well-being; knowing that medical practice based on the natural sciences is very different from sorcery, shamanism, and witch doctory, and so on.

All of this requires a great deal of conceptualized, detailed knowledge about things in nature, not for replication but to combine Spencer's poetics of nature with Broudy's interpretive use of knowledge. One can, for example, forget that the furthest known objects from the earth are 14 billion light years away (82 trillion billion miles) and how old the universe must be for this information to reach us; that there are 100,000 stars in our own galaxy, which is 100,000 light years across; or that there are millions of such galaxies in the universe, without losing the perspective that this information establishes and without losing the cosmic piety inspired by the grandeur of the vision.

Natural piety should ordinarily be a concomitant learning of the natural science curriculum. It should, however, become an explicit objective in ecology taught as the scientific study of the conditions under which the Earth can continue to be the home of humankind and accompanied by an environmental ethic based upon a biocentric viewpoint to help maintain these conditions. Just as every ethic is based upon some version of the fundamental principle of respect for persons to protect and enhance the value and dignity of individual human beings, so should an environmental ethic rest upon the explicit fundamental principle of respect for nature to disclose and protect the value and existence of living and nonliving things. With such a conceptualized principle, natural piety can be taught and learned in schools. Obligations and duties to the natural world can be conceptualized, reflected upon, and studied in cognitively valid ways. For example, in *Respect for Nature*, the distinguished ethical philosopher Paul Taylor (1986) justified four moral rules for an environmental ethic:

1. *Nonmaleficence.* One should not harm things in nature.
2. *Noninterference.* One should not interfere with natural ecosystems or biotic communities.
3. *Fidelity.* One should not betray the trust of wild animals.
4. *Restitutive justice.* Violations of these rules should be followed by restitution or reparation. (chaps. 4, 6)

Students can learn conceptually that if they respect nature, they incur obligations to repair whatever damage they do to the natural world and to make reparations for the exploitation of the natural world that occurs as human beings seek to maintain their own lives.

The intellectual study of these matters may be necessary to implement natural piety, but it is unlikely to promote its development as a fundamental attunement (or attitude) to the world. This requires the exploration of things in the manipulable and play world and an outdoor education that brings students directly in contact with the qualities of things. This contact is necessary if respect for nature is to be an emotionally deep structure of one's very being, that is, if it is to be the moral virtue of natural piety. Camping in the wilderness while learning about biotic communities on their own sites enables one to learn the rule of housekeeping in the wilderness: One ought to leave a campsite in as good a condition as one found it. One should remove all traces of one's presence, out of respect for the beauty of the place and for the next camper. This should become the first commandment of the religious, understood as the inner victory over cosmic homelessness that enables one to find and appreciate our home on Earth, for one cannot have a home without the housekeeping in which all take part. There may not be obligations to future generations as some environmentalists, like Abraham, believe, because one cannot have obligations to people who do not exist. There is, however, a clear obligation to the rising generation who will live after us. Essentially, however, the obligation to leave the earth in as good a condition as we found it is the duty to maintain and enhance the existence of things when the thing is Mother Earth herself.

The evidence that children and youth will respond to this obligation is that their openness to the world and experience of space lets them experience nature as a place of enchantment. The child, like Abraham and Woody Guthrie, is "exceptionally attuned to the full dimensionality of his places . . . and more receptive than most adults to the very fact, the ontological gift, of presencing as such" (Levin, 1985, p. 348). Outdoor education should not try to promote nature mysticism, "in which the highest state of human consciousness is understood as a matter of having one's self become one with the natural world," but such mysticism is "quite compatible with the moral attitude of respect for nature" (Taylor, 1986, p. 309). A love of nature will suffice as the motivational force for a willing adherence to an environmental ethic developed on a conceptual basis in classrooms in the context of the scientific knowledge of the biosphere that is needed to understand the natural conditions under which the earth can continue to be a home for the human race. From this knowledge will flow the duties and obligations that should be accepted to deserve the earth as our home.

Because the environmental ethic sketched is biocentric and heavily dependent upon science for its content, it should probably be part of the natural science curriculum. Two aspects, however, make its consideration appropriate to the social studies in the study of controversial issues related to human rights. One is the human right to have a home on Earth in the sense of William Blackstone's (1974) claim that "access to a livable environment must be conceived as a right which imposes upon everyone a correlative moral obligation to respect," and which requires legal control of natural resources (pp. 32ff.). A study of the problems of maintaining a livable environment for everyone as their human right cannot proceed very far without raising questions of justice and the fundamental rights to life, shelter, sustenance, freedom, and equal consideration. These in turn raise questions of modifications of the economic, political, and legal systems necessary to maintain the earth as the home of all the people of the earth, to which a great body of knowledge from the social sciences is relevant.

The Social World

Children and youth become aware of societal things through untutored experience in exploring the social world beyond their own neighborhood, but to feel and be at home in an advanced industrial society, they need familiarity with its economic, political, legal, and social institutions in a much greater depth. The things they should explore in the economic, political, and legal systems include the market, vocations, unemployment, inflation, representative government, taxation and public expenditures, political parties, civil and criminal law, and the court system. They should also explore and know something about the less dominant institutions such as the family, church, education, and medical and welfare systems. This listing may seem to be a justification for social studies, but Broudy seems right to propose the study of social institutions in developmental perspective. One can hardly become at home in a society without knowing its history, however, because a society is a historical thing. This history should subsume political and military events within the framework of the way in which the people of the land have made their homes within the natural setting of the place by establishing their own political, economic, legal, and social institutions, often by unjustly expropriating the homeland of the indigenous inhabitants.

The interrelatedness of institutions cannot really be adequately explored in interdisciplinary studies. These yield a static, cross-sectional view of the current state of affairs and create the impression that there is such a thing as the status quo by reifying it. Unless one of the disciplines is history, integrating it, such interdisciplinary study omits the most important aspect of societal things, their historicality. This makes it untrue to reality. To be at home in one's society requires foresight into one's own possibilities, which are inextricably intermeshed with societal possibilities. An imaginative projection into the future, supported by a confident trust in society's future, depends upon the imaginative sense of its past that has been established through historical studies. The adult without a historical consciousness lives in the present without much of a perspective on the future.

Although it is the societal things that should be explored in order to gain access to them and feel at home in society, the history of the country is the macro-ecosystem, so to speak, within which contemporary social institutions have their being. It should therefore furnish the intellectual context within which the things in society are studied, much as nature study should be the fundamental matrix of further study of the things in the natural world. No country's history, however, can be understood apart from the history of world civilization. The latter may be of secondary importance in learning how to become at home in one's native land, but it is very important for becoming at home on Earth and in the universe, particularly in countries with relatively short histories, such as Australia, Canada, and the United States.

This perspective resembles Dewey's equation of the historical and the social, but it does not dissolve it into the social and it retains chronology. Historical studies require considerable informational knowledge in order to disclose what actually happened in the sequence in which it happened, but this content should not be learned for the sake of replicating statements about what happened. It is, again, merely a temporary scaffolding that is necessary to obtain a sense of the past, without which there cannot be a sense of the present or a real present. Whereas the outcome of the study of the natural sciences in general education should be an interpretive schema, the historical study of one's own country should yield a temporal schema. One's place in the total scheme of things is a historical place, which must be understood as such for one to be at home in the universe. This purpose of history in the curriculum is more like Peters' than Broudy's view, but it differs because there is no claim that students should be initiated into history as a form of knowledge. Grappling with methods of historical research might be important pedagogically, but it is not essential to the process of gaining an understanding of the story of one's country's past in common, general education.

This concern for history in the school curriculum, moreover, does not exclude standard social studies subjects, such as civics, economics, and problems of democracy, that make available systematic bodies of knowledge that disclose the institutions of society. Previous statements by Mill and Russell about cosmic piety can be supplemented by a similar one by John Passmore (1980) regarding the societal region of the world:

> That at one time there were no men on the face of the earth; that men have lived, and still live, in conditions quite other than those to which we are accustomed, with different manners, different beliefs, different laws—none of this is information of which, ordinarily, the child will make any practical use. But it destroys his illusions, compels him to remake his picture of the world, helps him to understand it better, stimulates his imagination. And that is just why it is so important. (pp. 112–113)

Although the study of societal things should result in becoming at home in one's own society, this ought not be narcissistic, ingrown, narrowly patriotic, or politically partisan. If everyone has the human right to be at home on Earth, this is an equal right. The study of things in the societal world should therefore be compatible with the hymns of praise to Mother Earth across the political spectrum, from Kate Smith to Woody Guthrie. Loving one's country is also compatible with maintaining a critical perspective on it from either end of the political spectrum, so long as it encourages engagement in partisan politics within the system. To be at home on the earth in one's own country, moreover, is also compatible with celebrating the presencing of the earth in other countries.

The Lived World

Just as the immediate, familiar worlds of manipulation and play are overlooked by the methods of the natural sciences that distance themselves from the object of inquiry to obtain the proper objectivity and intersubjective validity of their knowledge, so, too, are the immediate, familiar human worlds of personal and interpersonal life overlooked by the methods of the behavioral and social sciences in their pursuit of knowledge with similar canons of inquiry. Just as things in the closer regions of the world should be explored in general education with materials drawn from the arts, crafts, trades, and sports to prevent an overdistancing from the world and a homeless mind through the study of the natural sciences, so, too, should things in the nearer regions of the personal and interpersonal worlds be opened up and explored with materials drawn from the humanities, such as history, literature, languages, art and music appreciation, ethics, religion, and philosophy, to prevent a similar overdistancing from the societal world that can result from study of the social sciences.

The kinds of things in the lived regions of the world that should be explored in general education include birth, growing up, love, marriage, inescapable suffering, mortality, jealousy, adventure, conquest, defeat, mystery, the struggle between good and evil, human hopes and aspirations, the comic and tragic elements of the human condition, cultural and scientific inventions, catastrophes, revolutions, and wars. The understanding of these things through the sensitively articulated conceptualizations of the humanities brings order and significance to one's own feelings, fears, hopes, and aspirations and helps one to become at home with one's own being as well as with the human condition in general.

The significance of the humanities considered as hermeneutical or interpretive sciences was discussed tangentially in Chapter 7. An example from poetry will therefore suffice. Adolescents are often as interested in exploring love intellectually as physically. This can be done through reading great love poetry. From Robert Burns's "A Red, Red Rose" they can get an idea of love being so intense one feels it will last until the seas run dry and "while the sands o' life shall run." From Elizabeth Barrett Browning's forty-third sonnet comes a vision of love that responds to "every day's most quiet need" and that promises to continue "with the breath, smiles, tears of all my life!" Add to these the great love stories from fiction and drama, such as *Cinderella*, *Wuthering Heights*, and *Romeo and Juliet*, and the view is like Broudy's exemplars, except these are not selected as examples of art objects, genres, or moral values. They are serious, profound treatments of a central feature of human existence, and they open up human possibilities. They lend themselves to classroom discussion of things that really matter and can bring a sense of significance to the student's own being in the world.

The idea is similar to what Peters and Hirst have in mind by including literature as a form of knowledge because a literary sensibility is a highly refined mode of awareness and knowledge. It differs, however, because it includes literature along with the other humanities because of what their knowledge is about. The objective is not to develop literary sensibility but an affective, moral, existential sensibility toward the things of the lived world, that is, toward one's participation in the human condition and being in the world with others. The idea is like Greene's (1978) recommendation that the hermeneutical interest should govern the emancipatory interest (pp. 102–106), but it is also like Broudy's interpretive use of knowledge. Such materials from the humanities develop an interpretive, evaluative perspective on life in addition to opening up genuine possibilities for one's own being.

Part of becoming at home in the lived, human world involves coming to know about some of the great events that have occurred, not merely to individuals but to humankind. This includes great cultural, scientific, and intellectual inventions, such as the Magna Carta; the abolition of slavery; women's suffrage; the Universal Declaration of Human Rights; the printing press; the telescope; the steam, internal-combustion, and nuclear-powered engines; the electric light bulb; and the achievements of Isaac Newton, Karl Marx, Charles Darwin, Sigmund Freud, Marie Curie, Jane Addams, Pearl Buck, and Eleanor Roosevelt (to name only a few). It includes all the things that make the study of history into one of the humanities rather than a social science, such as its catastrophes, revolutions, and wars. It concerns the successes and defeats, the false starts and the opportunities, that humankind has had in creating a human world in which one can be at home with oneself and in society, and in which one can also be quite homeless. These things offer countless opportunities for serious classroom reflection on the human condition, wondering if humankind has made progress, and, if so, whether it was worth it.

The World of Books

Dewey is frequently quoted as having said that the three Rs are always the basis of education, but the conceptual framework of *Democracy and Education* simply will not allow their inclusion. This shows the inadequacy of his theory. Broudy explicitly refers to the symbolic skills as being among the few things to be learned in school for their replicative use. The claim that written things ought to be explored in general education may seem to be empty schematizing, but we do speak of bookworms, who would understand the seriousness of the claim that one of the major areas of the world to be explored in general education is the world of books. Books worthy of exploration, of course, disclose things in the natural, societal, and human worlds (and in the worlds of the ACTS). Although the interest in a book may be the interest in the things disclosed, it is not the things themselves that are explored. It is the books that can be explored with a critical awareness that sorts out genuine from ungenuine disclosures. Small children who are read stories they enjoy look forward eagerly to exploring the world of books and the world opened up and made accessible through books. We might consider the elementary school practice where everything stops for fifteen minutes every day to allow for a free reading period in which everyone in the school participates, including maintenance staff, secretaries, and administrators. Reading is much more than a symbolic skill.

Although reading paraphernalia centered around basal readers now permit remarkably small children to learn to read, reading should not be reified as a self-subsisting process. For the purposes of mass, formal education, its isolation as a particular set of skills coordinating visual perception with the reception of nonvisual meanings may be programmatically justified. Reading, however, is in reality inseparable from the whole enterprise of education. Reading is always reading *about* something. Because it is the interpretation of marks on the page into meanings, however, it is one of the hermeneutical sciences, like language, linguistics, semantics, and logic. The symbolic skills of reading and writing therefore belong in the curriculum at the initiatory stage of the exploration of the world of books, which, because of the intentionality of consciousness, is inseparable from the exploration of the world itself.

The World of Numbers

It might be claimed that one must explore the world of numbers to feel at home in a society heavily dependent upon mathematics and in which many people know quite a lot of mathematics, but this assertion lacks the cogency of the utilitarian argument. Although only a very small amount of mathematics is necessary in general education if the criterion is the actual use of mathematics required by an average adult, many occupations and tertiary school programs do require considerable mathematics. Because many youth do not know until tenth or eleventh grade or later if they will go on to tertiary school, it is appropriate to keep the option open until the vocational choice is made. Without supporting the view that success in mathematics is an important predictor of success in tertiary schools, except for those programs that include mathematics, it can be said that keeping the options open as long as possible promotes the most realistic choice for the occupational home in society. Both the quantified and quantitative worlds should therefore be explored in general education. The former is coextensive with the regions of the natural, societal, and lived worlds that are mathematized in their disciplined study. Because the quantification of things in the world is an interpretive undertaking, mathematics belongs to the hermeneutical sciences. It is merely a universal, unspoken language that allows for extremely rigorous conceptual processes. When its concepts are reified as symbols, the cognizable objects are the numbers and other symbols themselves. When children learn their number facts in gamelike ways with clever teachers, it is a lesson in pure mathematics in which the world of numbers is itself explored. Just how the world of numbers should be related to the student's perceptual world is not a question of the curriculum but one of pedagogy and expertise in the teaching of mathematics. No more needs to be said about this because the argument for reading applies, *mutatis mutandis.*

CONCLUSION

To ascertain the central strands of the curriculum to which everyone should have access if education is a human right, this chapter began with a brief glance at the educational theories of Freire and Greene, who have been especially concerned with educating people who either do not have access to schools or whose access to them is not accompanied by access to education and who might be concerned with pressing a claim that education is their human right. These authors' theories differ from views of education like Dewey's or Broudy's because their use of phenomenology is an attempt to look out at the world with students to understand their educational search for their own being. Their recommendations encourage the search through establishing a transitive consciousness that freely transcends itself in exploring and investigating some region of the world and thereby transforming it.

The standard approach to determining the content of the education that is a human right is to define the human being as the rational animal, argue that rationality has to be developed educationally for people to become fully developed human beings, and then claim that education is a human right because it is a necessary means to becoming a rational human being (Crittenden, 1973, chap. 2; 1981, chap. 10). This approach begs the question unless rationality is defined in an intersubjectively valid manner, particularly in regard to the relation between theoretical reason (cf. Peters and Broudy) and practical reason (cf. Spencer and Dewey) in the life of the human being and consequently in education. Although Freire and Greene differ in regard to the theoretical components that can be allowed in education without deleterious effects on praxis, they agree on considering education from the perspectives of the students, especially in regard to maintaining the intentionality of consciousness, the carrier of any possible rationality, and in their efforts to develop the students' cognitive consciousness in their search for being and truth. This matter will be discussed more fully in the next chapter.

Suffice it to say that, instead of basing the claim that education is a human right upon the prior claim regarding human rationality, the approach here is in agreement with Freire that human beings "are able to detach themselves from the world in order to find their place in it and with it" (1969/1973b, p. 105). This depends upon rationality in the sense of being able to reflect upon oneself and one's activities self-consciously, but the point does not concern the kind of cognitive processes employed in this detachment. It is that *only* people can distance themselves from the world, and that they do so "in order to find their place in the world" by looking at it objectively, examining it deeply, and investigating it to discover the truth about it (Ibid.). The importance of having a place, or home, in the world is attested to by the prephilosophical understanding of its desirability in the role the great world religions have played in human history in fulfilling the ontological need to be at home in the cosmos.

In order to be at home with oneself and with others in society and in the universe, one has to explore the natural world first of all, for "the natural world is the horizon of all horizons" (Merleau-Ponty, 1945/ 1962, p. 330). With this as a basis, one should study the lived and societal worlds, not because the methods of studying the natural world suffice to study the human condition and society but because of the primacy of perception and the developmental primacy of tactile and motile perception. It therefore seems apparent that the school curriculum to which everyone has a human right should be constituted primarily by the knowledge from the natural and social sciences and humanities. This should enable the young to gain access to the natural, societal, and human worlds and become at home in them. These areas of study can easily become too abstract, conceptual, and theoretical unless their knowledge about the world is related to the perceptual world of students and preceded and accompanied by adequate exploration of, and contact with, things in the manipulative and play worlds. The problem is not merely to insure that the daily lesson is related to the perceptual world of students to insure there is a genuine disclosure of something in the world, but also, because of the embodiment of consciousness, to insure that students are related to the perceptual world with their whole being. Then school studies in the natural, societal, and human regions of the world will involve the explorations of these areas and not of reified academic disciplines. This is the reason for the emphasis upon learning something in the arts, crafts, trades, and sports (or the dance) throughout the school years.

The parallel of this division of the world into these three main provinces (natural, social, and human) can be found in a proposal by Brian Crittenden who argues that the study of each area should promote specific epistemic objectives. The natural sciences should seek to explain things through causal principles; the social sciences should seek to explain things through a combination of causal principles and accounts of reasons, purposes, and motives; and the humanities should offer expressive, normative interpretations of things (1981, p. 155). No view should exclude these epistemic characteristics, but the content of the subjects in the natural and social sciences can be distorted by concentrating on explanatory aspects at the expense of descriptive and interpretive aspects, just as it can be distorted by an overemphasis upon basic concepts, factual information, or inquiry methods.

For example, photosynthesis is a basic concept and an explanation, but it is also a phenomenon. The purposes of general education are best fulfilled if the phenomenon is understood and perceived as the wonderful basis of all life on Earth that it is. Of course it explains things, just as it is itself explained by reference to causal chemical processes. It is also true that the concept of photosynthesis is basic. Even more important than these understandings, however, is the sheer presence of photosynthesis as a phenomenon that is extremely important and a never-ending source of wonder. The conceptualized explanations ought not let this admiring amazement be explained away. This applies to all the things in the natural, social, and human worlds. Attention given to the domain-specific epistemic characteristics is appropriate insofar as it promotes the exploration of the region of the world, encourages wonder, discloses the phenomenon at hand more fully, and serves the epistemic functions related to the interpretive objectives of schooling. These are (1) an interpretive perspective on the natural world, (2) an interpretive and temporal (or historical) perspective on the social world, and (3) an interpretive and evaluative (or normative) perspective on the human condition.

The division of academic areas into the natural and social sciences and the humanities for heuristic purposes follows from the three regions of the world and does not imply the establishment of school subjects with these names. The standard academic disciplines in the secondary school are all right if this means English, history, biology, chemistry, physics, mathematics, geography, economics, social studies, foreign languages, and the arts. What is said is neither a defense of nor an attack upon a standard subject-matter curriculum. At best it indicates in general terms how the content within these subjects should be selected and arranged to enable the young to learn about the respective regions of the world in their general education regardless of whether they are completing their formal education with twelfth grade or going on to tertiary schooling. This makes the formulation practical in the sense that it can be implemented at the classroom level without waiting for the whole school system to change its program. The chapter is deliberately entitled "Knowledge in Education," rather than "Knowledge in the Curriculum," to indicate that actual curriculum design is beyond the scope of the present inquiry, which is concerned with the question of the knowledge we have available to enable the young to learn the truth and overcome nihilism, access to which is their human right.

It was claimed in Chapter 6 that we have such knowledge in each of the ACTS and disciplines. Peirce's criterion of a critical community of investigators was pluralized like Foucault's discursive practices to accommodate the empirical fact of the existence of a great variety of trade unions, professional associations, learned societies, and certification and registration procedures. This should now be supplemented with Peirce's (1878/1958b) ontological claim that the objects within a domain are reality when perceived by qualified investigators and when the investigation has been carried sufficiently far. If this means that reality is partly "socially constructed," there is nothing arbitrary about such construction, for it is partly given and discovered, too, especially by people who have the curiosity to employ disciplined methods of inquiry that let things disclose themselves in their search for truth, as illustrated in Figure 9.1. Peirce's precise view is that "the opinion which is fated to be ultimately agreed to by all who investigate is what we mean by truth and the object represented in this opinion is the real" (p. 133). "All who investigate" includes, of course, posterity, as well as the research methods that may be invented in the future. This implies that the present consensus within any of the ACTS and disciplines may not be the truth in that rigorous sense. It makes truth historically, but not individually or socially, relative. That truth is historically relative, however, does not make truth itself relative. As Sandra Rosenthal (1988) points out, "Truth is relative to interpretive context, not because truth itself is relative, but because without an interpretive context the concept of truth is meaningless. True knowledge is, by its very nature, perspectival, but also ontologically grounded" (p. 315).

The present estimate of which opinion is "fated to be ultimately agreed to" can be no better than the consensus of opinion that currently exists within the relevant community of investigators. This opinion contains truth to the extent that the schemata and informational knowledge of a discipline do in fact disclose characteristics of things as attested within the disclosure. The justification of this knowledge in the curriculum, moreover, is that children should be exploring things in the world, the same things that are studied in disciplined ways within the ACTS and disciplines. Their explorations can and should be facilitated by the latter in such a way as to disclose things truthfully. Any knowledge from the latter is tested in the opening of the world to the disclosive presence. This is enough for common, general education because it enables students to become more deeply aware of things in the world in a more truthful manner and progressively increases their access to the world.

A word should yet be said about how this chapter's outline of the elements of common general education is a synthesis of the other views examined. It accepts from Dewey, Broudy, and Greene their claims that there should be ample curriculum time for the study of issues to promote a reflective moral and civic education (cf. Chapter 5). It accepts from Peters, Broudy, and Greene their claims that it is the conceptual aspects, or theoretical knowledge, of the disciplines for which schools are needed and for which the teacher's presence may be helpful. It accepts from Spencer and Freire that the exploration of things in each of the regions of the world should begin with, or include, the perceptual awareness of the things, on the basis of which instruction can be as conceptualized as one likes so long as it continues to disclose possibilities, or features, of the thing being studied. This process can utilize pictures, slides, videos, models, or remembered or imagined perceptual images posited in imagination (in literature, for example), as well as the material object itself. This chapter also accepts the idea of perceptual cultivation from Spencer, particularly in the arts and crafts and tactile, textual perception. This coincides with the acceptance from Dewey of the idea that bodily activity is extremely important educationally, but this is channelled through the arts, crafts, trades, and sports that should occupy part of the time in elementary schools, and it is recommended that everyone participate in at least one art, craft, or trade, as well as a sport or dance, throughout high school. The chapter accepts from Greene the thesis that wherever knowledge in the school program comes from the disciplines, it should contain their conceptual components, but rearranged to parallel the common-sense objects in the perceptual world of students. This will enable students to deepen and discipline their understanding of these objects, that is, to make sense of them. Finally, this chapter agrees with Greene that pedagogy should help students search for being and truth while it helps them to make sense of themselves and their world. The synthesis of the views of Peters, Spencer, Dewey, and Broudy will continue at the pedagogical level through the examination of Greene's pedagogy in Chapter 10.

CHAPTER 10

Knowledge in Pedagogy

In one sense the epistemological difference among the educational views of Peters, Spencer, Dewey, Broudy, and Greene is very slight. They tend to agree that the knowledge from the natural and social sciences, humanities, and the arts belongs in the curriculum of general education. They tend to agree, too, that the educative aspects of knowledge are the concepts and conceptual schemata used to state, organize, explain, and interpret factual matters, and not the facts themselves. They disagree when defining the conceptual aspects of knowledge and when recommending how, when, and why they should be acquired in classrooms. Peters and Hirst want educated adults to think like experts in the several forms of knowledge, whereas Dewey wants them to think like experimental physicists. Broudy wants adults to be able to interpret and evaluate things and events in the world, whereas Greene not only wants them to be able to make sense of things but to struggle for their freedom. Spencer has more utilitarian goals for knowledge but does not exclude the interpretive understanding of social life honored by Dewey, Broudy, and Greene. Peters, Broudy, and Greene sharply distinguish general from vocational education, whereas Dewey focuses general education in vocations and Spencer regards vocational education of greater priority than general education.

These differences reflect fundamental disagreements about the relationship of the human being to the world that are manifested in beliefs about human rationality. Peters and Broudy tend to presuppose the Aristotelian view of the human being as the rational animal. Spencer and Dewey would agree if allowed to define reason biologically as intelligence. All four advocate educational programs to promote their particular interpretation of rationality: active theoretical reason, passive theoretical reason, passive practical intelligence, and active practical intelligence, respectively. This categorization may oversimplify, but it brings their assumptions about human nature out into the open and shows the need to consider generic claims before proceeding to their synthesis at the pedagogical level. There is no doubt that education has something to do with the development of reason. The question concerns a defensible definition.

GENERIC CLAIMS ABOUT HUMAN NATURE

ʹ Traditional considerations of man as a rational animal omit more than gender, for the human being is equally the social, political, economic, cultural, historical animal; or the tool-using, planting, artistic, scientific, musical, poetical, religious animal; or the valuing, laughing, crying, playing, loving, grieving, moral, suiciding, murdering, self-conscious animal; or the animal afflicted with cosmic homesickness. One might claim any of these aspects is the essence of human nature and formulate an educational program designed to develop it. In other words, the claim that the human being is the rational animal is a suppressed value judgment. It merely sounds more objective than saying, What I really like about people is their rationality. One can just as well prefer their sexuality, historicity, spirituality, or any of the other characteristics enumerated, like their sense of humor. That the human being is the humorous animal can be proven by tracing the common roots of the words *human* and *humor*. Although Peters (1977) recognizes that one cannot make these kinds of claims without expressing a value judgment, his educational proposals and definitions of the so-called educated person (pp. 10–18) assume a definition of the human being as the rational animal. That is why he finds most people uneducable. Dewey also capitalizes upon the human as a symbol-using animal, but he combines it with his technological preference for the human being as a tool-using animal in his claims that ideas and the human mind are instruments for controlling the environment.

The fairest judgment may be to note that these authors' educational proposals call attention to good things but not the only good things. It is unnecessary to challenge their views of human nature. It is good that some people have developed their reason as Peters honors it. It is good that others have developed theirs in the way Dewey honors. These are, however, not unmixed goods. It is also good that human nature is more manifold than is encompassed by either of their narrow-minded, provincial, patriarchal prejudices. It is good that Rembrandt developed his intelligence through painting; that Pavlova used her intelligence to become a great dancer; that we have had great humorists like Mark Twain and Will Rogers; that the world has known people whose spirituality was developed like that of St. Francis of Assissi, Gandhi, or

Mother Teresa. It is good that they, like many others, have developed their kinds of intelligence through learning, regardless of whether it helped them become more rational in the way ideologies define rationality. It is irrelevant, and perhaps even boorish, to wonder if they were educated persons. If a teacher adopts Peters' or Dewey's limited view of rationality or practices the pedagogy it justifies, it will tend to develop the kind of reason the theorist honors. Other human possibilities, however, will not be developed during the school time used for these. The question is why we should let Peters or Dewey decide what kind of people schoolchildren will become.

The question is not merely one of values. It is a matter of truth and authority to impose a view of the human being upon an educational process without the permission of the clients, who might have something to say about who they are becoming. The same problem arises if one starts with the view of human nature of Rousseau or Calvin. Rousseau (1762/1966) believes human nature is naturally good and therefore advocates negative or laissez-faire education to let the goodness of the child emerge according to its own nature. A view of original sin, on the other hand, leads to an authoritarian education to enable people to become good. The truth is that both Rousseau and Calvin are right: man as man has both good and evil possibilities throughout his life. It is not so clear about women, but men are both good and evil in the sense that anyone is capable of both.

Similarly, the truth is that both Peters and Dewey are right: The possibility to think in the ways they advocate belong to everyone. Generic presuppositions about human nature are therefore persuasive definitions, that is, propaganda. When embedded in a definition of education, as in Peters' idea of education as initiation or Dewey's of education as the reconstruction of experience, they become functioning programmatic definitions. Then we ought not argue about the assumptions but about the characteristics of the program conveyed, as we have done. When and where should students be initiated into public traditions? When and where should students learn by inquiry method? When and where should their theoretical reason or their technological mentality be developed? When and where should their sense of humor be developed?

THE EXISTENTIAL CONTEXT

What Sartre means by the slogan, "Existence precedes essence" is that even if the essence of human nature is rationality, each person must freely assume responsibility for being as reasonable as possible.

This is why the obligations to develop the virtue and intelligence in oneself and others were accepted earlier from Kant and Ross. What is strictly in accordance with human nature should happen purely as the result of maturation, without education, learning, or freely committed choice, as an acorn becomes a mighty oak whether it wants to or not. People ought to choose to become reasonable, of course, but only the possibility is written into the genetic codes, not the necessity. People like Sartre and Greene therefore reject generic claims about human nature, they say. Then they make them at a newer, deeper, and broader level. Such claims are inescapable. We can consider the characteristics already mentioned. Human beings are the symbol-using, social, political, economic, cultural, historical, tool-using, planting, artistic, scientific, musical, poetic, religious, valuing, meaningful, laughing, crying, playing, working, loving, hating, moral, suiciding, murdering, warring animals. Each aspect is distinctly human. Each anthropological claim is the basis of an art, craft, trade, profession, or university discipline. Each is learned. There is undoubtedly a genetic basis that creates possibilities and tendencies, but each of these characteristics embodies a mode of conduct that would not have to be chosen or developed. Ironically, when Sartre (1943/1956) says we are condemned to freedom, it is tantamount to saying that the human being is the choosing animal (pp. 438–441). Sartre is making the unacknowledged generic claim even while saying we ought not make them. Not rationality but choosing becomes for Sartre the generic trait of human existence. When we state that each of the claims about human beings given in the enumeration is learned, it is similarly assumed that we are condemned to learn. Learning is a generic trait of human existence. We are the learning animal. All of the features cited are learned because they are all acquired characteristics.

When animals acquire new behaviors, they are not learning in the sense that the word is used to refer to human learning. When humans learn to walk erect, use symbols or tools, and so forth, they are also learning to become more fully human, as Freire says. Human learning is humanizing. The feral children—the wolf children of Midnapore—prove that no one becomes a human being by maturation alone. Every characteristic that distinguishes members of the species as mature adults is learned. This may not have been true of *homo sapiens* a hundred thousand years ago, but this is not counterevidence because these people no longer exist. Although acquired characteristics are not inherited, the cultural evolution that has occurred has indeed changed human nature in the sense of changing what it means to be a human being. Today, consequently, one has to learn how to become a human being as we currently understand what it means to be a human being. If the human being is to be understood as the rational animal, the concept of rationality has to be sufficiently broad to encompass all of the distinctly human characteristics that are consciously learned. If so, we should merely claim that *homo sapiens* is the learning animal. This may be the truth inherent in Aristotle's definition of the human being as the rational animal when it is deconstructed by stripping it of historically contingent definitions of rationality.

Because the characteristics cited distinguish human beings from animals, they are a provisional taxonomy of human possibilities. When developed through learning, they become manifest in the arts, crafts, trades, sports, professions, university disciplines, and other cultural activities. Because of differential genetic endowments, no one knows what their own possibilities are except through the disciplined study and practice of some of the ACTS and disciplines. If individuals do not know their own mode of rationality except through learning and education, neither does the philosopher, who can only say that the human being is a creature of limitations and possibilities. The limitations are given by genetic endowment and historical, societal facticity. The possibilities are given the same way, but their realization requires projects of engaged action that involve learning, choice, and commitment. Among all the creatures, only human beings can ask who they are becoming and then choose and strive to realize their own possibilities.

Understanding the basis of this generalization in the human condition can deepen its meaning. The claim that the human being is the humorous animal is not refuted by the claim that hyenas and kookaburras laugh, for they are unable to laugh at themselves or deliberately choose to respond to a tense situation with levity. They do not have a sense of humor, but some people do. The claim that the human is the crying animal does not mean that animals do not shed tears, but it is doubtful that they can weep for the suffering of others or memorialize their grief in literature, anniversaries, and national holidays. Human beings are the only creatures that can make a promise, or who need to. Human beings are the only animal to commit suicide because only they can decide life is not worth living (which cannot be attributed to lemmings).

Laughing, crying, promising, and committing suicide are manifestations of human beings in their conscious, self-conscious awareness of their own existence and in their caring for who they are and who they are becoming. They not only manifest human dignity but human grandeur. They show transcendence over the facticity of bodily existence in a physical world. The transcendent self-consciousness of the human being is also shown in each of the other characteristics listed as distinctly human. For example, people plant crops and use tools because they are aware of the need they will have next winter for food and shelter, and so on. Consciousness of one's own possibilities, necessary for human dignity, is therefore the characteristic feature of human existence. Animals may be conscious of things in the world, but they lack consciousness of this primary, perceptual awareness. They lack self-consciousness and cannot transcend things in a free projection of being that converts the features of the world into their own possibilities. They lack praxis, which Mihailo Markovic says is "the specific characteristic of man and human history" (UNESCO, 1986, p. 121). They lack human agency.

This self-conscious awareness of one's own existence and the search for personal significance in one's life does not result from physiological maturation alone. It, too, is learned. The progressive deepening of consciousness and self-consciousness of things that occurs as the young seek the meaning of their being and the truth about things in the world is the educational process that guides them to an adult presence to the world. What it means to be an adult is to be fully aware of one's own existence in the world with other people, at least when one is wide awake. Adults know who they are and accept responsibility for their being. Education is the gradual assumption of this responsibility and the moral agency it involves (*cf.* Chapters 4 and 5).

The gradual acquisition of the awareness of who one is can occur through initiation into the disciplines in their secondary and tertiary schooling for some people. There is no need to doubt it. They can speak for themselves. For others it can occur through the development of their practical intelligence, but this is for them to say. For others it can occur in myriad other ways, depending upon which of the ACTS and disciplines they find enlarge their unique embodiment of rationality. It depends upon the specific methods of disciplined study in these areas that best facilitate the realization of their own possibilities and enable them to become who they can become.

This pluralism is necessitated by the openness of human existence. The open question of who someone is can be resolved only by personal decisions in one's own life, not in theory. The question each person should address in education is, Who will I become, given these bodily and historical factual conditions? This openness toward the future is the very ground of educability. It makes education both possible and necessary for human beings, who, alone among living creatures, find it necessary and desirable to educate their young. The openness toward the future that motivates the quests for being and truth is the subjective correlate of being in the world and of the concern for finding a place, or home, in the world. The difference is one of emphasis, that is, of whether the focus is on the inner horizons and the self or on the outer horizons and the world, on the openness to the future or on the outwardness to the world. People who know who they are are at home in the world. Conversely, people who are at home in the world know who they are and do not question their identity or the meaning of their lives. This is why pedagogy should help the young pursue their being and truth. It will enable them to achieve the aim of education, which, because the essence of human nature is being in the world, is finding a home in society and in the world.

The interpretation of human existence that places ultimate value upon becoming at home on Earth is attested to by the etymology of *homo sapiens*. The *homo* who is sapient was discussed in Chapter 4. The origin of the Latin *homo*, a man, according to *Webster's New World Dictionary*, is the Indo-European *ghom*, from the base *ghthem*, meaning earth or ground; and which is related to the Latin *humus* and the Greek *chthon*, both also meaning earth; and the Old English *guma*, meaning man. The Greek *chthon* is found in the English *autochthon*, taken from the Greek word of the same spelling, meaning sprung from the land itself, and in English referring to the earliest inhabitants of a place, its aboriginal people. These are the people who belong to the earth and whose homeland it is. The etymology suggests that the primordial, prephilosophical understanding of archaic people included a mystical connection between human existence and the earth such as that found, for example, in the culture of Australian Aborigines. It is also found in Genesis, where it says, "The Lord God formed man of dust from the ground" (2:7), and where Adam is destined to "return to ground, for out of it you were taken; you are dust, and to dust you shall return" (3:19). According to Eliade, images of the Earth Mother, as if early humans lived in the earth and were born from the earth, occurred everywhere in archaic societies, and the belief that human beings are born from the earth was universally distributed. He believes that the vague feelings of unity with the earth—with the land itself—that even Europeans feel today is one of having sprung from the earth, resulting in an autochthony that is understood as their being the people of this place in a deeper sense of cosmic relatedness than that of solidarity with family and ancestry (1968, p. 165). That is to say that the understanding of the earth as the origin and destiny of human beings is as primordial a grasp of the human condition as possible. It is, however, the essence of human existence to transcend the earth even while remaining rooted in it. Such transcendence of facticity is the origin of all that distinguishes human beings from other animals and all that embodies human dignity.

GREENE'S PEDAGOGY

Because of this transcendence, Greene (1973) also rejects definitions of human nature as a basis for pedagogy. A teacher with an image of the human being derived from such definitions is unable to perceive the student adequately as an individual human being who is open to a future in the world (p. 84). Greene believes the teacher should, on different occasions, function as a rationalist, empiricist, pragmatist, or liberationist, to be sure, but always guided by the futural orientations of specific students to help them explore and make sense of the world, not because of an a priori conception of what human beings should be like. This will involve emphasizing at different times conceptual schemes, propositional knowledge, experiential or experimental problem solving, and disciplined dialogue about things, respectively. Sometimes whispering helps.

Greene's (1973) recommendation is far from being an eclectic pluralism. She transfers to the teacher Sartre's statement about our being condemned to freedom: It is the teacher who is condemned to choose, not an ideology of knowledge, but the approach appropriate for each lesson. This choice should occur with an awareness of "the multiple untapped possibilities in each organism he [the teacher] is trying to teach" (p. 60). It may be impossible for a teacher to have personal encounters with students as individuals, but the obligation is nevertheless to help them realize their own possibilities within the common world (p. 82). The teacher cannot be guided directly by psychological theories, either. The students the teacher sees are not the scientific objects seen by empirical researchers. They are unique people, each with a particular life history (pp. 145–157). It is not enough, for Greene, to relate cognitive learnings to the world students perceive, for their present perceptual world is the product of previously sedimented meanings. Citing Merleau-Ponty, she claims the child's primary world "is constituted perceptually *before* the construction of cognitive structures" (p. 161). It is a rather developed, lived world, gained through play, handling things, and conversations and relations with other people. Some of the meanings that things in the student's world already have can be stated in common-sense language, while others are implicit, or tacit, and cannot. These meanings, however, are of personal, felt significance, value laden, and emotional as well as cognitive. Greene therefore recommends a reflection on things in the lived world to enable students to become aware of their own presence in the constitution of the objects perceived. This awareness is like what we felt when alternating between the empty box and the cube in Figure 9.1, an activity that drew attention to the constitution of the object.

To generate the necessary reflection, each unit of study should begin with dialogue about things in the relevant region of the lived world. This should break down the dogmatism of the taken-for-granted, everyday world by creating the awareness of the student's own presence to the world. The teacher already knows that what appears to the students to be given is not in fact given externally (e.g., the flat lines on the page in Figure 9.1 are not really given). It is only the common-sense meanings of the objects that are projected "out there." The initial dialogue should raise some of these meanings into explicit consciousness to enable students to explore the inner horizons. This involves reflecting on the accepted meanings as well as the way they formed them in their own experience. This loosens up their consciousness of what had seemed to be given perceptually, much as wondering where the movement occurs when alternating between the box and the cube in Figure 9.1 enables one to doubt that consciousness is an empty room in one's head. Students then become curious about the theme opened up and are freed to explore the outer horizons, using the intersubjectively valid concepts of a discipline to reconstitute the objects in the perceived world in epistemically valid ways, making sense of them (Greene, 1973, pp. 162–167).

The exploration of the outer horizons in the knowledge of the discipline should be motivated by the students' search for truth and for being after they are freed for this transcendence by the initiating discussion. Greene (1973) cites approvingly Alfred North Whitehead's insistence on acquiring and organizing facts as the route to knowledge to substantiate her claim that a properly initiated thematic investigation will lead students to generate the structures of the discipline as they organize its conceptual aspects into their own patterns of making sense of the world (p. 173). Her pedagogy is in fact a phenomenological version of Whitehead's pedagogy, comprising the three stages of romance, precision, and generalization (1929/1954, chap. 2). The initial dialogue that questions the student's everyday reality creates the romance. The thematic investigation is the precision stage, until it results in learning the generalization that makes sense out of something. When the thematic exploration combines the students' search for their own being with their search for truth, the new sense that is made of the world transforms the world (p. 175).

This has liberational overtones, but the emphasis upon the pupil's search for truth and being seems to heed Kierkegaard's (1846/1971) claim that "there is no objective truth, but the truth consists in personal appropriation" (p. 71). Greene wants students to appropriate personally the knowledge of the disciplines into their subjectivities, to integrate it into their life histories, rather than simply learning it conceptually without relating it to their own being. Using the knowledge of the disciplines to make sense of the world, however, is different from using it to learn the truth about the world. It seems to involve filtering the knowledge through one's self, rather than filtering oneself through the knowledge. If so, then this pedagogy, like Dewey's, may be guilty of what Russell called cosmic impiety.

Before we turn to the question of truth, we should consider motivation. Greene assumes students will indeed try to make sense of the world through the use of the knowledge in the disciplines if the teacher avoids the attitude that it is something to be learned and encourages seeing it as a possible source of perspectives on the world. She assumes that students want to be someone and will search for their own being, meaning, and truth if topics are begun with a dialogue not unlike that advocated by Freire, including problem-posing questions and the emergence of themes embedded in the students' background awareness. She assumes this search will prompt them to explore the concepts, generalizations, perspectives, and canons of inquiry of the disciplines and use them to make sense of the world. The question is whether this also assumes an Aristotelian innate desire to know and consequently a belief in the rationality of human nature. Greene (1973) claims, however, that something like Sartre's concept of praxis will emerge when students extend themselves to find answers to questions they pose for themselves in the course of the initiatory dialogue (p. 172). This seems warranted because of the intentionality of consciousness, or the projection of one's being into the future that one eagerly pursues when the world is safe enough to explore, for then its values draw consciousness out to it.

Greene's assumption that the initial dialogue will suffice to initiate praxis and existentially supported inquiry is like Freire's pedagogy, except she does not assume students are oppressed or need to be politicized. They need consciousness-raising dialogue to be awakened from everydayness and their belief that their common-sense knowledge of things is knowledge. Instead of a desire to know, then, Greene assumes people are fundamentally in search of meaning and significance. It is the quest for significance in one's life that urges one to try to make sense out of things. This is why the teacher must be committed to an ideal of truth and "must be concerned about his students' taking truth as seriously as they search for being" (p. 169).

The pluralism of Greene's (1973) claim that the teacher, while paying attention to the student's being, should function as a rationalist, empiricist, or pragmatist, depending upon the circumstances, is therefore more responsive to truth than any one of these ideologies. It exemplifies the truth of needing multiple perspectives within any domain of knowledge. Any insufficiency is due to the inadequate acknowledgment that truth occurs when the conceptual schemata or other aspects of the disciplines disclose aspects of reality. Greene denies epistemological realism; that is, she denies that the disciplines disclose the real nature of things (pp. 174–175). She says too little about the more limited claim that they disclose some of the real features of things or Peirce's claim that their kind of qualified investigation will eventually lead to the disclosure of the real nature of things. Unless they disclose some features or aspects of reality, however, there is no epistemic warrant for using them to make sense of things. She does not accept the disciplines' inherent organization as being pedagogically useful, but she has no doubt at all about their usefulness as sources of perspectives on the world, presumably because they disclose things truthfully. Otherwise there would be no epistemic basis for the claim that the teacher "always represents the public world with its institutions, its predefined forms, its categories and disciplines" (p. 175). The hands are the hands of Dewey, but the voice is the voice of Peters.

Greene's (1973) suggestion about how the teacher should enable students to make sense of the world in acts of free appropriation, however, is not as subjectivistic as it may seem. She claims the teacher must know the subject thoroughly and be committed to the ideal of truth embodied in its canons of inquiry. This is essential to being able to promote the students' search for truth and thereby their search for being. The teacher should also be aware of the students' need for a personal standpoint from which to constitute a meaningful world in the generation of the structures of the disciplines (pp. 169–170). Students should be encouraged to adopt the canons of inquiry from the disciplines and to try out various points of view from them to integrate them with existential meanings (p. 173). Presumably these canons of inquiry do in fact disclose real features of things in the world, compel phenomenological objectivity, and place epistemic limits upon the kinds of sense that can be made out of things. Her point seems merely to avoid studying a discipline as a reified body of knowledge, regardless of whether there is a continuing disclosure of things in the respective region of the world.

Greene's pedagogy can be understood as an application of Freire's to schools in the way Dewey's is an application of Spencer's. She cites Freire's phenomenology (but not his politics) along with primary sources of phenomenology to formulate a co-intentional pedagogy that would sometimes allow the conceptual apparatus of the disciplines to provide for the "disclosure of an aspect of the world" (Greene, 1973, p. 171). This is the same as Freire's "unveiling the world." The claim that the teacher can sometimes act as a rationalist, empiricist, pragmatist, or liberationist avoids overemphasizing the reified epistemic characteristics that distinguish the ideologies of Peters, Spencer, Dewey, and Freire from each other. Although she does not investigate the general structure of the curriculum, her incidental references to the standard academic subjects of the high school curriculum and her concern for students' generating the structures of the disciplines is compatible with students' acquiring an organized body of knowledge in their general education. The pedagogy can be used, for example, within the standard academic disciplines or within the schemes recommended by Peters, Broudy, or Adler. It would even adapt their proposals to the general education of youth who are not preparing for tertiary schools. A major difficulty in her view, however, and the need for further consideration of pedagogy can be shown through an examination of her illustrative application.

The teacher can begin the study of the history of the nineteenth century in the United States, Greene (1973) suggests, by asking the students questions about relations between the North and the South. A few themes can be selected from their replies and problematized by probing into the students' memories for the meanings that the themes already embody, some of which will have nuances of racial and regional prejudice. This exploration of the students' inner horizons should elicit reasons why the themes are significant and worth exploring to see their relation to the origins of the Civil War. This frees the students to become epistemic subjects who are concerned with the outer horizons and prepared to read historical materials to arrive at some resolution about the causes of the Civil War, thereby making sense of it (pp. 165–167). Because several macrocosmic social issues, such as industrialization versus agrarianism and federalism versus states' rights, are involved in addition to slavery, the study of the Civil War with its concluding release of five to six million unskilled Afro-Americans into society can lead to different ways of making sense, not only of the Civil War, but of interracial relations in the contemporary world.

Greene carefully distinguishes her view from Dewey's, which starts with a present social problem and probes its roots in the past. Hers is compatible with a basically chronological approach designed to develop the students' temporal perspective. It is generally compatible with the framework of any of the disciplines because it is concerned with tactics, not strategy. The illustration, however, does depend upon a deeply embedded, societal conundrum for its explication. Every student living in a racially mixed area is likely to have typifications embedded in the primary world that shape the everyday, taken-for-granted understanding of this particular region of the social world. This means it is not a good example from which to generalize. In a physics lesson, for instance, in which the things the students are to come to know more about are the four forces of the universe, they would have common-sense notions of gravity and perhaps of electromagnetism, but it seems unlikely they would have any ideas about weak and strong nuclear forces as physical phenomena. An initiatory dialogue might be as important here as elsewhere, but it would be more likely to discover what had been learned in previous schooling than to raise premature, inadequate meanings into consciousness to be amended by epistemically valid inquiry. In other words, Greene's pedagogy is more helpful in some regions of the societal and human worlds than in others, or in the exploration of the natural world.

There is also an ethical and epistemic question regarding the use of the classroom to modify students' existing beliefs. We concede the point in the illustration because we oppose racism and slavery and want to have the study of the Civil War result in certain moral effects as well as a deeper understanding of the United States. In other areas, however, the earlier typifications that make up the meanings of the students' everyday, primary world might have resulted from deliberate parental teaching in morality or religion. It is not obvious that a teacher has a right or obligation to raise these meanings into consciousness in order to demythologize them. It may not always be educationally productive, furthermore, for teachers to raise into consciousness previous school learnings that have become sedimented and are now used interpretively. We have to imagine what it would be like if every teacher, every year, in all subjects, began every unit of study with a focus upon some aspect of the students' life histories. The students might not experience the curriculum as a source of meanings with which to make sense of things once they realize that any conclusions they reach will be open to challenge by their next teacher.

This suggests that the exploration of the inner horizons can be educationally counterproductive. It can involve gross invasion of privacy and be a violation of human dignity. It can undo previously hard-won educative results. The initiatory dialogue may be necessary to enable the conceptualized materials of the subject to disclose things in the student's perceptual world, but this does not always require probing into the student's life history to insure that what is learned will be existentially significant. Just as Greene objects to the teacher having a fixed definition of rationality because it will not encompass the multitude of ways human intelligence manifests itself in students' possibilities, so should there be allowances for legitimate variations in the directions in which students choose to search for their being. One student might find history to be existentially relevant; another, biology; a third, literature and football; another, automechanics; and so on.

We need to distinguish between phenomenological and existential relevance. Knowledge in the curriculum is existentially relevant when integrated into the students' life histories and search for being, but it is phenomenologically relevant when it is related to the students' perceptual world and their search for truth. It can disclose things in the perceptual world without contributing to the search for being. If the purpose of general education is to enable the young to find a home in the human, societal, and natural worlds, it depends upon phenomenological rather than existential relevance. For the most part, existential relevance belongs with the specialization accompanying vocational preparation. What is not existentially relevant when it is learned, moreover, may very well be more relevant existentially in the student's subsequent life history, than that which is existentially relevant when it is learned. During learning, knowledge can only be integrated into the past and present life history. It only has to be perceptually relevant to establish the world as the home in which one dwells, which means it ought to be integrated within the student's search for truth.

This does not deny the pedagogical significance of the search for being. To the contrary, it merely claims it is not equally important for all the students in a given classroom. From the student's point of view, it is not equally important in all classrooms. Students who are attracted by the perceived qualities in the lived world, in society, in nature, or in one or more of the ACTS, should be allowed to realize value where they can and orient their search for being to the regions of the world in which they find themselves most at home. To discover these regions, however, requires an exploration of all the regions appropriate to general education. This requires phenomenological (i.e., perceptual) relevance and the search for truth.

WITNESSING THE TRUTH

Dialoging with students to help them articulate themes that will engage them in an investigation of sufficient intensity and direction to generate the structures of a discipline requires that the knowledge of the discipline be incorporated into the teacher's very being. If knowledge is to become existentially significant to students, in other words, it has to have obvious existential significance to the teacher. This means it has to have been learned as part of the teacher's own quest for being and truth and thoroughly integrated into the teacher's life history. The teacher should have explored the particular region of the world sufficiently to have become completely at home in it. This includes becoming aware of the qualities of the things in the region, caring for them, and wanting to preserve them and the knowledge about them. It involves something like Wildman's love of animals (see Chapter 5), Spencer's poetics of science, or whatever is appropriate to the domain. Teachers should not, then, be one of Greene's strangers or outsiders. The teacher's love for the things may involve an estrangement from everyday, common-sense convictions about them, and from people who hold them, but this occurs only because of being deeply at home in the cosmos through the rooting in the specific region of the world of the teaching specialization.

To avoid reifying knowledge and to recognize that it exists only in the processes of someone's being, perhaps we should say that when the knowledge of one of the ACTS or a discipline is thoroughly integrated into the teacher's being, the teacher is the knowledge. Just as it is ontologically wrong to say that one has a body because one is one's body, or one exists one's body, so is it wrong to say that the teacher has knowledge as a possession. When it is thoroughly incorporated into the teacher's very being, the teacher is the knowledge, or exists the knowledge. When the teacher brings knowledge into being by speaking the truth about something, the teacher is the truth, existing in the truth. To avoid reifying truth, it should be said that the dialogical teacher should speak truthfully, but one can speak the truth by rote memory, without understanding what one is saying, and without disclosing anything. Because truth, like knowledge, exists only in the projection of someone's being, and only during the occurrence of the disclosure of something in the world, we should say that the teacher should be the truth. The teacher should exist in the truth of what is taught because the disclosure of things in the world manifests the teacher's being in the world as well as things in the world.

The ontological independence of truth and knowledge has to be retained, however, because they do not exist in the teacher as if he or she were not intentionally related to the world. Truth and knowledge exist in the disclosure in the world. The words refer to what happens in the disclosure, making them independent of the existence of any particular person. For example, what is said about the boxes in Figure 9.1 could be said by anyone and discloses something to others, or it is truthless. To account for the intersubjectively valid disclosures authorized by the respective communities of investigators, we should perhaps say that the teacher should be a witness to the truth. For knowledge in schooling to have existential significance for students, then, the teacher should bear witness to its truth.

To bear witness in a court case, one swears publicly, by all one holds sacred, to tell the truth, the whole truth, and nothing but the truth. The oath puts one's personal existence on trial, "So help me God," under pain of perjury. One's very being is at stake in every single word of one's testimony. A concern for being a witness to the truth is part of Kierkegaard's (1854/1957) criticism of those clergy who make excellent livings preaching doctrines opposite to those of the New Testament. They do not bear witness to the alleged truth of Christianity (pp. 2–26). Freire refers to being a witness of one's radicalism, but never of sectarianism, in liberatory education, but this is to bear testimony to respect for democracy, freedom, and the virtue of living with and respecting differences (Freire & Shor, 1987, p. 34). Gabriel Marcel (1946/1964) suggests that we give testimony about something independent of ourselves and therefore objective and real, but doing so commits us to be answerable for what we say and for ourselves. This involves a very high degree of existential "tension between the commitment and the objective end" (p. 95).

What is pedagogically important is bearing witness to human dignity and the things in the specific region of the world explored in the school subject. The biology teacher should love animals and the beauty of plants; the historian should critically venerate the previous struggles of humanity; the English teacher should appreciate the noble aspects of life depicted in literature; and so on. Teachers in the arts, crafts, and trades should love good materials and fine objects made with them. Objective knowledge and skills, or intersubjectively established and recognized conceptualizations, should not be replaced with something more subjectivistic in an epistemic sense. To the contrary, the teacher's intellectual grasp of knowledge should be supplemented, not replaced, with dialogical, I–Thou relations with things in the region of the world taught about. It is, after all, the personal encounter with them that makes them so important that one becomes willing to devote a lifetime to teaching about them and able to be a witness to their truth. Witnessing the truth of things shows students they are important to the teacher and encourages them to seek out their values for themselves. Disclosing them perceptually as well as conceptually, moreover, shows their values to students.

Bearing witness to the truth of the canons of inquiry and knowledge in one's teaching specialization is manifested in pedagogic enthusiasm and dedication. When students sense a teacher's lack of engagement in the content of instruction, they are deprived of the most fundamental catalyst of their own enthusiasm. The word *enthusiasm* originally meant not merely intense interest and ardent zeal but divinely inspired (*en theos*: possessed by a god). The teacher can know the truth of what is taught on the purely cognitive level of conceptual consciousness, or with the passion that accompanies a whole-hearted commitment to it. With an exuberant devotion to the things in the world and the canons of inquiry necessary to investigate them, the teacher can help to overcome cognitive nihilism and cosmic impiety. It merely requires the teacher to be in the truth (Heidegger, 1927/1962, p. 263).

The incorporation of the canons of inquiry and knowledge of the teaching specialization into the teacher's very being may seem more appropriate to secondary or tertiary schooling, but it is needed in the elementary school, too. It appears in elementary school science in object lessons, in the "hands-on" approach to connecting the concepts with the perceptual world, and even in the legibility with which everything is written on the chalkboard. Legibility is a canon of inquiry, so to speak, or at least a norm, that, like correct spelling, is bound into the content of the cognitive skills of reading and writing. Another norm to be learned in the elementary school is a respect for reading and for books themselves. The importance of books can be explicated through analogy with the Bible. When the books of the Judeo-Christian tradition were brought together at the end of the second century, they were simply known as books, *biblas*. This was mistaken for the singular noun, and the collection became known as the book. Its subsequent sacralization was an accidental, historical mystification that merely exaggerated a very high regard for the book that contains the best knowledge of the early Hebrews and Christians. Within their community, the book was thought to contain the best knowledge of their own history.

There is no difference between this respect for their book and a similar respect for the books that contain the best knowledge available today. Just as the popular education of the sixteenth and seventeenth centuries was oriented toward enabling everyone to read that book, so do today's efforts at common, general education have the same goal. The books are different, but learning to read is still the route to gain access to the best knowledge, which is to be found in the books stored in the modern surrogate for the Holy of Holies, the main library at the university. The knowledge in these books is as worthy of reverence as that stored in the book called the *Bible* because Spencer is right: Personal and group survival depend upon it. In any case, it is extremely important for elementary school teachers to teach reading in such a way that children come to love books. When teachers show their own love for books, they bear witness to the truth of the cognitive skills they transmit with reading. Their very presence in the classroom bears witness to the truth of what Freire says: "We must work to have some good classroom experiences in reading texts. . . . We must continue to study books as another way of reading the world" (Freire & Shor, 1987, p. 182). Freire, however, was referring to all teachers.

Knowledge and existence should therefore be synthesized in the teacher's being, that is, in the teacher's presence to the class. When the teacher knows things with such great thoroughness that the knowledge and skills permeate his relation to the world as revealed in all his actions, then whatever the teacher says or does discloses things in the world. One cannot have truth like a pocketful of buttons, but one can bear witness to it by allowing it to be present in one's speech, action, and general orientation to the world. One can allow it to shine forth in one's presence to the world.

Many educationists have avoided the word *truth* in this century because, like Dewey, they have had an interpretation of science that has emphasized its tentativeness, corrigibility, relativity, and so on. If people of this persuasion would object to the idea of witnessing the truth on the grounds that doing so is authoritarian, the objection would criticize something that was not said. The problem is to understand the role of knowledge in education and existence without using the words *knowledge, science,* and *scientific method.* These words reify aspects of human knowing and have historically generated the dualism between the subjective knower and the objective thing known. If the subject/object relation that is distinctly cognitive should be structured by scientific methods, for example, in order to discover the best knowledge, it is because these methods allow things in the world to be most adequately disclosed to the subject. If they are superior to other ways of knowing things in the natural world, it is because they are better ways of obtaining truth. This means that the criterion by which to judge the value of a method of knowing things is disclosedness, or truth. If the result is a qualified rather than an absolute or unqualified truth, then the qualifications are an essential aspect of the truth. Science is not a sacred cow, but cosmic impiety cannot be avoided without the sacralization of truth and the methods that both allow us to become present to objects that exist in the world and allow those objects to become present to us. It is the power of methods of inquiry, whether in the ACTS, natural sciences, social sciences, or humanities, to allow things in the world to disclose themselves—to let truth be—that makes them valuable and worthy of our very highest respect.

The idea of truth, furthermore, overcomes a possible misinterpretation in the use of the word *subjectivity* to refer to a person's inwardness rather than to the inadequacy of knowledge. The issue is the way in which knowledge structures a person's consciousness and very being, not the abandonment of objective knowledge in favor of everyone having their own opinion. The problem is how science can be learned so as to avoid the development of a conceptualized mode of thought that is alienated from the perceptual world and its own being. It is how knowledge can be acquired so as to open up consciousness to the world in genuine acts of knowing, or how conceptual consciousness of things can maintain its connections with the perceptual world. How consciousness opens to the world and lets the world open toward oneself is a matter of truthfulness. This openness to truth, to being, suggests that the locus of truth is in the very process or event of consciousness becoming conscious of something in the world. If so, one cannot have truth as if it were the content of consciousness. One can only witness the truth by being open to the world and letting the world open to one. One can be the truth by being disclosive of things in the world.

Teachers who bear witness to the truth, furthermore, no longer have to teach the truth. They only have to talk seriously about what matters the most to them. If science and knowledge do not exist, because only people who know things do, then teachers can teach only what they know. They cannot teach science, knowledge, or an academic discipline, but only what they know as a result of their own search for truth and being in the regions of the world investigated by people using the methods of the ACTS and disciplines. They do not have to make didactic presentations, for it suffices to talk with and to students about texts and about the things in the world.

Such talk will be the co-intentional dialogue Freire, for one, advocates, because of the teacher's strong orientation to the highly valued things in the world. There need be no concern about whether such talk will be sufficiently intellectual, for such a witness cannot talk about valued things except in the modes that have been structured by the conceptualizations of the respective ACTS or discipline. These schemata will discipline everything such a witness to the truth says, does, and is. That is to say that when a teacher bears witness to the truth, pedagogy is simply a disciplined dialogue about the things in the region of the world under study. In this kind of dialogue, both teacher and students are truthful. Such truthfulness involves being loyal both to what is common to both perceptions—that is, to what is intersubjectively valid (as in Peters, Dewey, or Broudy)—and to what appears within their own horizons (as in Spencer, Freire, or Greene). It synthesizes the conceptual understanding of things with the things in the world as perceived by students.

Teachers who bear witness to the truth can help students acquire and maintain dialogical relations with, for example,

1. Natural objects, particularly those involved in biotic communities and terrestrial ecosystems, but not excluding celestial things
2. Social objects, such as one's own country and its institutions, other cultures, and previous civilizations
3. Human creations, such as works of art, literature, music, scientific discoveries, religions, and moral principles.

They can give existential significance to the acquisition of literacy and numeracy through manifesting their own love of and enthusiasm for reading and arithmetical precision. They can insure that the learning of the ACTS has existential significance through insuring that students enjoy them for the value inherent in making things and in playing.

Such disciplined dialogue can be as conceptualized as possible, and as teacher controlled as one likes, and it will not violate the conditions of dialogue so long as the students' attention remains focused upon the things in the world that are disclosed by the conceptual schemata embodied in the teacher's talk. Such attention maintains the needed transcendence to the world. The dynamism, enthusiasm, and gusto with which one teaches do not deny it its status as teaching or as dialogue so long as students witness the truth.

DOMAIN- AND LESSON-SPECIFIC PHENOMENOLOGICAL RESEARCH

We should accept Dewey's (1916) dictum that the best method of teaching and learning is that arrangement of subject matter that makes it most effective in use (p. 194), while believing that one criterion of effectiveness is enabling students to become sufficiently familiar with the qualities of things in the world to establish harmony with them and a deeper sense of being at home in the universe. Appreciating their qualities should arouse obligations to care for and preserve them as students develop the love for the world that eventuates in natural piety. To secure this outcome, pedagogical methods should rely heavily upon the perceptual awareness of things through object lessons involving photographs, slides, demonstrations, videos, movies, and the use of real-world objects in constructive activities, laboratories, shops, studios, kitchens, theaters, gymnasiums, and athletic fields.

The educational justification for these perceptual materials in schools, however, is to enable the young to submit the things of the everyday world to disciplined study through the use of the conceptualizations of the ACTS and disciplines. Each of these has emerged precisely to employ the most disciplined and reliable methods of investigating and creating the objects in the respective region of the world. As Dewey (1916) says, formal education should open the young to experiences that would not otherwise be accessible to them (p. 9). The emphasis upon disciplined dialogue in pedagogy lets teachers bear witness to things in the world by embodying the facts, generalizations, and conceptualizations of the ACTS and disciplines in conversation about them. The use of the expression "the disciplined study of things" is more general and more fundamental than terms from epistemology or philosophy of science and than questions of whether pedagogy should focus upon the procedures for discovering knowledge in a domain (as in Spencer, Dewey), initiate students into the conceptual schemata of the disciplines (as in Peters), or use expository methods to transmit the substantive content of a domain (as in Broudy). It allows for their use without prescribing any of them, depending upon the exigencies of the lesson or topic (as in Greene). The alternatives are based upon reified aspects of knowledge and arrest attention on something other than the fundamental phenomena in the respective region of the world. Greene correctly intimates they are each epistemically inadequate when taken by themselves when she claims the teacher should emphasize the various epistemic characteristics when appropriate.

The focus upon "disciplined dialogue" is compatible with Greene's pedagogical pluralism, but this phrase in its more generalized expression frankly recognizes that what a teacher has to work with is words. All any knowledge in any of the disciplines is, is words. Even when the teachers of the ACTS demonstrate how to do something by physically showing how to do it, they say things about what they are doing while they are doing it. The concepts in their words disclose finer perceptual discriminations than would be visible to students if they remain silent. Epistemologies and philosophies of science merely prescribe various ways the words of the disciplines should be formalized and organized into logical structures to promote the further discovery and organization of knowledge. Their prescriptions for the words of the disciplines are not directly germane to the pedagogical question in general education, which is how students can become aware of the things in the various regions of the world by using these words. In any case, it is the words that house the factual and conceptual components of the ACTS and disciplines that enable the teacher to talk with students in disciplined ways and exercise their pedagogical responsibility for opening the things of the region to students.

The question of how the teacher's words can disclose things in the world, however, is much too general. This can be seen in Greene's example of the Civil War and the observation that her proposal is not applicable to physics (or other domains), where the necessity of beginning with an exploration of the student's inner horizons is not obvious. The reason is that physical and historical phenomena have very different kinds of characteristics. The methods for becoming aware of them vary accordingly. Because this is true for all the regions of the world and all the disciplines, the epistemic characteristics of good knowledge should vary according to the essential characteristics of the fundamental phenomena of the respective region. To ascertain how students can become aware of the things in a particular region of the world therefore requires *domain-specific* research.

This research should discover the precise relations of perceptual to conceptual consciousness of things in a specific domain. The techniques, methods, and canons of inquiry for insuring that the perceptual and conceptual components of knowledge interact in the disclosure of truth should vary according to the characteristics of the phenomena in a domain. The knowledge in some domains is consequently more perceptual; and in others, more conceptual. Things are even more complex than this, however, as can be shown in Greene's example. The exploration of the inner horizons in preparation for the study of the Civil War should be very different from the preparatory exploration for the American Revolutionary War and World War II. These wars are very different kinds of phenomena with very different characteristics of which the student should become aware. In other words, *lesson-specific* phenomenological research is needed to determine how much the inner horizons need to be explored in relation to the particular topic to free students for the praxis of genuine investigation. It is also needed to determine the kinds of perceptual and conceptual materials necessary to disclose to students the things at the center of the lesson.

The kind of research needed for a grounded pedagogy, then, is similar to that which should be undertaken by the basic theorists in each domain. It should be phenomenological research that establishes how qualified investigators become aware of the essential characteristics of the phenomena distinctive to a specific domain. This involves the establishment of basic perceptual and conceptual schemata in the formulation of a regional ontology (Husserl, 1913/1952, pp. 411–412; Heidegger, 1927/1962, pp. 30–31, 408–415). The pedagogical significance of how consciousness in general constitutes its objects in general is limited. Whether it is oppressed or not, this consciousness is the uneducated, common-sense consciousness of the everyday world, precisely what all education tries to transcend. Nor is it of general pedagogic significance, *pace* Freire, to know how the oppressed consciousness can be liberated to constitute its objects freely. This is the proper concern for a kind of remedial education that is appropriate for some people in some classrooms as a kind of special education that should be preceded by an adequate diagnosis of its necessity.

What is pedagogically important for general education is the development of consciousness of things in the world structured by the refined schemata of the ACTS and disciplines. This requires domain-specific phenomenological research to answer the following kinds of questions: How can one become aware of historical events that no longer exist? How can one become aware of physical objects or events the way physicists see them (cf. Arons, 1982; Striley, 1988)? How can classroom and laboratory learning coalesce to enable a consciousness of chemical things and events? What is the role of field and laboratory experience in becoming aware of living things the way biologists see them? How can one become aware of the ongoing historical reality of social, legal, and political institutions? Of economic things such as the market, inflation, unemployment, and primary industries? Of love, anguish, and victory as seen by poets and dramatists? Of human aspirations and tragedies as depicted in *belles lettres*? How can one become aware of mathematical objects?

These kinds of questions should be investigated in each of the major regions of the world that should be explored in common, general education, that is, in the manipulable and play worlds; in the natural, societal, and lived worlds; and in the worlds of reading and mathematics. Because these categories concern distinct regions of the world and particular modes of access to the things located within them, they involve various modes of knowing that nurture specific, embodied, intellectual powers as their schemata come to structure the consciousness of the things in the region through disciplined study (as in Peters, Hirst). It is not the aim of common, general education to develop these modes of intelligence as such, however, except as this happens concomitantly with the establishment of equal access to the things in the world, for it is this that provides, to the extent that it is educationally possible, the equal access to the home in the world that is everyone's human right.

To avoid reifying modes of knowing, which do not exist apart from what is known, this phenomenological research should focus on the most important things within each of the major regions and on the way in which perceptual and conceptual consciousness of them should coincide in the dialogue needed to promote their disciplined study. This does not necessarily have to replicate the standard patterns of the logic of the discovery of new knowledge in the respective domain. It also needs to be supplemented from the pedagogical side. Because the precise relation between perceptual and conceptual consciousness of something is not merely domain-specific but also lesson-specific, depending upon the students' experiential backgrounds and the way in which a specific teacher can open things up, there should also be phenomenological research conducted within pedagogy itself. This should begin with some fact, concept, theory, issue, or phenomenon in the curriculum and investigate the ways in which students can become aware of the corresponding thing in the world. This should begin with the pretheoretical understanding of the teacher who has learned through experience (1) how students are enabled to become aware of the objects in the particular region of the world and (2) how to explicate the constitution of the object from the learner's perspective. Such explication should involve the conceptual schemata of the respective art, craft, trade, sport, or discipline, but only as they become transformed pedagogically. Because domain- and lesson-specific research requires expertise in the respective domain of knowledge and its pedagogy in the elementary and secondary schools, the present investigation can proceed no further.

CONCLUSION

There are a number of things this chapter on knowledge in pedagogy does not attempt to do. It does not attempt to supply a magical formula, such as Dewey's method of reflective experience or Herbart's formal steps of instruction. Such methods are based on ideologies of knowledge that omit domain-specific considerations and distort the content of instruction in seriously miseducative ways. It does not

furnish a model of thinking because thinking is always thinking of
something. Whatever it is about has already been investigated and
thought about in one of the ACTS or disciplines. Students should learn
what is already known about things so they can employ the conceptual
schemata of the appropriate ACTS or disciplines and have something to
think with, that is, with which to structure their conceptual consciousness of the thing. There is no reference to brain research, for if there is
a relation between the hemispheres of the brain and the perceptual and
conceptual aspects of knowledge, both aspects are needed in all domains. If some domains are more perceptual and others more conceptual, their pedagogies should reflect these epistemic characteristics.
The appropriate hemispheres of the brain can be assumed to be involved.

There is in this chapter no use of cognitive science to develop a
model for use in all domains, for such a model necessarily abstracts
from domain-specific considerations in search of the Golden Fleece.
Such a model is therefore necessarily not about the cognitive structures
actually involved in knowing something, which is always knowledge
about some specific region of the world with its own characteristics.
E. D. Hirsch (1987) is phenomenologically correct when he denies that
there are any transferable cognitive skills. He even claims that "all
cognitive skills depend on procedural and substantive schemata that are
highly specific to the task at hand" (pp. 60–61; also see Ennis, 1989;
Foucault, 1969/1972; and Perkins & Salomon, 1989). He has to be
correct because the belief in transferable cognitive skills presupposes
faculty psychology and mental discipline, which are no longer meta-
physically tenable. It matters little whether these models are proffered
by philosophers, brain researchers, or cognitive scientists; or whether
they are advocated by genuine theorists who are honestly wrestling
with the problems of education or by misguided idealists, ambitious
entrepreneurs, or outright charlatans. In any case, they are both symptoms and causes of intellectual nihilism. Their use in pedagogy distracts
attention from learning about things in the world and is therefore
inimical to the co-intentional dialogue about the things in the world, to
truthful disclosure of these things, and to the students' search for truth
and being.

Greene's central pedagogic principle, however, is supported. The
idea of exploring the students' inner horizons at the beginning of each
unit of instruction, thereby enabling praxis, parallels Dewey's beginning a learning episode with the sense of a problem and Herbart's first
step of preparation as well as Whitehead's stage of romance. It allows
for the transition from the perceptual world to the horizons within a

domain to acquire its knowledge in domain-specific ways. The acceptance of the principle is qualified, however, by broadening it to allow for the modification of the exploration of the inner horizons to fit domain-specific characteristics of knowledge, particularly the relation between perceptual and conceptual consciousness. The acceptable principle is that the teacher should begin with whatever perceptual awareness of the thing to be studied that the pupils already possess or can be induced to have, and then build up its conceptual understanding by involving the conceptual schemata from the relevant ACTS or discipline to let the thing be studied in a disciplined manner.

This pedagogy is based on the interpretation of the Enlightenment heritage that the basic role of the schools is to enable the young to learn about things in the world and come to be at home in the world. The emphasis on knowing about things is not a retreat to factual knowledge, propositional knowledge, or "knowing that," each of which can result in verbal memorizing. It does not involve "teaching the" or "teaching that," but teaching about things in order to promote learning about things in the world, which is what most people believe schools are for. Very complicated conceptual schemata can be required to disclose the truth about things (e.g., the viscosity of water). The concern, moreover, is not for knowing facts about the world for the sake of knowing facts. That would involve the replicative use of schooling. The concern is for the interpretive use of knowledge, for how learning about things in school will be used tacitly in adult life. Some evidence for this is in the different vocabularies of educated people. One's reading vocabulary is larger than one's listening vocabulary, which is larger than one's writing vocabulary, which is larger than one's speaking vocabulary. One can read and listen to things with understanding that one cannot replicate in one's writing or speaking because of the tacit knowledge involved in the allusionary base, or "the complex of images, concepts, memories of all sorts available to provide meaning to words and events" (Broudy, 1988, p. 65). The knowledge about things comprising general education should not be learned for replication but for recognition. It should serve as the shared background information that Hirsch (1987) calls *cultural literacy* (chap. 2) and that makes it possible to feel at home in a pluralistic, urbanized society.

The elucidation of the teacher as a witness to the truth within the framework of co-intentional dialogue is midway between inquiry and didactic pedagogies, either of which might be employed by such a witness. It articulates what Buber (1926/1965a) seems to mean when he says the effective world should be "concentrated and manifested in the educator" and that it is the world that educates the person (p. 89).

Nor is the emphasis upon knowledge about the world as conservative as it may seem, for it is an attempt to formulate a program of common, general education that is the human right of all students. It articulates what Freire (1968/1970) seems to mean when he says that pedagogic dialogue should be mediated by cognizable objects (pp. 67f.) by establishing a macrocosmic framework for the kinds of cognizable objects that belong in the curriculum when education is understood to be a human right. An adequate assessment of whether the concern for knowledge about things in the world and the teacher as a witness is progressive or conservative, or whether this matters at all, should measure the syntheses provided in Chapters 4, 5, 9, and 10 by the ideals of the Enlightenment and by the criteria for schooling inherent in these 1934 words of Dewey's (1934/1966):

> Ours is the responsibility of conserving, transmitting, rectifying, and expanding the heritage of values we have received that those who come after us may receive it more solid and secure, more widely accessible and more generously shared than we have received it. (p. 87)

References

Adler, M. J. (1982). *The paideia proposal: An educational manifesto.* New York: Macmillan.

Apple, M. W. (1987). [Review of D. F. Walker & J. F. Soltis, *Curriculum and aims.*] *Teachers College Record, 88,* 598–603.

Apple, M. W. (1988). Social crisis and curriculum accords. *Educational Theory, 38,* 191–201.

Arons, A. B. (1982). Phenomenology and logical reasoning in introductory physics courses. *American Journal of Physics, 50*(11), 13–20.

Bacon, F. (1939a). The great instauration. In E. A. Burtt (Ed.), *The English philosophers from Bacon to Mill* (pp. 5–27). New York: Random House. (Original work published 1605)

Bacon, F. (1939b). Novum organum. In E. A. Burtt (Ed.), *The English philosophers from Bacon to Mill* (pp. 28–123). New York: Random House. (Original work published 1620)

Belenky, M. F., Clinchy, B. M., Goldberger, N. R., & Tarule, J. M. (1986). *Women's ways of knowing.* New York: Basic Books.

Bell, D. (1974). *The coming of the post-industrial society.* New York: Basic Books.

Bell, D. (1976). *The cultural contradictions of capitalism.* New York: Basic Books.

Benn, S. (1981). Human rights and human nature. In A. E. Tay (Ed.), *Teaching human rights* (pp. 103–109). Canberra: Australian Government Printing Service.

Bennett, B. J. (1989). Representation and reality in quantum mechanics. *Journal of Speculative Philosophy, 3,* 67–85.

Bentham, J. (1939). An introduction to the principles of morals and legislation. In E. A. Burtt (Ed.), *The English philosophers from Bacon to Mill* (pp. 791–852). New York: Random House. (Original work published 1789)

Berger, P. L., Berger, B., & Kellner, H. (1981). *The homeless mind: Modernization and consciousness.* New York: Penguin. (Original work published 1973)

Bernstein, R. T. (1983). *Beyond objectivism and relativism: Science, hermeneutics, and praxis.* Oxford: Basil Blackwell.

Blackstone, W. (1970). Human rights and dignity. In R. Gotesky & E. Laszlo (Eds.), *Human dignity, this century and the next* (pp. 3–37). New York: Gordon & Breach.

Blackstone, W. (1974). Ethics and ecology. In W. Blackstone (Ed.), *Philosophy and environmental crisis* (pp. 16–43). Athens: University of Georgia Press.

Bloch, E. (1986). *Natural law and human dignity* (D. J. Schmidt, Trans.). Cambridge, MA: MIT Press. (Original work published 1961)

Bloom, A. (1987). *The closing of the American mind*. New York: Simon & Schuster.

Bode, B. H. (1938). *Progressive education at the crossroads*. New York: Newson.

Bollnow, O. F. (1989). The pedagogic atmosphere: The perspective of the child (M. van Manen and P. Mueller, Eds. & Trans.). *Phenomenology & Pedagogy, 7*, 12–36. (Original work published 1968)

Bowles, G. (1984). The use of hermeneutics for feminist scholarship. *Women's Studies International Forum, 7*, 185–188.

Brady, L. (1975a). *Do we dare: A dilemmas approach to moral development*. Sydney: Dymocks.

Brady, L. (1975b). *Values—taught or caught: Personal development for secondary schools*. Sydney: Dymocks.

Brameld, T. (1965). *Education for the emerging age: Newer ends and stronger means*. New York: Harper & Row.

Brinton, C. (1967). Enlightenment. In P. Edwards (Ed.), *The encyclopedia of philosophy* (Vol. 2, pp. 518–525). New York: Macmillan.

Broudy, H. S. (1976). Science, technology, and the diminished mind. *Journal of College Science Teaching, 5*, 292–296.

Broudy, H. S. (1977). Criteria for a humane society. *Educational Studies, 8*, 37–50.

Broudy, H. S. (1988). *The uses of schooling*. New York: Routledge.

Broudy, H. S., Parsons, M. J., Snook, I. A., & Szoke, R. D. (1967). *Philosophy of education: An organization of topics and selected sources*. Urbana: University of Illinois Press.

Broudy, H. S., Smith, B. O., & Burnett, J. R. (1964). *Democracy and excellence in American secondary education*. Chicago: Rand McNally.

Buber, M. (1956a). The man of today and the Jewish Bible (O. Marx, Trans.). In W. Herberg (Ed.), *The writings of Martin Buber* (pp. 239–250). New York: Meridian. (Original work published 1936)

Buber, M. (1956b). Teaching and deed (O. Marx, Trans.). In W. Herberg (Ed.), *The writings of Martin Buber* (pp. 317–324). New York: Meridian. (Original work published 1936)

Buber, M. (1965a). Education. In R. G. Smith (Ed. & Trans.), *Between man and man* (pp. 83–103). New York: Macmillan. (Original work published 1926)

Buber, M. (1965b). The education of character. In R. G. Smith (Ed. & Trans.), *Between man and man* (pp. 104–117). New York: Macmillan. (Original work published 1939)

Buber, M. (1965c). Elements of the interhuman. In M. Friedman & R. G. Smith (Eds. & Trans.), *The knowledge of man* (pp. 72–88). New York: Harper & Row. (Original work published 1957)

Burnett, J. R. (1988). Dewey's educational thought and his mature philosophy. *Educational Theory, 38*, 203–213.

Caputo, J. (1987). *Radical hermeneutics: Repetition, deconstruction, and the hermeneutic project.* Bloomington: Indiana University Press.

Cassirer, E. (1961). *The philosophy of the Enlightenment* (F. C. A. Koelln & J. P. Pettegrove, Trans.). Boston: Beacon. (Original work published 1932)

Concise Oxford dictionary (6th Ed.). (1976). Oxford, England: Clarenden Press.

Crittenden, B. (1973). *Education and social ideals: A study in philosophy of education.* Don Mills, Ont.: Longmans Canada.

Crittenden, B. (1981). *Education for rational understanding: Philosophical perspectives in the study and practice of education.* Hawthorn: Australian Council for Educational Research.

Degenhardt, M. A. B. (1982). *Education and the value of knowledge.* London: Allen & Unwin.

Descartes, R. (1931). *Rules for the direction of the mind.* In E. Haldane & G. R. T. Ross (Eds. & Trans.), *The philosophical works of Descartes* (pp. 1–77). Cambridge, England: Cambridge University Press. (Original work published 1628)

Desmond, W. (1988). Philosophy and failure. *Journal of Speculative Philosophy, 2*, 288–305.

Dewey, J. (1916). *Democracy and education.* New York: Macmillan.

Dewey, J. (1938). *Experience and education.* New York: Macmillan.

Dewey, J. (1939). *Theory of valuation.* Chicago: University of Chicago Press.

Dewey, J. (1960). *The quest for certainty.* New York: Putnams. (Original work published 1929)

Dewey, J. (1961). *Philosophy of education (Problems of men).* Paterson, NJ: Littlefield, Adams. (Original work published 1948)

Dewey, J. (1966). *A common faith.* New Haven: Yale University Press. (Original work published 1934)

Dreyfus, H. L. (1981). Knowledge and human values: A genealogy of nihilism. *Teachers College Record, 82*, 507–520.

Edel, A. (1969). Humanistic ethics and the meaning of human dignity. In P. Kurtz (Ed.), *Problems in contemporary society: Essays in humanistic ethics* (pp. 227–240). Englewood Cliffs, NJ: Prentice-Hall.

Eliade, M. (1968). *Myths, dreams, and mysteries: The encounter between contemporary faiths and archaic reality* (P. Mairet, Trans.). London: Collins.

Eliade, M. (1969). *The quest: History and meaning in religion.* Chicago: University of Chicago Press.

Ennis, R. H. (1989). Critical thinking and subject specificity: Clarification and needed research. *Educational Researcher, 18*(3), 4–10.

Foucault, M. (1972). *The archaeology of knowledge* (A. M. Sheridan Smith, Trans.). New York: Pantheon. (Original work published 1969)

Frankena, W. (1966). Toward a philosophy of moral education. In I. Scheffler (Ed.), *Philosophy and education* (2nd Ed., pp. 225–244). Boston: Allyn & Bacon.

Freire, P. (1970). *Pedagogy of the oppressed* (M. B. Ramos, Trans.). New York: Herder & Herder. (Original work published 1968)

Freire, P. (1973a). Education as the practice of freedom (M. B. Ramos, Trans.). In *Education for critical consciousness* (pp. 1–84). London: Sheed and Ward. (Original work published 1967)

Freire, P. (1973b). Extension or communication (L. Bigwood & M. Marshall, Trans.). In *Education for critical consciousness* (pp. 93–164). London: Sheed & Ward. (Original work published 1969)

Freire, P. (1985a). Education, liberation, and the church (W. Bloom, Trans.). In D. Macedo (Ed.), *The politics of education: Culture, power, and liberation* (pp. 121–142). South Hadley, MA: Bergin & Garvey. (Original work published 1973)

Freire, P. (1985b). *The politics of education: Culture, power, and liberation* (D. Macedo, Trans.). South Hadley, MA: Bergin & Garvey.

Freire, P., & Shor, I. (1987). *A pedagogy for liberation: Dialogues on transforming education.* South Hadley, MA: Bergin & Garvey.

French, M. (1985). *Beyond power: On women, men, and morals.* London: Cape.

Gadamer, H. G. (1975). *Truth and method* (W. Glen-Doepel, Trans.). London: Sheed & Ward. (Original work published 1960)

Gadamer, H. G. (1985). On the origins of philosophical hermeneutics. In H. G. Gadamer, *Philosophical apprenticeships* (R. R. Sullivan, Trans.) (pp. 177–193). Cambridge: MIT Press. (Original work published 1977)

Gadamer, H. G. (1988). On the circle of understanding. In J. M. Connolly & T. Teutner (Eds. and Trans.), *Hermeneutics versus science? Three German views* (pp. 68–78). Notre Dame, IN: Notre Dame University Press. (Original work published 1959)

Gewirth, A. (1984). The epistemology of human rights. *Social philosophy and policy, 1*(2), 1–24.

Gilligan, C. (1982). *In a different voice.* Cambridge: Harvard University Press.

Götz, I. L. (1987). Camus and the art of teaching. *Educational Theory, 37,* 265–276.

Greene, M. (1972). Towards a reciprocity of perspectives. In M. A. Raywid (Ed.), *Philosophy of education, 1972* (pp. 275–284). Edwardsville, IL: Studies in Philosophy and Education.

Greene, M. (1973). *Teacher as stranger: Educational philosophy for the modern age.* Belmont, CA: Wadsworth.

Greene, M. (1974). Countering privatism. *Educational Theory, 24,* 209–218.

Greene, M. (1978). *Landscapes of learning.* New York: Teachers College Press.

Greene, M. (1986). In search of a critical pedagogy. *Harvard Educational Review, 56,* 427–441.

Greene, M. (1988). *The dialectic of freedom.* New York: Teachers College Press.

Guardini, R. (1959). *Die Lebensalter: Ihre ethische und pädagogische Bedeutung* [The stages of life: Their ethical and educational significance]. Wurzburg, Germany: Werkbund.

Habermas, J. (1971). *Toward a rational society* (J. Shapiro, Trans.). London: Heinemann. (Original work published 1968)

Hahn, G. L. (1987). The right to a political education. In N. B. Tarrow (Ed.), *Human rights and education* (pp. 173–187). New York: Pergamon.

Heidegger, M. (1958). *The question of being* (W. Kluback & J. T. Wilde, Trans.). New York: Twayne. (Original work published 1956)

Heidegger, M. (1962). *Being and time* (J. Macquarrie & E. Robinson, Trans.). New York: Harper & Row. (Original work published 1927)

Heidegger, M. (1977). On the essence of truth (J. Sollis, Trans.). In D. F. Krell (Ed.), *Martin Heidegger: Basic Writings* (pp. 117–141). New York: Harper & Row.

Heidel, A. (1967). *The Babylonian genesis: The story of creation.* Chicago: University of Chicago Press.

Henry, M. (1975). *Philosophy and phenomenology of the body* (G. Etzkorn, Trans.). The Hague: Martinus Nijhoff.

Hirsch, E. D. (1987). *Cultural literacy: What every American needs to know.* Boston: Houghton Mifflin.

Hirst, P. H. (1965). Liberal education and the nature of knowledge. In R. D. Archambault (Ed.), *Philosophical analysis and education* (pp. 113–138). New York: Humanities Press.

Hirst, P. H. (1974). *Knowledge and the curriculum.* London: Routledge & Kegan Paul.

Hirst, P. H. (1986). Richard Peters' contribution to the philosophy of education. In D. E. Cooper (Ed.), *Education, values, and mind: Essays for R. S. Peters* (pp. 8–40). London: Routledge & Kegan Paul.

Hirst, P. H., & Peters, R. S. (1970). *The logic of education.* London: Routledge & Kegan Paul.

Hobbes, T. (1839). *Elements of philosophy.* In W. Molesworth (Ed.), *The English works of Thomas Hobbes Volume 1.* London: John Bohn. (Original work published 1655)

Holy Bible (Revised Standard Version). (1952). New York: Thomas Nelson.

Hume, D. (1965). *A treatise of human nature* (L. A. Selby-Bigge, Ed.). Oxford: Clarendon Press. (Original work published 1739)

Husserl, E. (1952). *Ideas: General introduction to pure phenomenology* (W. R. B. Gibson, Trans.). London: Allen & Unwin. (Original work published 1913)

Husserl, E. (1970). *The crisis of European sciences and transcendental phenomenology* (D. Carr, Trans.). Evanston, IL: Northwestern University Press. (Original work published 1936)

Jagodzinski, J. (1988). Reawakening aesthetic insight. *Phenomenology & Pedagogy, 6,* 119–146.

James, W. (1958). *Talks to teachers on psychology, and to students on some of life's ideals.* New York: Norton. (Original work published 1899)

Kant, I. (1949). *Critique of practical reason and other writings in moral philosophy*

(L. W. Beck, Trans.). Chicago: University of Chicago Press. (Original work published 1788)

Kant, I. (1955). *The metaphysical elements of justice: Part I of the metaphysics of morals* (J. Ladd, Trans.). New York: Bobbs-Merrill. (Original work published 1797)

Kant, I. (1959). *Foundations of the metaphysics of morals* (L. W. Beck, Trans.). New York: Bobbs-Merrill. (Original work published 1785)

Kant, I. (1964). *The doctrine of virtue: Part II of the metaphysics of morals* (M. J. Gregor, Trans.). New York: Harper & Row. (Original work published 1797)

Kant, I. (1965). *Critique of pure reason* (N. K. Smith, Trans.). New York: St. Martins Press. (Original work published 1781)

Karier, C. J. (1987). Some reflections on the coming of American fascism. *Educational Theory, 37,* 251–263.

Kierkegaard, S. (1954). *Fear and trembling;* and *The sickness unto death* (W. Lowrie, Trans.). New York: Doubleday. (Original work published 1843 and 1849)

Kierkegaard, S. (1956). *Purity of heart is to will one thing* (D. V. Steere, Trans.). New York: Harper. (Original work published 1847)

Kierkegaard, S. (1957). *Attack upon Christendom* (W. Lowrie, Trans.). Boston: Beacon. (Original work published 1854–1855)

Kierkegaard, S. (1967). *Stages on life's way* (W. Lowrie, Trans.). New York: Schocken. (Original work published 1845)

Kierkegaard, S. (1971). *Concluding unscientific postscript* (D. F. Swenson & W. Lowrie, Trans.). Princeton, NJ: Princeton University Press. (Original work published 1846)

Kierkegaard, S. (1987a). *Either/or: Part I* (H. V. Hong & E. H. Hong, Trans.). Princeton, NJ: Princeton University Press. (Original work published 1843)

Kierkegaard, S. (1987b). *Either/or: Part II* (H. V. Hong & E. H. Hong, Trans.). Princeton, NJ: Princeton University Press. (Original work published 1843)

Kilpatrick, W. H. (1951). *Philosophy of education.* New York: Macmillan.

Kohlberg, L. (1976). The cognitive developmental approach to moral education. In D. Purpel & K. Ryan (Eds.), *Moral education: It comes with the territory* (pp. 176–195). Berkeley: McCutchan.

Kohlberg, L. (1984). *The psychology of moral development.* New York: Harper & Row.

Kroll, F. R. (1988). From the inside out—personal history as educational research. *Educational Theory, 38,* 467–479.

Levin, D. W. (1985). *The body's recollection of being: Phenomenological psychology and deconstruction of nihilism.* London: Routledge & Kegan Paul.

Lingis, A. (1971). Intentionality and corporeity. In A. Tymieniecka (Ed.), *Analecta Husserliana: The yearbook of phenomenological research* (Vol. 1, pp. 75–90). Dordrecht, Holland: Reidel.

Liston, D. (1988). Faith and evidence: Examining Marxists' explanations of schools. *American Journal of Education, 96,* 323–350.

Locke, J. (1939). An essay concerning human understanding. In E. A. Burtt (Ed.), *The English philosophers from Bacon to Mill* (pp. 238–402). New York: Random House. (Original work published 1689)

Marcel, G. (1964). Testimony and existentialism. In M. Harari (Trans.), *The philosophy of existentialism* (pp. 91–103). New York: Citadel. (Original work published 1946)

Marcel, G. (1972). Human dignity. In H. Y. Jung (Ed.), *Existential phenomenology and political theory* (pp. 294–315). Chicago: Regnery. (Original work published 1963)

Maritain, J. (1960). *Education at the crossroads.* New Haven: Yale University Press. (Original work published 1943)

Martin, J. R. (1981). Needed: A new paradigm for liberal education. In J. F. Soltis (Ed.), *Philosophy and education* (pp. 37–59). Chicago: University of Chicago Press.

Marx, K. (1967). The Jewish question. In L. D. Easton & K. H. Guddat (Eds. & Trans.), *Writings of the young Marx on philosophy and society* (pp. 216–241). Garden City, NY: Doubleday. (Original work published 1843)

McClosky, H. J. (1981). What ought to be taught about human rights. In A. E. Tay (Ed.), *Teaching human rights* (pp. 83–93). Canberra: Australian Government Printing Service.

Melden, A. (1977). *Rights and persons.* Oxford, England: Blackwell.

Merleau-Ponty, M. (1962). *Phenomenology of perception* (C. Smith, Trans.). London: Routledge & Kegan Paul. (Original work published 1945)

Merleau-Ponty, M. (1964). The child's relations with others (W. Cobb, Trans.). In J. M. Edie (Ed.), *The primacy of perception and other essays* (pp. 96–155). Evanston, IL: Northwestern University Press. (Original work published 1960)

Mill, J. S. (1939a). On liberty. In E. A. Burtt (Ed.), *The English philosophers from Bacon to Mill* (pp. 947–1041). New York: Random House. (Original work published 1859)

Mill, J. S. (1939b). Utilitarianism. In E. A. Burtt (Ed.), *The English philosophers from Bacon to Mill* (pp. 895–948). New York: Random House. (Original work published 1863)

Moore, G. E. (1966). *Principia ethica.* Cambridge, England: Cambridge University Press. (Original work published 1903)

Nabert, J. (1969). *Elements for an ethic* (W. Petrak, Trans.). Evanston, IL: Northwestern University Press. (Original work published 1943)

Naisbitt, J. (1984). *Megatrends.* New York: Warner.

Neill, A. S. (1960). *Summerhill: A radical approach to child rearing.* New York: Hart.

Nelson, L. (1956). *System of ethics* (N. Guterman, Trans.). New Haven: Yale University Press. (Original work published 1932)

Nietzsche, F. n.d. *Thus spoke Zarathustra* (T. Common, Trans.). New York: Random House. (Original work published 1885)

Noddings, N. (1984). *Caring: A feminine approach to ethics and moral education.* Berkeley: University of California Press.

O'Hear, A. (1981). *Education, society, and human nature: An introduction to the philosophy of education.* London: Routledge & Kegan Paul.

Olson, R. (1967a). Nihilism. In P. Edwards (Ed.), *The encyclopedia of philosophy* (Vol. 5, pp. 515–517). New York: Macmillan.

Olson, R. (1967b). Teleological ethics. In P. Edwards (Ed.), *The encyclopedia of philosophy* (Vol. 8, p. 88). New York: Macmillan.

Ortega y Gasset, J. (1957). *Man and people* (W. R. Trask, Trans.). New York: Norton.

Ortega y Gasset, J. (1958). *Man and crisis* (M. Adams, Trans.). New York: Norton. (Original work published 1933)

Packer, M. J. (1985). Hermeneutical inquiry in the study of human conduct. *American Psychologist, 40,* 1081–1093.

Passmore, J. (1980). *The philosophy of teaching.* London: Duckworth.

Peirce, C. S. (1958a). Critical review of Berkeley's idealism. In P. P. Wiener (Ed.), *Values in a universe of chance: Selected writings of Charles S. Peirce* (pp. 73–88). Garden City, NY: Doubleday. (Original work published 1871)

Peirce, C. S. (1958b). How to make our ideas clear. In P. P. Wiener (Ed.), *Values in a universe of chance: Selected writings of Charles S. Peirce* (pp. 113–136). Garden City, NY: Doubleday. (Original work published 1878)

Peirce, C. S. (1958c). *Science and philosophy: Collected papers of Charles Sanders Peirce, Volume VII.* Cambridge: Harvard University Press.

Peirce, C. S. (1958d). Some consequences of four incapacities. In P. P. Wiener (Ed.), *Values in a universe of chance: Selected writings of Charles S. Peirce* (pp. 39–72). Garden City, NY: Doubleday. (Original work published 1868)

Perkins, D. N., & Salomon, G. (1989). Are cognitive skills context-bound? *Educational Researcher, 18*(1), 16–25.

Peters, R. S. (1964). *Education as initiation.* London: University of London Institute of Education.

Peters, R. S. (1966). *Ethics and education.* London: Allen & Unwin.

Peters, R. S. (1977). *Education and the education of teachers.* London: Routledge & Kegan Paul.

Piaget, J. (1965). *Logic and psychology.* Manchester, England: Manchester University Press. (Original work published 1953)

Plato. (1974). *The republic* (D. Lee, Trans.). Middlesex, England: Penguin. (Original work published c. 375 B.C.E.)

Prichard, H. A. (1955). Does moral philosophy rest on a mistake? In A. I. Melden (Ed.), *Ethical theories* (pp. 469–481). Englewood Cliffs, NJ: Prentice-Hall. (Original work published 1912)

Purpel, D. E. (1989). *The moral and spiritual crisis in education. A curriculum for justice and compassion in education.* Granby, MA: Bergin & Garvey.

Raths, L. E., Harmin, M., & Simon, S. B. (1966). *Values and teaching: Working with values in the classroom.* Columbus: Merrill.

Raywid, M. A. (1973). The politicalization of education. *Educational Theory,* 23, 119–132.

Reich, C. A. (1970). *The greening of America.* New York: Random House.

Ricoeur, P. (1965). *Fallible man* (C. Kelbley, Trans.). Chicago: Regnery. (Original work published 1960)

Ricoeur, P. (1981). *Hermeneutics and the human sciences: Essays on language, actions and interpretation* (J. B. Thompson, Trans.). New York: Cambridge University Press.

Rochowiak, D. (1988). Extensibility and completeness: An essay on scientific reasoning. *Journal of Speculative Philosophy,* 2, 241–266.

Rosen, S. (1969). *Nihilism: A philosophical essay.* New Haven: Yale University Press.

Rosenthal, S. B. (1988). Third alternative: Speculative pragmatism. *Journal of Speculative Philosophy,* 2, 312–317.

Ross, W. D. (1930). *The right and the good.* Oxford, England: Clarendon Press.

Rousseau, J. (1966). *Emile* (B. Foxley, Trans.). New York: Dutton. (Original work published 1762)

Russell, B. (1918). The place of science in a liberal education. In *Mysticism and logic* (pp. 33–45). London: Longmans, Green.

Russell, B. (1984). *A history of western philosophy* (2nd ed.). London: Allen & Unwin. (Original work published 1946)

Ryle, G. (1949). *The concept of mind.* New York: Barnes & Noble.

Sartre, J. P. (1956). *Being and nothingness: An essay in phenomenological ontology* (H. E. Barnes, Trans.). New York: Philosophical Library. (Original work published 1943)

Scheffler, I. (1960). *The language of education.* Springfield, IL: Charles C Thomas.

Schneider, P. (1967). Social rights and the concept of human rights. In D. D. Raphael (Ed.), *Political theory and the rights of man* (pp. 81–94). London: Macmillan.

Schutz, A., & Luckman, T. (1974). *The structures of the life-world* (R. M. Zaner & H. T. Engelhardt, Jr., Trans.). London: Heinemann.

Schweitzer, A. (1956). *The quest of the historical Jesus.* London: Black.

Scudder, J. R., & Mickunas, A. (1985). *Meaning, dialogue, and enculturation: Phenomenological philosophy of education.* Lanham: University Press of America.

Seguin, C. (1965). *Love and psychotherapy.* New York: Libra.

Shafer, S. M. (1987). Human rights in schools. In N. R. Tarrow (Ed.), *Human rights and education* (pp. 191–205). New York: Pergamon.

Simon, S. R., Howe, L. W., & Kirschenbaum, H. (1972). *Values clarification: A handbook of practical strategies for teachers and students.* New York: Hart.

Skinner, B. F. (1948). *Walden two.* New York: Macmillan.

Smith, B. O. (1945). The normative unit of instruction. *Teachers College Record,* 45, 219–229.

Smith, B. O., & Ennis, R. H. (Eds.). (1961). *Language and concepts in education: Analytic study of educational ideas.* Chicago: Rand McNally.

Sollberger, E. (1971). *The Babylonian legend of the flood.* London: British Museum.

Soltis, J. F. (1969). On defining education: An apology. In D. Arnstine (Ed.), *Philosophy of education, 1969* (pp. 172–176). Edwardsville, IL: Studies in Philosophy and Education.

Soltis, J. F. (1971). Analysis and anomalies in philosophy of education. In R. D. Heslep (Ed.), *Philosophy of education, 1971* (pp. 28–46). Edwardsville, IL: Studies in Philosophy and Education.

Soltis, J. F. (1985). Logic and languages of pedagogical research. In E. E. Robertson (Ed.), *Philosophy of education, 1984* (pp. 273–282). Normal, IL: Philosophy of Education Society.

Spencer, H. (1963). *Education: Intellectual, moral, and physical.* Paterson, NJ: Littlefield, Adams. (Original work published 1860)

Spiegelberg, H. (1970). Human dignity: A challenge to contemporary philosophy. In R. Gotesky & E. Laszlo (Eds.), *Human dignity, this century and the next* (pp. 39–63). New York: Gordon & Breach.

Striley, J. (1988). Physics for the rest of us. *Educational Researcher, 17*(6), 7–10.

Taylor, C. (1987). Overcoming epistemology. In K. Baynes, J. Bohman, & T. McCarthy (Eds.), *After philosophy: End or transformation?* (pp. 464–488). Cambridge, MA: MIT Press.

Taylor, P. W. (1986). *Respect for nature: A theory of environmental ethics.* Princeton, NJ: Princeton University Press.

Toulmin, S. (1985). *The return to cosmology: Postmodern science and theology of nature.* Berkeley: University of California Press.

UNESCO. (1959). Two versions of the Universal Declaration of Human Rights prepared by school pupils. In *Education for international understanding: Examples and suggestions for class-room use* (pp. 106–108). Paris: Author.

UNESCO. (1986). *Philosophical foundations of human rights.* Paris: Author.

Vandenberg, D. (1969). Non-violent power in education. *Educational Theory, 19,* 49–57.

Vandenberg, D. (1971). *Being and education: An essay in existential phenomenology.* Englewood Cliffs, NJ: Prentice-Hall.

Vandenberg, D. (1974). Phenomenology and educational research. In D. E. Denton (Ed.), *Existentialism and phenomenology in education: Collected essays* (pp. 183–220). New York: Teachers College Press.

Vandenberg, D. (1980). Education or experience? *Educational Theory, 30,* 235–251.

Vandenberg, D. (1983). *Human rights in education.* New York: Philosophical Library.

Vandenberg, D. (1984a). Charlatans, knowledge, curriculum, and phenomenological research. In R. E. Roemer (Ed.), *Philosophy of Education, 1983* (pp. 201–211). Normal: Illinois State University Press.

Vandenberg, D. (1984b). Human rights in the curriculum. In *The teaching of human rights: Proceedings of the conference held by the Human Rights Commission and UNESCO* (pp. 28–41). Canberra: Australian Government Printing Service. Also in *Educational Research and Perspectives, 11*, 85–91.

Vandenberg, D. (1986). Human dignity, three human rights, and pedagogy. *Educational Theory, 36*, 33–44.

Vandenberg, D. (1987a). Education and the religious. *Teachers College Record, 89*, 69–90.

Vandenberg, D. (1987b). Interpretive, normative theory of education. *Educational Philosophy and Theory, 19*(1), 1–11.

Vandenberg, D. (1988). Knowledge in schooling. *Phenomenology & Pedagogy, 6*, 63–78.

Van Manen, M. (1984). Practicing phenomenological writing. *Phenomenology & Pedagogy, 2*, 36–69.

Veblen, T. (1943). *The theory of the leisure class.* New York: Viking. (Original work published 1899)

Waks, L. J. (1988). Three contexts of philosophy of education: Intellectual, institutional, and ideological. *Educational Theory, 38*, 167–174.

Weaver, J. F. (1972). Crisis as a coercive metaphor. In M. A. Raywid (Ed.), *Philosophy of education, 1972* (pp. 84–91). Edwardsville, IL: Studies in Philosophy and Education.

Webster's new world dictionary of the American language (2nd College Ed.). (1974). New York: Collins & World.

Whitehead, A. N. (1954). *The aims of education and other essays.* New York: The New American Library. (Original work published 1929)

Zuurdeeg, W. (1958). *An analytic philosophy of religion.* Nashville: Abingdon Press.

Index

Abraham, 36, 39, 87, 195–198, 206, 209
ACTS, 132–134, 137, 181, 202, 218, 219, 237, 241
  and disciplines, 180, 219–220, 225, 226, 240, 242, 244, 245, 246, 247
  required, 203, 218, 220
Adler, Mortimer J., 178, 233
Agriculture, 169
Allusionary base, 172, 175, 247
Anarchism, 178
Anthropological claims, 223, 225, 226
Anthropology, 173
Apple, Michael, 128, 129
Aristotle, 177, 226
  influence on Peters, 157–158, 160–161
Arons, A. B., 244
Art, 146, 173, 185, 219
Art education, 173, 174
Astronomy, 173
Attunement, 199, 209
Autochthony, xii, 228

Bacon, Francis, 125, 130, 156
Basic concepts, 172
Being in the truth, 236, 238
Belenky, M. F., 162
Bell, Daniel, 134–135
Beneficence, 22, 25, 34, 48, 71, 81, 88, 111
Benn, S., 82
Bennett, B. J., 190
Bentham, Jeremy, 47–49, 51, 93, 143, 144, 156
  evaluated, 60, 65, 82
Berger, B., 200

Berger, P. L., 200
Berkeley, George, 156
Bernstein, Richard, 131, 144
Bill of Rights, 38, 113, 115
Binswanger, Ludwig, 199
Biology, 207, 235, 237
Blackstone, William, 68, 210
Bloch, Ernst, 82, 83
Bloom, Allan, xi, 8, 10, 116, 117
Bode, Boyd, 118
Bollnow, Otto F., 95, 205
Books, world of, 214–215
Bosanquet, Bernard, 156
Bowles, Gloria, 135, 136, 192
Brady, Laurie, 109
Brameld, Theodore, 118
Brinton, Crane, xi
Brotherly/sisterly love, 30, 61, 62, 80–82, 85, 86, 93, 110
Broudy, Harry S., 153, 171–176, 177, 178, 179–180, 181, 222, 247
  mentioned, 144, 188, 191, 207, 211, 212, 213, 214, 216, 217, 220, 221, 233, 241, 242, 247
Buber, Martin, 41, 42, 108, 116, 175, 247
  experiencing the other side, 87
  on revelation, 38
  on the teachings, 39, 40
Burnett, Joe R., 170, 171

Calvin, John, 224
Caputo, John, 65
Canons of inquiry, 132, 142, 152–153, 187, 213, 219, 232, 238, 240, 243
Cassirer, Ernst, 30
Choice, existential, 13, 16, 36–37

Civics, 212
Civil liberties, 78
Clinchy, B. M., 162
Cognitive science, 246
Comedy, 5, 145–146, 213, 223, 225, 226
Common world, 162, 163, 181, 199
Community of investigators, 131–132, 133, 155, 162, 219–220
Community of scholars under law, 32–34, 37, 42, 53, 85, 86–89, 91–92, 100, 101
Competitive classrooms, 103–104
Conceptual consciousness, 156, 184, 185, 243, 245, 246, 247
Conceptual schemata, 222, 229, 232, 241, 247
  as curriculum content, 163, 172, 246
Consciousness, 158. *See also* Conceptual consciousness; Perceptual consciousness
Connoisseurs, in Mill, 51, 52
Consensus of the learned, 175–176, 220
Constitution of objects, 189, 190, 230, 245
Cooperative classrooms, 100
Copernicus, 194
Cosmic homelessness, 200
Cosmic impiety, 231, 238, 240
Counterexamples, 23, 42–43, 77
Critical theorists, xi, 123
Crittenden, Brian, 216, 218
Cultural literacy, 247

Decalogue, 8, 38–39, 61–62
Declaration of Independence, 8, 20–21
Declaration of the Rights of Man, 82
Degenhardt, M. A. B., xii
Democratic ideals, 82, 83, 84–86, 115
Demoralization, 17
  of education, 89–90
  of Western civilization, 90
Deontology, 17, 19–20, 38–39, 64, 66, 87, 102, 103, 107, 149
  in education, 34, 35, 74, 114
  in teleological ethics, 49, 53, 56, 118
  mentioned, 45, 84, 146
Descartes, Rene, xi, 130, 156, 167, 179, 203

Desmond, W., 145
Develop self and others, 22, 25, 34, 41, 43, 71, 119, 225
Developmental studies, 173
Dewey, John, 8, 142, 177, 178, 181, 222, 223, 224
  cooperative classroom, 33, 93, 100
  embodiment, 201, 203, 204
  ethics of, 54–56, 58, 60, 117
  evaluation of, 125, 131–132, 134
  on philosophy of education, 153–154
  and the religious, 194–195, 197
  theory of knowledge of, 133, 134, 167–171, 245, 246, 248
  mentioned, 143, 144, 162, 184, 188, 191, 199, 207, 208, 211, 214, 216, 217, 220, 231, 232, 233, 234, 239, 241, 242
Dialogical relations
  with others, 73, 116, 184, 203
  between students, 86–87
  with things, 98, 199, 237–238
Dialogue, 15, 108, 230, 231, 246, 247
  with author of text, 144, 147
  disciplined, 229, 241, 242
Didactic pedagogy, 176, 185, 247
Diemar, Alwin, 115
Dilthey, Wilhelm, 143–144
Disclosure, 114, 180, 184–185, 190, 192, 193, 201, 203, 218, 219–220, 233, 235, 236–237, 238, 239–240, 243, 246
  attunement for, 194, 199
  countering nihilism, 108, 192–193
  by teachers, 98, 100, 116
  through texts, 145–146, 147, 215
Discovery learning, 165
Dissociation of sensibility, 71, 167
Distributive justice, 22, 31, 41
Domain-specific epistemology, 218, 243, 244–245
Dostoevsky, Fyodor, 6
Dreyfus, H. L., 43

Ecology, 173, 198–199, 206, 207, 208
Economics, 163, 187, 212, 219
Edel, Abraham, 76
Education, 3
  as a human right, xiii, 43, 51, 119–120, 137, 193, 216–220, 248

Egalitarianism, 26, 53, 127, 132
Eliade, Mercia, 198, 228
Embodiment of consciousness, 181, 201, 218
Empiricism, 57, 59, 155–156, 171, 191, 229, 232, 233
Enlightened self-interest, 48, 52, 82
Enlightenment, 125, 192, 248
  goal of, xi
  heritage, xi, xii, 115, 116, 144, 247
Ennis, Robert, 148, 246
Environmental ethics, 208–210
Equal consideration, 23, 84–85
Equal freedom, 27, 41
  as a human right, 79–80
  to learn, 80, 84
Esthetic phase, 35–36, 37
Esthetics, 158
Ethical phase, 17, 35, 36, 37
Ethics, as school subject, 158, 213
Exemplars, 173, 213
Existentialism, xii
Exodus, 38
Experiential vocabulary, 182

Fairness
  in classroom rules, 30, 44, 93
  in society, 174
Fallacy
  axiological, 59–60, 90, 140
  of composition, 130
  epistemological, 134
  genetic, 129, 161
  naturalistic, 56–58, 59, 65, 93
Feminine principle, 167
Fichte, Johann G., 156
Fine arts, 164, 176, 187, 213
Formal logic, 149, 158
Forms of knowledge, 158–160, 171
Foucault, Michel, 120, 141, 219, 246
Foundationalism, demise of, 156, 191, 193
Frankena, William, 115
Franklin, Benjamin, xi
Fraternity, 30, 31, 85, 127
Freedom
  equal, to learn, 34, 150
  laws of, for Kant, 24, 27
  of thought, speech, action, 78
Freire, Paulo, 179, 182–187, 193, 204, 237, 239, 248

  mentioned, 144, 188, 190, 191, 192, 207, 216, 217, 220, 225, 231, 233, 240, 241, 244
French, Marilyn, 161, 167, 173
Froebel, F. W., 142
Fundamentalism, 178
Fusion of science and technology, 170

Gadamer, Hans-Georg, 143, 144–146, 149, 152
Galileo, 194
Gardening, 169
Genesis, 195–197, 228
Geography, 169, 173, 219
Gewirth, Alan, 76
Gilligan, Carol, 110
God, death of, 5, 6, 197
Goldberger, N. R., 162
Good, usage of, 12–14, 17, 44–45, 56, 69–71
Goodness, experienced, 13, 23
Good will, 11, 31, 32, 81, 88, 117
Gotz, I., 151
Greek cosmology, 197
Greene, Maxine, xi, xii, 10, 104, 115, 146, 151, 187–188, 190–192, 193, 222, 225, 229–235, 243, 246
  mentioned, 144, 207, 214, 216, 217, 220, 221, 236, 241, 242
Group projects, 54–55, 86, 100, 168–169
Guardini, Romano, 98
Guthrie, Woody, 206, 209, 212

Habermas, Jurgen, 125–126
Hahn, G. L., 114
Hammurabi, Code of, 38, 61
Happiness, 21, 22, 24, 25, 48, 50, 51, 52–53, 63, 64, 65, 66, 82, 93, 118
Harmin, M., 104–105, 107, 112
Health, 163
Hedonism, 7, 45–47, 58, 62–63, 69, 70, 74, 90, 93, 140
  in childhood and youth, 16, 35
  the logic of, 53, 56
Hegel, Georg W. F., 156, 159
Heidegger, Martin, 36, 203
  and hermeneutics, 144, 146, 244
  on nihilism, xii, 43, 194, 199
  on truth, 192, 238

Heidel, A., 197
Henry, Michel, 189, 201, 202
Herbart, Johann F., 142, 245, 246
Hermeneutical circle, 144, 152, 175, 194
Hermeneutics, xii, 139, 141, 143–147,
    148, 149, 152–153, 155, 183, 213,
    214, 215, 216
Hirsch, E. D., 246, 247
Hirst, Paul, 158–159, 162, 167, 178,
    214, 222, 245
Historical consciousness, 211, 212
History, 146, 159, 162–163, 163–164,
    169, 173, 176, 178, 179, 211, 212,
    213, 219, 233–234, 235, 237,
    244–245
Hobbes, Thomas, 45, 100, 156
Home
    in advanced industrial society, 200,
        210, 211, 213, 214, 247
    on Earth, 181, 195, 196, 197,
        198–199, 200, 203, 210, 228
    in foreground, 203, 204, 205, 207
    in playworld, 201
    in teaching specialization, 98, 99, 236
    in universe, 3, 74, 92, 196–198, 203,
        209, 217, 242, 245, 246
Howe, L. W., 105–107, 113
Human dignity, 3, 11, 72, 75, 76, 84,
    85, 164, 178, 190, 199, 226, 228,
    229, 237
    as criterion of rightness, 26, 50, 51,
        65, 67–68, 73, 93, 102, 114,
        115–116, 117, 118
Humanities, 143, 145–146, 176, 199,
    213, 217–218, 244–245
Human rights
    covenants of United Nations, 39
    in Declaration of Independence, 21
    necessity to affirm them, 76
    See also Rights, human
Human sciences, 159
Hume, David, 71, 156
Humor, sense of, 223, 225, 226
Husserl, Edmund, 129, 160, 244
Hygiene, 163
Hymns of praise, 212

Ideological critique, xiii, 139, 147, 148
Ideology, bourgeois, 82, 83, 107, 128,
    187

Inquiry pedagogy, 247
Initiation, education as, 158, 159
Intentionality, 160, 183, 188, 189, 193,
    217, 231
Interpretive schema, 211–212, 218
Intuitionism, 20–23, 34, 40, 67, 69–71,
    87, 111, 141
    in hedonism, 45–46
    in Moore, 57
    mentioned, 28, 29, 31, 33, 42, 146

Jagodzinski, Jan, 204
James, William, 184
Jefferson, Thomas, xi, 20–21
Jesus, 60–62, 93, 187, 197
Justice, 117

Kant, Immanuel, xi, 24–27, 29, 30–31,
    32, 42
    categorical and hypothetical
        imperatives, 86, 102
    compared to others, 47, 52, 53, 58,
        73, 74
    duty to humanity in self, others,
        34, 35, 37, 67, 75, 88, 119,
        225
    good will, 81, 88
    on lying, 67
    mentioned, 28, 41, 65, 80, 86, 91, 92,
        93, 117, 118, 143, 144, 156, 159,
        178
Karier, Clarence, 8
Kellner, H., 200
Kierkegaard, Soren, 7, 42, 87, 88, 111,
    143, 152–153, 231, 237
    ethical phase, 117
    phases of existence, 35–37
    truth as appropriation, 231
Kilpatrick, William Heard, 19, 142
Kirschenbaum, H., 105–107, 113
Knowing about, 151, 163, 178,
    180–181, 193, 200, 207, 214, 215,
    246, 247, 248
Knowing how, 150, 168, 180
Knowing that, 150, 168, 180, 247
Knowing with, 119, 175, 180, 246
Knowledge, 133–134, 135, 136, 160,
    185, 187, 236–239, 242, 243
    applicative use, 163, 171, 172, 177,
        178

associative use, 172, 173, 175, 177, 178
diffusion of, xi
interpretive use, 163–164, 171, 172, 173, 175, 177, 178, 180, 208, 214, 247
for leisure, 164
in literature, 145, 146
propositional, 192–193, 229
recognitive use, 247
reification of, 128, 130–131, 193, 236–237, 242
replicative use, 171, 172, 173, 177, 178, 247
for vocational use, 163, 168, 169–170, 186
Kohlberg, Lawrence, 28–30, 41, 86, 109, 112, 113, 158
research limitations, 29, 110
Kroll, F. R., 143

Languages, 213, 219
Law, 31–32, 33, 40, 51, 61
role of, in values clarification, 108
Laws, just, 79–80, 84, 92
Learning, autonomy of, 64, 225–226
Lectures, 185
Leibniz, Gottfried W., 130, 156
Lesson-specific research, 243, 245
Levin, David, 198, 202, 203, 204
Leviticus, 61, 62, 170, 171
Liberal education, 176–177
Liberationism, 229, 233
Liberty, equality, and fraternity, 82, 83, 115, 174
Lingis, Alphonso, 189
Liston, D., 148
Literature, 145–146, 159, 164, 173, 176, 178, 187, 213–214, 219, 235, 237
Lived world, 212–214
Locke, John, 156, 167, 179, 181
Logocentrism, 42, 135, 179, 192

McKlosky, H. J., 75
Magellan, 194
Magna Carta, 214
Manipulable world, 201–203
Marcel, Gabriel, 68, 237
Maritain, Jacques, 83, 142

Markovic, Mihailo, 227
Martin, Jane Roland, 134, 161, 162
Marx, Karl, 82, 83, 198, 214
Masculine principle, 167
Mathematics, 123, 158, 163, 176, 178, 215–216
Matthew, 60–62
Melden, Abraham, 8
Meritocracy, 135
Merleau-Ponty, Maurice, 201, 202, 203, 206, 229
Mill, John Stuart, 8, 49–52, 56, 119, 212
compared to Moore, 60
qualitative distinctions among pleasures, 88, 93
on sense of dignity, 50, 67
as social philosophy, 65
mentioned, 117, 118, 143, 144, 156, 192
Montessori, Maria, 142
Moore, G. E., 56–60, 68, 69–70, 73, 143, 144, 149
on naturalistic fallacy, 93
Moral and civic education, 220
Moral agency, 21, 23, 24, 26, 37, 81, 85, 86, 88, 90, 92, 119, 120, 194, 227
as a human right, 74–77
Moral autonomy, 75
Moral community, 24, 65, 77, 86, 102–103
in counterculture, 32
in Kant, 26–27, 30–31
Moral dilemmas in learning human rights, 114
Moral good, 60
Morality delimited, 10–11, 26, 90
Moral law, 24, 32, 33
Moral sensibility, xii, 30, 31, 33, 43, 80, 87, 93, 114, 175, 214
absent in teleological ethics, 60, 64
developed in classrooms, 89
Moral training, 29, 33
Moses, 38, 61, 62, 93
Mother Earth, 198, 200, 206, 209, 212, 228
Multiple perspectives, xii, 146, 154, 190, 191, 232
Multipartisan classroom, 113

Nabert, Jean, 75, 88
Naisbitt, John, 34
Natural sciences, 123, 150, 159, 163,
    169, 172, 173, 187, 197, 199, 207,
    208, 217–218, 219, 244–245
Natural world, 201, 205–210
Nature mysticism, 209–210
Nature study, 169, 206
Neill, A. S., 46
Nelson, Leonard, 75
Newton, Isaac, xi, 214
Nietzsche, Friedrich, xii, 5, 6, 7, 10, 17
Nihilism, xii, 4–7, 8, 43, 126, 194, 198,
    203
    in educational literature, xiii, 107,
        118, 127–128, 181, 246
    in loss of truth, 4, 123, 137
    in moral relativism, 4, 7
    its educational overcoming, 17, 137,
        166, 192, 219, 238
    in teleological ethics, 60, 64, 90
Noddings, Nel, 62
Nonmaleficence, 22, 31, 39, 41, 71, 78,
    209
    in classrooms, 34, 92
    regarding things in nature, 71
Normative research, 139
Numbers, world of, 215–216

Oakeshott, Michael J., 159
Objectivity, phenomenological,
    174–175, 181, 190, 232
Object lesson, 165, 166, 183, 184, 204
Obligations, 11, 14, 20, 58, 60, 87, 90,
    92, 108, 117, 118, 242
    as concomitant learnings, 19, 33, 34,
        43, 44, 63–64, 84, 86, 87, 89,
        91–92, 99, 101
    to develop self and others, 43, 225
    disclosed conceptually in lessons,
        113, 114, 119, 208–209
    feelings of, 23, 24, 27, 39–40, 42, 43,
        50, 65, 68, 70, 71, 72, 81, 87, 90,
        102, 108, 117, 118–119, 167
    to natural world, 69, 70, 71, 167,
        208, 209, 210
    as prima facie duties, 22–23
    in teleological ethics, 44–45, 56, 60,
        90

O'Hear, Anthony, 178
Olson, R., 4, 44–45
Openness, 192, 197, 209, 220,
    227–228, 240
Ordinary language philosophy, 139
Ortega y Gasset, J., xi, 201
Outdoor education, 165, 166, 181, 206,
    209

Packer, M. J., 143
Paine, Thomas, xi
Passmore, John, 212
Patriarchy, 161, 167, 186, 198, 207
Pedagogic love, 86
Pedagogic relation, 91, 183–185
Peirce, Charles Sanders, 132, 133, 171,
    177, 219, 232
Perception, primacy of, 70, 217
Perceptual consciousness, 21, 34, 69,
    70, 73, 87, 105, 111, 156, 166, 182,
    184, 185, 201, 202, 203–204, 206,
    217–218, 220, 229, 235, 242, 243,
    245, 246, 247
Perceptual cultivation, 166, 174–175,
    179, 181
Perkins, D. N., 249
Pestalozzi, Johann H., 142, 165
Peters, R. S., 157–162, 167, 171, 175,
    176, 177, 178, 181
    compared to Dewey, 222, 223–224
    on moral training, 29, 100–101
    mentioned, 144, 166, 183, 188,
        191, 207, 212, 214, 217,
        220, 221, 232, 233, 241,
        242, 245
Phenomenology, xii, 139, 152, 160,
    188, 190, 216, 233, 244
Philosophy, 41, 42, 130, 132, 138–139,
    146, 151, 153, 154, 158, 159, 173,
    190, 213
Physicalism, 131
Physiology, 163
Piaget, Jean, 29, 183
Piety, 203, 208, 209
    cosmic, 195, 197, 199, 200
    natural, 194, 198–199, 242
Plato, 43, 53, 118, 134, 142, 145, 153,
    160, 177
Play world, 201, 204–205

Pleasure
  as concomitant of good, value, 13
  as goal of right action, 22, 45–50
  qualitatively different, 49–51, 67
Poetry, 213
Popper, Karl, 156, 159
Positivism and noncognitive values,
  4, 7
Postindustrial society, 134–135
Postmodernism, xi, 6, 123, 191
Pragmatism, 171, 191, 229, 232, 233
Praxis, 54, 72, 89, 183, 189, 217, 227,
  231, 243, 246
Prephilosophical understanding, 141,
  142, 146–147, 149, 152, 228
Prichard, H. A., 42
Prima facie duties, 22–23, 42
Primary qualities, 69, 71, 94, 166–167,
  179
Progressive pedagogy, 165
Promise keeping, 22–23, 24, 26, 27, 41,
  45, 50, 58, 60, 73, 102, 226
  in classrooms, 91–92
  as dialogical, 81, 87
Problem-posing, 183, 184, 231
Problem-solving, 54, 168, 169, 170, 229
Propositional knowledge, 168, 192,
  229, 247
Psychology, developmental, 163
Public world, 158, 160–161
Purpel, David, 8, 10

Raths, L. E., 104–105, 107, 112
Rationalism, xi, 24–27, 42–43, 53, 156,
  157, 171, 191, 222, 223–224, 229,
  232, 233
  mentioned, 29, 31, 37, 146
Raywid, Mary Ann, 186
Reading, 173, 182, 183, 185–186,
  214–215, 238, 239
Recovery of being, 88
Region of the world, 99, 119, 120, 160,
  163, 181, 193, 199, 200–201, 205,
  207, 213, 218–219, 237, 244
Regional ontology, 244
Reich, Charles A., 31–32, 33, 41
Relativism, moral, xii, 4, 8, 194
Relevance, existential/
  phenomenological, 235

Religion, 146, 158, 159, 173, 186–187,
  194–198, 213
Repairing wrongs, damages, 22, 38, 41,
  50, 209
  in classrooms, 85, 88, 92
Respect
  for law, 27, 32, 85, 102
  for nature, 208
  for others in school, 32, 34, 84, 86
  for persons, 30–31, 41, 72, 76, 83,
  208
  for self, 67, 80, 87
  for students, 108
Responsibility, 78, 83, 84, 85, 224, 227,
  248
Returning services received, 22, 41, 50
Revelation, 38, 146
Ricoeur, Paul, 77, 148
Rightness, 19–20, 21–23, 27, 33, 39,
  42, 90, 102, 103
  as dependent upon consequences, 44,
  47, 52, 54, 57–58, 62
  in ordinary usage, 11–12, 14–15, 17
Rights, human, 53, 68, 116, 117
  derivative human rights, 78, 82, 83,
  92, 93, 118, 210
  learned concomitantly, 83–86
  learned in lesson content, 111–114
  to a livable environment, 210, 245
  See also Human Rights
Rochowiak, D., 193
Rosen, Stanley, 4
Rosenthal, Sandra B., 70–71, 219–220
Ross, W. D., 21–23, 26, 27, 39
  beneficence, 22, 88, 93
  obligation to develop self, 22, 25, 34,
  35, 119, 225
  mentioned, 28, 29, 31, 33, 41, 42, 58,
  60, 65, 85, 88, 143, 144, 149
Rousseau, Jean Jacques, 30, 142, 165,
  177, 224
Rule utilitarianism, 51, 52, 53, 101–102
Russell, Bertrand, 156, 180–181, 192,
  195, 199, 212, 231

Salomon, G., 249
Sartre, Jean-Paul, 31, 94, 224, 225, 229,
  231
Scheffler, Israel, 148

Schemata, 176, 178, 181, 244, 246
  cognitive, developmental, evaluative,
    174, 218
  corporeal, 201, 202–203, 204–205,
    206
  of disciplines, 188, 190, 192, 232,
    242, 245
  temporal, 162–163, 212, 218
Schneider, P., 82
Schutz, Alfred, 159–160, 162
Schweitzer, Albert, 187
Science, 130, 132, 176, 178, 185
  critique of, 123–127
  physical, 158, 159
  poetics of, 164, 165, 208
Scudder, John, 187
Search for being, 151–153, 228, 230,
    235
Secondary properties, 71, 166–167,
    179, 181
Sectarianism, 186
Seguin, C., 76
Self-consciousness, 226–227
Shafer, S. M., 114
Shor, Ira, 185
Simon, S. B., 104–105, 107, 112
Simon, S. R., 105–107, 113
Skinner, B. F., 46, 156
Smith, B. Othanel, 113, 148, 171
Smith, Kate, 212
Social sciences, 199, 217–218, 244–245
Social studies, 173, 212
Social world, 201, 210–212
Sociology, 163, 173
Socrates, 40, 42, 50, 93, 111
Sollberger, E., 197
Soltis, Jonas F., 139, 148–149
Sophists, 111
Spencer, Herbert, 156, 163–167, 171,
    177, 178, 180, 181, 222
  mentioned, 144, 162, 184, 191, 204,
    207, 208, 217, 220, 221, 233,
    236, 241, 242
Spiegelberg, Herbert, 68, 76
Spinoza, Baruch, xi, 156
Sports, 159, 163
  required, 204, 220
Spranger, Edward, 142
Striley, J., 244
Summerhill, 46, 140

Tarule, J. M., 162
Taylor, Charles, 193
Taylor, Paul, 71, 208–209
Technological consciousness, 125–127,
    135, 170, 192, 207
Teleological ethics, 17, 44–45, 64, 66,
    90, 118, 146, 149
Teleological suspension of the ethical,
    35, 36, 87
Thematic investigation, 114, 230
Tillich, Paul, 5, 6
Time, experienced existentially, 36
Toulmin, S., 197, 198
Tragedy, 145–146, 213, 223, 225, 244
Transcendence, 24, 31, 72, 183,
    189–190, 203, 226, 228, 229, 230,
    241
Transitive consciousness, 183
True words, 184
Truth, 13, 15, 59, 144, 159, 190, 191,
    192–193, 194, 195, 219–220, 230,
    231, 232, 246
  criterion of, 160, 166, 170–171, 175
  as disclosedness, 146, 147, 179–180,
    185, 239–240
  search for, 153, 175, 228, 230–231,
    232, 235
Truth telling, 22, 24, 41, 42, 45, 73, 78,
    81, 104, 117
  in the classroom, 91, 92, 236–237, 239
  as dialogical, 87, 108
  and human dignity, 50, 60, 67

UNESCO, 114, 115, 227
Universal Declaration of Human
    Rights, 113, 115, 214
Urbanization, 4, 6, 7, 33, 134, 200
Utilitarianism, 47–54, 56, 58, 102–103
Utility, principle of, 48

Value
  clarification, 104–108, 109, 110, 111,
    112, 114, 140
  distinguished from rightness, 11, 71
  education, 203–204
  reified, 94, 95, 104, 105–106
  sensibility, 167
Vandenberg, Donald, xv, 114, 152, 177,
    187, 194
Van Manen, Max, 152

Veblen, Thorstein, 161
Vocational education, 159, 164,
    168–169, 170, 186, 222, 235
Voltaire, xi

Waks, Leonard, 129
Walden II, 46, 140

Weaver, Jan, 8
Welfare rights, 82, 83, 93
Whitehead, Alfred North, 142, 230,
    247
Witness, 237–238

Zuurdeeg, W., 197, 199, 200

About the Author

Donald Vandenberg delivered morning newspapers and worked as a drug store clerk and soda jerk in Milwaukee before serving as a photographer in U.S. naval aviation. He was a gardener/handyman on an estate in northern Wisconsin for six summers before and while earning his bachelor's in arts at Maryville College in Tennessee, where he won the English Prize. He taught high school in western Michigan while completing a masters degree at the University of Wisconsin, having already benefitted from a year in American Studies at the University of Wyoming under a Coe Fellowship. The doctorate from the University of Illinois was followed by teaching philosophy of education at the University of Calgary, Penn State, University of California-Los Angeles, and the University of Santiago. His papers have been published in *Educational Theory, Teachers College Record, Harvard Educational Review, Educational Philosophy and Theory, Journal of Educational Thought, Journal of Educational Administration, Educational Forum, UCLA Educator, Educational Research and Perspectives, Phenomenology & Pedagogy,* and *Discourse.* He is a consulting editor for *Educational Philosophy and Theory* and *Phenomenology & Pedagogy.*

Vandenberg has also edited two volumes of readings in the philosophy of education in the Broudy series with the University of Illinois Press (1969) and has written *Being and Education* (1971) and *Human Rights in Education* (1983). He has been a Reader in Education at The University of Queensland in Brisbane since 1976.